D1117491

DATE DUE			

Robert Stone

Twayne's United States Authors Series

Frank Day, Editor

Clemson University

TUSAS 632

ROBERT STONE
Gigi Kaeser

Robert Stone

Robert Solotaroff

University of Minnesota

Twayne Publishers • New York
Maxwell Macmillan Canada • Toronto
Maxwell Macmillan International • New York Oxford Singapore Sydney

Twayne's United States Authors Series No. 632

Robert Stone
Robert Solotaroff

Twayne Publishers   Maxwell Macmillan Canada, Inc.
Macmillan Publishing Company   1200 Eglinton Avenue East
866 Third Avenue   Suite 200
New York, New York 10022   Don Mills, Ontario M3C 3N1

Library of Congress Cataloging-in-Publication Data
Solotaroff, Robert
  Robert Stone / Robert Solotaroff.
     p. cm.—(Twayne's United States authors series ; TUSAS 632)
  Includes bibliographical references and index.
  ISBN 0-8057-4011-2
  1. Stone, Robert—Criticism and interpretation. I. Title
  II. Series.
  PS3569.T6418Z86   1994
  813'.54—dc20   93-32300
                                                               CIP

The paper used in this publication meets the minimum requirements of American
National Standard for Information Sciences—Permanence of Paper for Printed Library
Materials. ANSI Z3948-1984. ∞ ™

10 9 8 7 6 5 4 3 2 1 (hc)

Printed in the United States of America

For Rose Weiss Solotaroff,
1904–1972

Contents

Preface

One way of placing Robert Stone's fiction among the larger continuities of American literature is to position him in a line with those American authors like Crane, Hemingway, Dos Passos, and Mailer who believe that, at bottom, life is war. In a contribution to a 1985 conference on the relationship between the writer and American society, Stone—using the phrase from the Civil War—wrote of the first time that he went "to see the elephant": when he saw combat. This occurred about 14 months into his three-year hitch in the navy, in October 1956, when he was a radioman on the *U.S.S. Chilton*. The ship was an AKA (attack troop carrier) assigned to the Suez Canal to pick up American civilians during the crisis there. On the day French Mirage jets blew apart Port Said, as well as a great many Egyptians in the harbor in their little reed boats, the *Chilton* was tied to the quay, and on the *Chilton* was the 19-year-old Robert Stone, for a while hugely enjoying the beauty of the illumination rounds and the spectacle of flying rubble and bodies. Eventually, one Mirage violated the Americans' sense of the sanctity of the space *they* occupied by blowing away the quay. Stone's pleasure turned to anger at the French in their planes, "and we really wanted to kill them, because it began to penetrate our consciousness that the harbor was filled with dead people." So far all of this is relatively collective: a good many of his shipmates joined Stone in his modulation from experiencing combat as entertainment to finding it a morally dubious activity. But how many felt, as Stone did, that his new sense of combat-as-horror was absolutely recognizable? As he put it in 1985, "I always thought that the world was filled with evil spirits, that people's minds teemed with depravity and craziness and murderousness, that that basically was an implicit condition, an uncurable condition of mankind." And if there were any like sensibilities, did any of them try to deal with the familiar sense of the frequent horror of unmediated experience by thinking something like the following: "This is the way it is. There is no cure for this. There is only one thing you can do with this. You can transcend it. You can take it and you make it art."[1]

One can only begin to understand how it was that this 19-year-old had arrived at both this appraisal of humankind's murderous quotient and the strategy he might employ to deal with it by confronting the relatively sensational facts of Stone's early years: a wholly absent father; a schizophrenic mother; and a three-and-a-half-year residency, between his sixth and tenth years, at St. Ann's in Manhattan, a school that the only character Stone ever created whose experience closely followed his own recalled as "a physical and moral chaos of all against all."[2] After I wrote about two-thirds of this book, it occurred to me that in each of his first three novels Stone, to varying degrees, recasts the power dynamics of St. Ann's. There the "scholars," as the variously abandoned children were ironically called, were pitted against unfairly empowered authorities, who were often sadistic and arbitrary. So it is with at least one of the principals in the New Orleans of *A Hall of Mirrors* (1967), in the California and the fantasy terrain in the American Southwest of *Dog Soldiers* (1974), and in the Nicaragua-like Tecan, so affected by American influence, in *A Flag for Sunrise* (1981). A few years after Stone completed *Flag*, an interviewer asked him if he consciously tried to write about America. In the three novels he had published, Stone had woven enough relevant American detail into the accountings of his principals' struggles to justify his response: "Yes, I do. That is my subject. America and Americans."[3]

But then Stone began working his way out of this partial recasting of his abused past. What social orderings surface in his fourth novel, *Children of Light* (1986), are not particularly malevolent, but the principals are so afflicted and destructively involved with each other that Stone needed no unjust collective structures to bring them to—or close to—death. *Children of Light* is not particularly "about America," but Stone's fifth and best novel, *Outerbridge Reach* (1992), very much is. With St. Ann's much less present in the author's synapses, however, the sense of America as destroyer of its citizens or collaborator with other repressive regimes does not emerge. Correspondingly, although Stone fits his protagonist to a situation that drives him to psychological disintegration and suicide, the characters of *Outerbridge Reach* are, as a whole, much less socially and/or emotionally marginal than the drug smugglers, gun runners, alcoholics, drug addicts, schizophrenics, murderers, and sadistic law enforcers who largely occupy the pages of the preceding novels.

To a considerable degree, Stone has worked his way free from the need to write about damaged people in diseased settings. When, during a May 1992 radio interview, I asked him if he found this evolution in his career, Stone began nodding before I finished the question, then said, "One tries to get a handle. One tries to get in control if you spent some of your childhood feeling completely out of control and pitted against

forces at whose mercy you were. I'm still tremendously angry; I've never
been able to get away from that. I just never stopped being angry about
that, I now realize."[4]

But the violent injustice that Stone suffered as a child shaped his writing only inasmuch as it was supported by a great deal else that he saw or
read or heard about as an adult; his response to the Port Said bombing is
just one example. Of course, a good deal of what happens in the world is
not particularly violent or unjust or destructive, but, at least through
Stone's first three novels, happenings of this order did not fire his fictional imagination. His assertion of the healthy resiliency of the
American psyche surfaced in an interview he gave in 1983, less than two
years after he published *Flag*, but not in any prior story or novel.[5] All of
this is not to suggest that someone with as ironic and skeptical a sensibility as Stone created fictions that are univocal laments about the crushing of the good, sensitive people by sadistic authorities. Indeed, sadistic
brutes do contribute to the deaths of the sympathetic heroines of his first
and third novels, but, as we shall see, the heroines' characterizations are
interestingly qualified. In 1981 Stone approvingly quoted a character in
a V. S. Naipaul novel who said, " 'It isn't that there isn't any right and
wrong, it's that there isn't any right.' " Then he continued: "It is
extremely difficult to discover where right is. It keeps disappearing—
you think you see it and you've got it in your hands, and then you
don't—that old ambivalence comes down and you're compromised. It's
just that the ambiguities of life are infinite."[6]

However elusive Stone might find the absolutely appropriate act in
life, he has always had a powerfully developed sense of what is proper
behavior at his writing desk. One part of his burden is, in a sense, to add
the words "about how bad things can get" to Hemingway's frequently
uttered "A writer's job is telling the truth." Another part is to celebrate
the struggles of characters to transcend the often desperate and demeaning situations in which they find themselves. Often the struggle is for a
glimpse of the numinous, for the spiritually transcendent. Approached
from one point of view, Stone is an old-fashioned writer. Although he
may talk about the distance between what is on the pages and what is in
the world, compelling verisimilitude is, with the exception of a few sections in *Hall*, a demand shaping his creation of sharply, often complexly
depicted characters, who usually interact in a swiftly developing
sequence of events. And Roger Sale has called Stone "a nineteenth century moralist, as eager as Carlyle or George Eliot to make the precise
assessments required to judge the choices made by an individual or soci-

ety."[7] But Stone is quite au courant in his ability to capture the accents and appearances of a good many of the eruptions and disruptions, both internal and political, of the contemporary world while thinking up incidents, narrative description, and dialogue that are often simultaneously surprising and absolutely appropriate.

As an explanation for what he is about stylistically, Stone has several times invoked the opening sentence of Conrad's preface to *The Nigger of the "Narcissus"* (1897): "A work that aspires, however humbly, to the condition of art should carry its justification in every line."[8] In the first chapter I discuss Stone's theories concerning the stylistic precision he feels he must attain if his fiction is to justify its existence. Here I will only hint at how much Stone has succeeded in his goals by quoting the first two sentences of A. Alvarez's fine review of *Children of Light:* "In just four novels in almost twenty years Robert Stone has established a world and style and tone of voice of great originality and authority. It is a world without grace or comfort, bleak, dangerous and continually threatening."[9]

In the chapters that follow I touch upon some of the ways that Stone's individual experiences helped to bring into being the particular worlds of the novels, which I discuss in the second through the sixth chapters. Because his evolution from an abused child raised by a schizophrenic, a West Side gang member who was thrown out of high school, into an internationally respected author was so improbable and, at least to me, so interesting, in the first chapter I follow his life from birth to the publication of *Hall of Mirrors.* After that I confront his life only inasmuch as his later actions immediately shaped the creation of the novels or stories. In the seventh chapter I discuss Stone's four stories as well as some of his nonfiction, an extremely suggestive and intelligent body of work in its own right.

Acknowledgments

From *Children of Light* by Robert Stone. Copyright © 1985, 1986 by Robert Stone. Reprinted by permission of Alfred A. Knopf, Inc.

From *A Flag for Sunrise* by Robert Stone. Copyright © 1977, 1980, 1981 by Robert Stone. Reprinted by permission of Alfred A. Knopf, Inc.

From *Conversations with American Authors* by Charles Ruas. Copyright © 1985 by Alfred A. Knopf, Inc. Reprinted by permission of Alfred A. Knopf, Inc.

From "Robert Stone," in *Writers at Work, Eighth Series*, ed. George Plimpton, intro. Joyce Carol Oates. Copyright © 1988 by The Paris Review, Inc. Used by permission of Viking Books USA, Inc.

Permission for the following were granted by Houghton Mifflin Company: excerpts from *Dog Soldiers*, Copyright © 1973, 1974 by Robert Stone; excerpts from *A Hall of Mirrors*, Copyright © 1964, 1966 by Robert Stone; excerpts from *Outerbridge Reach*, Copyright © by Robert Stone. All rights reserved.

Excerpts from "An Interview with Robert Stone" by Kay Bonetti reprinted by permission of American Audio Prose Library, Inc. This work is a print version of a recorded interview with Robert Stone, which is available on audiocassette from the American Audio Prose Library, P.O. Box 842, Columbia, Missouri 65205, along with recorded interviews of over 120 other contemporary authors.

Excerpts from "Helping" (*New Yorker*), "Absence of Mercy" (*Harper's*), "Aquarius Obscured" (*American Review*), "Porque No Tiene, Porque Le Falta" (*New American Review*), and "Havana Then and Now" (*Harper's*) by Robert Stone, by permission of Robert Stone.

Excerpts from "A Higher Horror of the Whiteness" by Robert Stone, Copyright © 1986 by *Harper's* magazine. All rights reserved. Reprinted from the December 1986 issue by special permission.

Excerpts from "The Reason for Stories: Toward a Moral Fiction" by Robert Stone, Copyright © 1988 by *Harper's* magazine. All rights reserved. Reprinted from the June 1988 issue by special permission.

I would also like to thank Robert Stone, almost as much for his generosity in granting interviews and his patience during them as for producing such an arresting body of writing; Janice Stone for her kindness and helpfulness; Steve Hagen for some background on Zen; Bill

Malandra for a translation from the Sanskrit; Frank Day, Cindy Buck, and Mark Zadrozny for their editorial corrections; the University of Minnesota for the quarter leave that enabled me to get two of the chapters written; and my wife Claudia and my brother Ted for their encouragement during the project.

Chronology

1937	Robert Anthony Stone born 21 August in Brooklyn, New York, to C. Homer Stone and Gladys Catherine Grant.
1939	Moves to Manhattan with his mother.
1942–1955	Goes to St. Ann's School in Manhattan; a resident there from 1943 to 1946.
1955–1958	Serves in U.S. Navy.
1958–1959	Works as copyboy and caption writer for *New York Daily News*; reads his poetry in coffeehouses.
1958–1959	Goes to New York University.
1959	Marries Janice G. Burr on 11 December.
1960	Lives in New Orleans from February to October, working in a coffee factory, as a census taker, and as a sailor in the Merchant Marine. Reads poetry in bars. Daughter Deidre born on 15 June.
1961	Back in New York, works as an advertising copywriter and begins writing *A Hall of Mirrors*.
1962–1964	Stegner Fellow at Stanford University.
1963	Son Ian born on 24 May.
1964	Awarded Houghton Mifflin Literary Fellowship.
1965–1967	Back in New York, works as a writer for *National Mirror* and as a clerk in an art gallery.
1967	*A Hall of Mirrors* is published.
1967–1971	Works as a free-lance writer in Hollywood, London, and Saigon; lives in England.
1968	Awarded William Faulkner Foundation Prize for the best first novel of 1967.
1970	Writes "WUSA," a screenplay based on *Hall of Mirrors*.
1971	Guggenheim Fellow.
1971–1972	Writer-in-residence, Princeton University.

1972–1975   Teaches at Amherst College.

1974   *Dog Soldiers* is published.

1975   Wins National Book Award for *Dog Soldiers*.

1978   Writes "Who'll Stop the Rain," screenplay (with Judith Rascoe) based on *Dog Soldiers*.

1979   "Who'll Stop the Rain" nominated by the Writers' Guild of America for best script adapted from another medium.

1979–1980   Teaches at Stanford University and at the University of Hawaii-Manoa.

1981–1983   Teaches at Harvard University, the University of California-Irvine, and New York University.

1981   *A Flag for Sunrise* is published.

1982   Receives John Dos Passos Prize for Literature, as well as American Academy and Institute of Arts and Letters Award; receives *Los Angeles Times* Book Prize for *A Flag for Sunrise*.

1983   Receives NEH fellowship.

1986   *Children of Light* is published.

1987   Receives Mildred and Harold Strauss Living Award.

1992   *Outerbridge Reach* is published. Edits *Best American Short Stories: 1992*.

Chapter One

Toward a First Novel

Unpromising Origins

Robert Anthony Stone was born in Good Samaritan Hospital in Brooklyn on 21 August 1937 to C. Homer Stone and Gladys Catherine Grant. His mother's family had "lived and worked around New York Harbor for a couple of generations. My [maternal] grandfather was a Conradian figure—he was a Scottish ships' engineer who settled in the Port of New York and became the captain of a tugboat."[1] Of his father, Stone knows only that he had been a railroad detective and then worked on tugs, and that through his work he met and eventually impregnated Gladys Grant, who gave her son his father's last name. To this day Stone doesn't know—nor has he ever tried to find out—what happened to his progenitor after 1937. As with the relationship between God and the adult Robert Stone, the relationship between Homer Stone and his son was one of nonpresence.

The consequences of his father's absence were intensified by the fact that, though his mother was "well-spoken and refined . . . very fond of me and educated [she was] completely batty": a schizophrenic.[2] Stone has traced his abiding sense of the distance between the verbal structures of novels and the physical structures of the world to "the curious luck to be raised by a schizophrenic, which gives one a tremendous advantage in understanding the relationship of language to reality. I had to develop a model of reality in the face of being conditioned to a schizophrenic world. I had to sort out causality for myself. My mother's world was pure magic. . . . Realism wasn't an issue to me because there wasn't any. I always had a vague dreamlike sense of things. There was no strong distinction for me between objective and imaginative worlds. . . . Life wasn't providing [coherent] narrative so I had to" (Woods, 43).

The mix is an interesting one. For Stone, as for most children, his mother was his "contact person for reality, for information about the world." But because she was schizophrenic, "I got some confusing signals" (Woods, 35). "Confusing" is a euphemism. When I asked Stone in

October 1991 whether his mother, in her illness, ever occupied anything like the continuous alternative terrain that Lu Anne Bourgeois of *Children of Light* (1986) does when she consorts with the delusional Long Friends, he replied, "Yes, but she was reticent about it with me. It was something she didn't really want me getting into and she would get cryptic. There was a sense of something, an ongoing reality I was not supposed to know about, at least not yet. I didn't like it and I didn't want to get a sense of details."[3]

The last sentence was uttered with an angry resentment quite uncharacteristic of the easy graciousness that characterized the rest of Stone's comments during the three-hour interview, and it hinted strongly at how alarming Gladys Grant's schizophrenic depths were to her young son. The intensity of his need for a more accurate account of the external than the one offered by his "contact person for reality" helps to account for the preternatural clarity and vividness of most of Stone's pages—in particular, the settings, the conversations, and the renderings of physical movement. Paul Gray's phrase about almost all of *Dog Soldiers* (1974)—"as precise as the cross hairs on a rifle sight"—describes most of Stone's fiction.[4]

In other interviews Stone has also spoken of his sense of the interpenetration of the objective and imaginative worlds: the external was something he could play with, could to some extent master with imaginative strategies. And since he was a relatively solitary child, "radio fashioned my imagination. Radio narrative always has to embody a full account of action and scene. I began to do that myself. When I was seven or eight, I'd walk through Central Park like Sam Spade, describing aloud what I was doing, becoming both the actor and the writer setting him in the scene. That was where I developed an inner ear" (Woods, 34).

Stone has described in different ways the moment late in 1961 when, as a 24-year-old college dropout with a wife, a child, and a job writing copy for low-end furniture stores, he finished rereading *The Great Gatsby* and said to himself: "This is what I want to do. I want to write novels" (Solotaroff 1991). The declaration of oneself as a writer is often as complex in motivation as it is crucial in the assertion of one's sense of self-worth and purpose. Surely Stone wanted to create something that would reach for the insight, the beauty of language, and the triumphant structure of *Gatsby*, and surely he had to make a living. But his 1984 response to William Crawford Woods's comment about his characters' frequent uncertainty about their identity hints at how enduring were the consequences of his difficult childhood: "Yes. And my becoming a writer was my answer to that question. It was an absolute necessity. I had to create somebody significant or I would have been swept away" (Woods, 43). Swept away into a mediocre existence? Or into substantial and chronic emotional disturbance? The degree to which Stone feared the latter has also contributed mightily to his tenacity as a novelist and to the force of what he has produced.

A Real Little-Orphan Place

"Cross hairs on a rifle sight" captures more than Stone's characteristic clarity; there is also a sense of menace, of immediately impending violence. For his sense of life as war, Stone needed St. Ann's, a school, run by brothers of the Marist Order, on Lexington Avenue in the Seventies in Manhattan. Stone and his mother had moved from Brooklyn to Manhattan when he was about two, and when the time came for him to start school, at age five, they lived in the Yorkville section, at Lexington and Eighty-fifth. Although Gladys Grant, the daughter of a Presbyterian father and a Catholic mother, was herself offended by Catholic doctrine and clergy, she thought that the rigor of the Catholic educational system would be good for her son, and so Stone went to kindergarten at St. Ann's, a bit down Lexington Avenue. He has described the conditions of the first five years of his life as "a kind of lost paradise. My mother taught in the public school system and we lived in comfortable, middle class apartments" (Solotaroff 1991). But shortly after his sixth birthday, his mother's symptoms became so severe that she had to be hospitalized, at Creedmore Hospital on Long Island. There was no extended family to take in her son; St. Ann's had a boarding as well as a day school, and so, working with the network of Catholic charities, the family court system placed Stone in a setting where, as he put it in his 1987 story "Absence of Mercy," "a good beating was forever at hand," in a locale with "the social dynamic of a coral reef" ("AM," 61–62). There are differences between the experiences of Mackay, the protagonist of the story, and Stone—Mackay was placed in St. Michael's when he was five, and his virgin schoolteacher aunt, not the Catholic charities, paid his tuition—but unfortunately, the differences are trivial.

From the time he began giving interviews in 1967, Stone has seemed appalled at any suggestion of self-pity. Consequently, his comments about St. Ann's have revealed little about the impression the place made upon him. When, in 1980, Maureen Karagueuzian asked him if St. Ann's was strict, Stone replied, "They were strict in the sense that they hit you. As those orders were in the forties and fifties, they were strict and they were a bit physical."[5] He conceded a bit more to Charles Ruas a year later; even so, St. Ann's was primarily a useful locale for the embry-onic novelist: "I grew up, in those years [in St. Ann's], with people who were going that way—these affectless, institutionalized sociopaths were the people right around me. When I was in the navy at seventeen, there again I ran into military people like that. Those things frightened and fascinated me" (Ruas, 275).[6] To Steve Chapple in 1984, Stone barely hinted at how much he still resented his vulnerability there: "This was a real little-orphan place, for little orphans holding hands two-by-two. I'll never forget it. Never. Ever" (Chapple, 40). Talking to Sybil Steinberg in 1986, Stone described the school as merely "the last vestige of the old fashioned orphanage."[7]

But by 1986 he decided that it was time to write up as a short story an anecdote, in which St. Ann's figured, that he felt compelled to tell friends. The anecdote concerned the way in which the consequences of a fight he had had in a subway station a bit more than two decades earlier cemented the sense he'd acquired at St. Ann's of the fundamental unfair-ness of things. Since he was for once trying to write fiction closely based on autobiography, and since Mackay's sense of being "the last orphan" ("AM," 61) is at the center of "Absence of Mercy," the appalling dynam-ics of aggression at St. Ann's stand out clearly.

The violence was wreaked upon Stone-Mackay by other students, by priests in class, and, most memorably, at night by the school disciplinar-ian, "implacable as a shark or a hurricane" to the boys who, as young as six and sick with terror, had been waiting outside his room. Each palm was lashed three times by the priest as implacable shark, "St. Michael's children would fly weeping toward their pillows, their burning hands tucked under their armpits, scuttling barefoot over the wooden floor like skinny little wingless birds. In bed, in the darkness, they would moan with pain and rage against the state of things, against Brother Francis and God's will. . . . Children can never imagine a suffering greater than their own" ("AM," 63).

Like Mackay, Stone was "an intelligent child who liked books and so was able to mythologize his experience. One of the favorite myths informing his early childhood was the Dickensian one of the highborn orphan, fallen among brutish commoners. Sometimes he would try to identify and encourage in himself those traits of character that gave evi-dence of his lost eminence" ("AM," 63). Among these traits were sympa-thy for the helpless, a willingness to speak out, and eloquence. Of course, at St. Ann's, courageous and eloquent defiance of the priests was out of the question, but by the time Stone was seven and a half he was permitted to walk away from the school by himself for a while, and he could cast himself as an observant, dominating Sam Spade figure, or as a children-avenging Zorro, in the peace of nearby Central Park.

Stone's acquaintance with God's will coincided with his first day at St. Ann's day school, which fell just after his fifth birthday. Stone has neatly laid out the contour of his religious responses for the next 11 or 12 years: "First I resisted, then I was kind of won over by it, then I became enthusiastic, and then [I] turned around," when he converted to atheism at the age of 17 (Karagueuzian, 254). Though he was much taken with the ritual, faith at St. Ann's was complicated by the fact that the brothers claimed to be the representatives of God's will—the sadistic disciplinarian would advise his victims "to offer their humiliations to the Holy Ghost" ("AM," 62). In 1974 Stone explained that he had "felt very rebellious. Every once in a while I would get very angry at the whole structure, although I guess I believed it. I was in that very difficult position you get in when you really believe in God, and at the same time you are very angry: God is this huge creature who we must know, love and serve, though actually you feel like you want to kick the son of a bitch. The effect on me was I felt I was just doing things wrong" (Woods, 48). Writing a few years later about Mackay, Stone remembers the complex of his feelings more vividly:

> Mackay's religous allegiances shifted with his daily fortunes. One day he would find himself in transports of love for his Father in Heaven, who was after all the only one he knew, and he would pray that God's will be done on earth. At other times he would desire nothing so much as the defeat and ruin of the United States, on the theory that even the conquering Japanese were bound to be an improvement on the Pauline Brothers. On such days he would address his prayers to Satan, Hitler, and Stalin. It would seem at these times that the right side was not for him. ("AM," 62)

But Stone does have positive things to say about the education he received there. For a while he was given piano lessons, which he loved, and though he has complained about St. Ann's essential anti-intellectuality, he "credits the school with deepening his respect for literature, initially instilled by his mother" (Steinberg, 72), and for giving him a training in the study of grammar and the writing of grammatical, strongly organized paragraphs that was "practical, down-to-earth, and basic—in its way, good" (Karagueuzian, 254). Stone, who was reading Ovid—"in the expurgated version, of course" (Steinberg, 72)—by the time he left St. Ann's, "really enjoyed learning Latin and I still read poetry in Latin" (Chapple, 40).

A More Secular Existence

A bit before Stone's tenth birthday, his mother was released from the hospital, and he began living with her, staying on at the St. Ann's day school. Since Gladys Grant could no longer gain a teaching position, she supported herself and her son with low-paying jobs, first as a maid in a hotel, then as an addresser of envelopes. No longer able to afford the comfortable apartments of her life before hospitalization, she rented rooms in seedy hotels in the West Seventies and Nineties. But sometimes she would get a bit of money together and confess to her son that she had always wanted to try life anew in a certain place. Excited by the prospect, Stone would then talk his mother into the quest, and, with very little money, the disturbed woman with the vulnerable son who had just left full-time occupancy on the coral reef of St. Ann's would journey to New Mexico or Montreal or Chicago, in search of a new, richer life.

The most prolonged and influential trip was their four-month sojourn in Chicago when Stone was eleven. After a few weeks their money ran out, and so they lived for three of those months in a Booth shelter on the North Side. Stone's recollections, offered more than 40 years later, are worth repeating:

> That hostel made a tremendous impression on me and I always go back to it in my mind. Basically it was for women who didn't have any man and the kids there were gypsy-kids in a way that I was sometimes but not always: I went in and out of that life. In a way there was a lot of stability in mine. This was a taste of what happened and what you came up with when there weren't any systems. Those kids were interesting; they were from all over. This place was interracial: black kids, black families were there at a time—this was in 1948—when this was relatively uncommon. Chicago in 1948 was a relatively segregated city and it got us in a lot of trouble with other kids. To be associated with that shelter was to be of low status and the fact that there were black kids in there made it all the more troublesome. I always held on to all that. (Solotaroff 1991)

As we shall see, Stone certainly held onto it in the creation of one of his most overwhelming characters, Raymond Hicks of *Dog Soldiers*.

Eventually Stone and his mother got back to New York, and for a few days, until some assistance came through from welfare, they lived on the roof of a building on Lexington Avenue. There was one more sojourn the next year, and then, his fear of chaos having won out over the romance of the road, Stone refused to go on any more. This was two years after he had begun to write stories—the first was a science-fiction effort, written when he was ten, and from time to time over the next five or six years, "I'd get a notion to write one." (Although he is exceptionally forthcoming about his published work, Stone is reluctant to say much about his juvenilia.) He did win a contest as a junior in high school, for a story "probably written a couple of weeks after I finished reading *The Catcher in the Rye,* and I have a feeling that if I read it now I would find it intensely Salingeresque. The story was published in something called *Good Themes.* I don't remember who sponsored the contest, maybe *Scholastic* magazine." Stone did remember, though, that his mother sent the story to the *New Yorker,* "and while they refused it they also asked to see more of my writing. That really set me up" (Solotaroff 1991). He also wrote a short play—a dialogue between Napoleon and a cancer researcher—that won a contest sponsored by the American Cancer Society.

He had first read about Napoleon in eighth grade in Thomas Carlyle's *History of the French Revolution* (1837), and he credits the author with being

> the first person who gave me what I would call a literary experience, who taught me something about how language works and what writing is about. . . . My first reaction to it was "I can't understand a word of this, it doesn't make sense to me, what a strange way of writing this is." But as I read it, I began to really enjoy it and I began to understand it more. It really struck me as most unfamiliar, provocative, and strange. That was the first time I was really struck with language. I learned about the variety of textures that prose could have, about the liberties that could be taken with language, that one could depart from the conventional rhetoric of English and in so doing produce a strong effect. (Ruas, 283)

Though he wanted to be a writer almost from the time he began reading, and though his writing, mostly of compositions, was all that got Stone favorable attention in school, he did not feel that it was possible:

> There was no opposition from my mother, a kind of maverick in this blue-collar milieu I was in, who always liked, looked favorably upon

bohemians and eccentrics. But I think that with a very few exceptions the teachers and friends I had really didn't look at the life of arts except as an excuse for not working. Also, I didn't think that being a writer was economically possible: I'd come to share from somewhere, not from my mother, the idea that you had to make a living in a more solid way. A writing career was unstable, and what I was really after on some level was stability. I really wanted to be something absolutely solid, something uneccentric, perfectly acceptable and secure. (Solotaroff 1991)

But like most adolescents, Stone's yearnings were contradictory. From whatever blend of his hatred of authority, his desire to impress his friends, his loyalty to his mother, and his self-destructiveness, he often did not act like someone seeking a secure place in a stable organization. For example, "one of my party tricks to amaze my friends, to show that nobody was crazier or more out to lunch than I was, was to drink four or five cans of beer in the morning and show up for school completely plastered. That was my way of demonstrating my disinterestedness, my self-destructiveness and willingness to do any crazy shit" (Solotaroff 1991).

Stone also sought peer approval, when he was 15, by becoming a "junior" in the Saxons, a mostly Irish, West Side gang. One night, within a year of joining, Stone was in Central Park, drinking with some other members on what they felt was their turf—the Egyptian obelisk behind the Metropolitan Museum of Art. Members of another gang appeared, knives were taken out, and "a lot of people got cut, not me, but I figured, this is foolish. If I'm going to get killed, I'm going to get killed over something worthwhile" (Chapple, 40). By the next year, he was hanging out with members of a largely Italian, fascist youth group in East Harlem. "They would do things like exchange fascist salutes and paint 'Viva Il Duce' on walls, more to bust balls than anything else . . . but also as a reaction to the pressure of the general black and Puerto Rican takeover of Central Park." All of this deepened Stone's understanding of the workings of right-wing resentment, an interest that would prove useful when he wrote his first novel. There were also substantial consequences in his immediate life: in his senior year of high school he more or less converted Fred Vassi, a member of the East Harlem group and a classmate who also became a novelist, to the atheism he had recently reasoned his way into. One Sunday Vassi refused to go to church with his parents. When asked whom he'd been talking to, Vassi fingered Stone. The Vassis went to the authorities at St. Ann's, other friends of Stone's were called in, and, though he had recently won a New York State Regents' Scholarship, Stone was expelled during May of his senior year. When asked how he took all this, Stone responded, "I felt pretty good when they called me on the carpet and were accusing me. I felt like Martin Luther."[8]

The Navy Years

He would soon be 18 and eligible for the draft, he loved the sea, the navy had a three-year hitch for enlistees younger than 18, and so Stone tried to enlist immediately. Since there was a waiting list, he was not taken until early August 1955. Boot camp was at Bainbridge, Maryland, and being submerged again for 24 hours a day in an authoritarian locale was "too familiar, absolute hell." That it was summer made the experience particularly traumatic: "We wore summer whites and the only way you could clean them was with a brush and Ivory soap. . . . My mother was an old lady, I wasn't very handy at keeping my gear together. I was also kind of dreamy and unfocused, not ideal navy material. It was really traumatic for me" (Solotaroff 1991).

As with Mackay in "Absence of Mercy," the instinctive cringe Stone had picked up at St. Ann's reasserted itself until, with great difficulty and humiliation, it was pounded out of him by his drillmasters. Stone had to repeat part of boot camp, and it was not until November that he was sent to a technical air patrol squadron at Norfolk Naval Air Station , where he was transferred to radio school. It was as a radioman that Stone shipped out on the *U.S.S. Mulliphen*, an AKA. With the Suez crisis, he was transferred to the *U.S.S. Chilton*, but when it subsided he was returned to the *Mulliphen*, which he remained on through two Mediterranean cruises. By spring 1956 he had passed a high school equivalency test as well as a competitive examination to become a navy journalist, third-class petty officer. He did a story on the Marine residence station in Beirut, but his main reportage was between December 1957 and March 1958 with Operation Deep Freeze III in Antarctica. For his two two-month duties—there was a liberty in Melbourne in February—Stone wrote articles, for service newspapers, on the base at Cape Hallett on the Pacific side, and on the operation's particular scientific mission: tracing cosmic waves in accordance with a course prepared by scientists from the University of Chicago. Since Stone was there during the Antarctic summer, "the weather often didn't get much colder than a winter day in New York. Sometimes we would have these shore parties where we'd go and hang out, drink a couple of cans of beer, and look at the penguins" (Solotaroff 1991). By April he was back in the

United States, and he was discharged, as he likes to remember, on Bastille Day 1958.

Save for boot camp and an extremely unpleasant detail during his last weeks as a prisoner guard, Stone's navy years were, if occasionally uneasy, quite tolerable:

> I really had a pretty good time of it. I was fairly lucky in getting to travel a lot. I got to the Mediterranean. In the fifties, especially, the eastern Mediterranean was a pretty exotic location. People in the midfifties didn't often get to go to Greece, for example. It was interesting. And, certainly, Operation Deep Freeze III was wonderful. And I felt fairly successful. I got rated, got the badge of junior petty officer; it gave me a certain sense of attainment, a sense of being productive.

When I asked him if he would say, then, that he had learned to shed the self-destructive ways of high school, Stone responded, "The navy did not engage my tendency to fuck up. They didn't bring that out in me" (Solotaroff 1991).

He did a great deal of reading—*Moby-Dick* and *Ulysses* were the two novels that most absorbed him—began writing poetry, and wrote a story, "a neighborhood thing, a boy-girl story that was kind of an idealized version of my girlfriend and me at the time, which I sent to *Esquire* and which they refused" (Solotaroff 1991). He also felt that his later writing was much enriched by his "being thrown together with a whole lot of people from all over the country, especially since this was at a time, in the midfifties, when the country was less homogeneous, when, for example, the South was still the South and all that it entailed, and people from Appalachia were much more distinct, regional types, a time when there was much more contrast between New York kids and kids from West Virginia. It was very interesting and tremendously helpful."[9]

A Manhattan Beatnik

Once back in New York, and trying out a journalistic career, Stone got a job with the *Daily News* at $60 a week. Though he was hired as a copyboy, "the idea with the copyboys was that they were also a kind of talent reserve: some people did features for the big, thick Sunday section. Sometimes they would send you out as a kind of substitute reporter. They would send you to places they didn't want to go, like the morgue. I did a lot of sports and wrote some sports captions" (Solotaroff

1991). Most memorably, he once watched and reported on the wrestling matches in Madison Square Garden shortly after he had taken peyote.

Though Stone was much taken with some of the hard-boiled reporters who had been newspapermen since the 1920s—while he was there two of them disguised themselves as a doctor and a nurse and photographed Ruth Snyder in the electric chair—he was in retrospect grateful to the *News* for having enough repellent aspects to scare him off a newspaper career forever. First there was what seemed to him the same kind of working-class authoritarianism that he had loathed at St. Ann's, a brand exercised by "a not altogether dissimilar kind of person." But the *News* brought to this generalized "police department ethos" its own "paranoid and vicious political stances. . . . If they had their choice of coming out for life or coming out for death, they'd come out for death" (Solotaroff 1991).

In September 1958 Stone entered New York University, taking courses in Spanish, economics, composition, and (he thinks) communication arts. His wife, Janice Burr Stone, whom he met in the one course he took spring semester—creative writing—summarized his career as a college student in this way: "Bob always wanted to write, not to be a student, but he had no way of making a living. We were both committed to the idea that you had to get through college if you were going to make something of yourself. But Bob wasn't too good at making classes, taking notes, giving the professor what he wanted. It wasn't necessary for him to go to college at all."[10] To this Stone added that he was much more interested in the characters at the *News* and his new career of hanging out as a late 1950s beatnik. Early on, he began reading his poems in coffeehouses in Greenwich Village; after he met Janice, he would get off work at 1:00 A.M. and go to the Seven Arts Gallery, a midtown coffeehouse. Having left her first job as a "guidette" at the RCA Building, Janice put on her black tights and became a waitress at the Seven Arts. At that time the coffeehouse was frequented by stars like Jack Kerouac, Allen Ginsberg, Gregory Corso, and LeRoi Jones (now Imamu Amiri Baraka): "They were very important, famous, central people at the scene and I was basically Janice's boyfriend" (Solotaroff 1991).

But Janice's boyfriend had already written a story for the writing course. The instructor, M. L. Rosenthal, immediately recognized Stone's great promise and suggested that he apply for a fellowship to the Wallace Stegner Writing Program at Stanford, which required no degree. The story was about a guard in a naval prison. It was based on a brief experience I had just before I got out of the navy. . . . I'd go to the brig at Camp Allen, where the marines had the court-martialed prisoners. I had to march them along a military highway to breakfast. We'd have ours, and we'd see that they had their breakfast. They'd relax and get out of hand, and I was always afraid they'd pull some disastrous thing on us when we were bringing them back while admirals would be going to work. We wanted to make it look good, and we had these .45s on. It was stressful to have these .45s, which we were supposed to be ready to use on these guys who were fighting us. This was no way to have breakfast. (Solotaroff 1991)

Readers of *Dog Soldiers* will remember the fearful Converse's recollection of when he was a guard at the Yokasuka brig.

The New Orleans Experience

Stone's formal academic career dwindled down to sitting in on a course with Rosenthal during the fall semester of 1959. On 11 December he and Janice were married. About a month later he quit his job at the *News*, and, in Janice Stone's recollection, with barely enough money for bus fare, they traveled to New Orleans, arriving just before Mardi Gras. About a fifth of Stone's "Keeping the Future at Bay" (1988), a piece on the 1988 Republican National Convention (held in New Orleans), is a reminiscence of his nine-month stay in the city:

The last thing Louisiana needed in 1960 was a few more beatniks, but there we were. It was existential. We got by with odd jobs and passing the goblet after poetry readings. . . . In those days, the *vie de bohème* was undertaken without state assistance. The only thing forthcoming from the municipal welfare authorities, should we have been rash enough to approach them in our penury, would have been a couple of expletives and the advice to get out of town. We went from day to day, eating when we worked, fasting otherwise. Our poverty was not a game; there were no rich relatives back home to bail us out. On the other hand we always felt just on the edge of vision, an available cop-out.[11]

Stone had so many jobs, often for only a few days each, that 30 years later he and Janice could not remember all of them. Some that they could recall, like brief stints repairing drums or working in a bookstore, would not figure in his first novel, *A Hall of Mirrors* (1967), which Stone set in New Orleans. But some did: Rheinhardt, the protagonist, works for a week or two on the assembly line of a soap factory, and so did Stone. The author, who also worked for a bit in a coffee factory, reminisced that "no tour of American life is complete without a stint on an assembly line. You can learn a lot about what America's about on an assembly line." Though the Stones mostly associated with like-minded counterculture types, what he learned in the jobs in factories, in boiler rooms, and on the docks contributed to his later realization that "we were really seeing the horrid side of white Louisiana, the sweet side of black Louisiana" (Solotaroff 1991).

One of Stone's early jobs, trying to sell encyclopedias in the towns outside New Orleans, quickly introduced him to the least amiable side of the Deep South. No northern civil rights workers had yet started organizing Louisiana, but the local constabulary were ready enough to think that they had. He was arrested twice, in Covington and in Bogalusa, for peddling door to door without a license. Although Stone was never able to sell any encyclopedias—the few who said they would buy invariably changed their minds a few days later—his northern accent entitled him to a special sort of interrogation: "The police would ask us if we were selling encyclopedias to blacks; they kept asking us in what way they might concern blacks. They seemed to doubt that we were selling encyclopedias at all" (Solotaroff 1991). This was simply the most flamboyant example of the hostility toward northerners that he and Janice frequently encountered, part of a volatile racial paranoia that struck deep responses in a young man who, for most of his 23 years, had never lacked the ability to imagine disaster.

Stone's faculty for finding his way to where the action was or was going to be—whether in the Suez, or in the Deep South of the United States, or in Vietnam, or in Central America—had brought him to New Orleans just a few days after 1 February 1960, when four black students from North Carolina Agricultural and Technical College sat down at the lunch counter of the F. W. Woolworth store in Greensboro, North Carolina, and touched off the wave of sit-ins that swept through the South and the border states for the next few years. On 28–29 March, toward the end of the Stones' second month in Louisiana, the wave reached Baton Rouge, 70 miles from New Orleans. Sixteen blacks, students of Southern University, tried to integrate a lunch counter at a downtown department store; they were arrested, and close to 5,000 of their classmates demonstrated on the steps of the state capitol. The sit-ins did not reach New Orleans until 9 September, when seven members of CORE (Congress of Racial Equality), five blacks and two white grad-

uate students from Tulane, requested service at the lunch counter of a
department store on the fringe of the French Quarter. "Six hours later
police arrested them for being in violation of a law which prevents people from 'temporarily taking possession of a business.' "[12] (The law had
been passed earlier in the year in anticipation of just such events.) On the
next day black pickets marched in front of the department store as well
as in front of two nearby Woolworths, on the border of the French
Quarter where Stone lived. The demonstrations continued into October,
Stone's last month in the city, when arrests and failing funds weakened
the resolve of CORE, which had staged the protests. Two letters to
Mayor DeLesseps Morrison, referred to in Edward Haas's biography of
the mayor, capture some of the range of civic response. One urged
Morrison to have the courage to let the police "turn a machine-gun on a
bunch of niggers to break up their threatened riot"; another pleaded
with the mayor to recognize "that Negroes have legitimate demands,
and to negotiate with them, rather than to open the city to embarrassment in the national news media."[13] If the first position had more white
advocates, the second proved more predictive of the consequences of the
events of 4 November, when four black girls, escorted by U.S. marshals,
entered two elementary schools in an all-white, working-class ward of
New Orleans. The Stones were back in New York by this time, but, like
tens of millions of other Americans, they learned from the media about
the consequences:

> When the white mothers of the neighborhood learned that their two
> schools were the targets for integration, they reacted with fear and
> hatred. They rushed to the schools and removed their children, then
> remained to shout obscenities, spit, and hurl stones at the four little black
> girls. . . . One white man screamed, "Kill the niggers! . . . At the end of
> the day Mayor Morrison stated that the crowd behaved quite well and
> attempted no violence. The booing and jeering and the applauding is all
> part of the American way of life and is the ordinary human tendency for
> people to express themselves (Haas, 269).

On 15 November William Rainach, a state senator and the most
flamboyantly racist candidate in the recent gubernatorial contest, and
Leander Perez, the political boss of adjoining St. Bernard Parish,

> addressed a crowd of five thousand persons at the Municipal Auditorium.
> In his speech Perez demanded demonstrations against the NAACP,
> Communists, the "Zionist Jews," [Federal District] Judge [J. Skelley]

Wright, [who had ordered the public schools to begin desegregation with the first grade in September,] and "the real culprit, malefactor and double-crosser—the weasel, snake-head mayor of yours." In classic form the segregationist continued: "Don't wait for your daughter to be raped by these Congolese. Don't wait until the burr-heads are forced into your schools. Do something about it now." One witness described the meeting as "a gathering straight out of Nazi Germany" (Haas, 269–70).

If Perez wanted to foment riot, he got his wish. On the next day about 3,000 unruly teenagers marched through the city and invaded city hall, where they demanded to see the mayor. They then tried to invade the education building, but police and firemen with high-pressure hoses turned them back, and so off they went through the business district, hurling cans, bricks, and bottles at buses and cars that carried blacks. When blacks took to the streets in retaliation that evening, the police arrested 250—most of them black. In the following weeks mobs sometimes followed the girls and their parents home from school, where they smashed windows, slashed tires, and screamed threats. The father of one of the children was told by his supervisor that his wife and daughter had been shot; when one of the CORE workers who had demonstrated in September appeared at one of the integrated schools, he was attacked by the mob of screaming mothers. The police rescued him but for a year did nothing to dispel the mob of cursing mothers. They became such a celebrated part of the local entertainment industry that a cab driver correctly assumed that "the cheerleaders," as the mothers were called, were the first thing John Steinbeck wanted to see when, in December and on the last leg of his travels with Charlie, he drove in from Texas.

Stone would have to follow all this from afar, but he and Janice had felt the city percolating with particular vehemence after 15 May, when Judge Wright had issued his order. The segregationist school board then appealed to Jimmie Davis, who had just replaced the far more liberal Earl Long as governor, to intervene, and the state legislature countered Wright's order by prohibiting the allocation of any funds to integrated schools and by allowing Davis to close all the schools in the state if one of them became integrated. This is not the place to follow through the complex series of judicial stays and new racist fiats from governor and legislature, save to say that the base appeals of the elected officials were not lost on Stone.

Nor did Stone miss either the increasing pressure coming from federal challenges to the discriminatory practices of voter registration throughout the state during his nine months in Louisiana or, above all, the announcement in early August that the "newly formed state welfare board had approved a welfare spending cutback of $7,640,000, made possible by the purge of 22,650 children . . . from the state aid rosters because they live in common-law marriage homes or because their mothers bore illegitimate children after taking state aid . . . about 90 per cent of the children taken from the rolls were Negroes."[14] Stone recently remembered his response: "What was especially infuriating was that the people who were proclaiming their morality were so obviously corrupt and demagogic and in the wrong. . . . It was plainly traditional, racial demagoguery" (Solotaroff 1991).

The immediate victims of this demagoguery were mostly poor blacks, but it also helped to keep deformed the poor whites, who fervently accepted it. Looking back in 1988 at the 1960 workings of southern poverty, Stone wrote that his understandings of the political causes and consequences of poverty came later; at the time, "because I was young and male, the aspect of the poor South that most arrested my attention then was its anger and violence" ("KFB," 58). One suspects that there were a fair number of young male visitors to New Orleans in the early 1960s who moved through the streets without much thought of the city's violence and its potential for much greater violence. But they had not had to work through an overt bodily cringe acquired during those three and a half years at St. Ann's, where a good beating was always near at hand. When Robert and Janice Stone on weekend nights sat out on the balcony of their small apartment in the Quarter, they occasionally heard the pop of Saturday night specials. In 1967 Stone referred to the "small arms fire" as justification of his sense that "no one had any assurance of getting out of town alive."[15] Reminded of this in 1991, Janice Stone smiled and said that at the time she didn't feel that the shots in any way related to their future (JBS interview). Her husband still seemed to feel that his sense of endangerment was appropriate.[16]

Stone's immersion in black New Orleans came in May, when he began working on the 1960 census. Janice, who had been gathering census reports since the preceding month, worked largely in the white French Quarter, but her husband most often knocked on the doors of homes, apartments, and rented rooms in black sections of town. The short-term benefit of these jobs was that they bailed the Stones out economically. The long-term benefits were only fully realized with the publication of *A Hall of Mirrors*. Some of Stone's black respondents would sit him down with a cool drink and tell him their life's story. Apart from the way in which these encounters deepened his sense of the unfairness of much of American society and gave him the setting for five chapters of *A Hall of Mirrors*, Stone in part attributes the jumpy, colloquial feel of much of the language throughout the novel to the way black speech was, in 1960, "ringing my young literary bells . . . the rhythms and the raps . . . [were] sounding in my dreams; I [thought,] I'm ready to signify." The early chapters of *Hall* also owe a good deal to some of the whites Stone tracked down for the census: "the hard cases—the brothels, skid row, the B-girl dorms, the transvestites who scared the last census taker away" ("KFB," 59). A story in the paper about a woman who hanged herself in jail was a key source for Geraldine Crosby, the novel's second most important character. Some of the beatniks Stone hung out with contributed to the three entertaining and important *isolatoes* in the apartment below Rheinhardt's, and a few of the con men Stone met in his stint as an encyclopedia salesman, as well as "a kind of psychopathic hustler, part-time actor" (Solotaroff 1991), were ingredients of the different scam artists who populate the novel. Between the people he met, the racial struggle, the city's cresting violence potential, and the one-of-a-kind locale—seedy yet exotic, "like a cross between Paterson, N.J. and Port-au-Prince," in A. J. Liebling's words (61)—New Orleans was a windfall for someone who wanted to write about immediate experience but had grown up somehow feeling that authentic experience could be found only outside of New York ("IF," 24).

The economic relief of the census gathering proved temporary, for Stone's work was finished by the end of June. Though their daughter Deidre was delivered free at the Huey Long Charity Hospital on 15 June, Janice could not work for some weeks, and there were, of course, additional expenses. During the last months of the summer Stone spent most of the time trying to find work; finally, in September, he got into the seamen's union. His wife and daughter returned to New York while Stone stayed on to clear up expenses, mostly doing stevedore work on the docks, though he did take two short voyages to Curaçao and the Antilles. In October he joined his wife and daughter in New York.

"I Want to Write Novels"

In New Orleans Stone had written no fiction, just some poetry that he read to jazz accompaniment, in an attempt to feed his newly enlarged family. He thought about writing plays but never considered attempting a novel. As Stone told Charles Ruas 20 years later, "I wasn't ready to write a novel at that point in my life. I started the novel when I must have been about twenty-six [actually, twenty-four], and prior to that I had not enough sense of life lived in time, the shape of people's lives; there was no pattern that I saw in things until I got to be that age. When I was twenty-one, twenty-two, I was no Carson McCullers—I did not have any vision, I just didn't know enough" (Ruas, 269).

If, as Dr. Johnson observed, the prospect of immediate hanging marvelously concentrates one's faculties, so too might intense economic pressure have accelerated Stone's sense that he did know enough to begin a novel—and just a bit more than a year after his return to New York, not the three or four years that he would recall later with Ruas. Once back in the city, Stone got a job writing copy, mostly for stores that sold cheap furniture. He hated the work and did it for the five or six months that enabled him to get five or six months of unemployment compensation, which was at that time about $35 a week. Meanwhile, Janice Stone had returned to waitressing and then gotten into keypunching, a skill that often kept them afloat for the next six or seven years. As she remembers the time: "There was no money to return to college; it was enough to pay the rent and put food on the table" (JBS interview).

And so, one day late in 1961, Stone put down *The Great Gatsby* and decided that "I understood patterns in life. I figured, I can't sell this understanding, or smoke it, so I will write a novel. I then started to write *A Hall of Mirrors*" (Woods, 27). To kick off the project, Stone took a bus to Stroudsburg, Pennsylvania, on the Delaware Water Gap, stayed at an old inn in the town, and spent the weekend walking about, contemplating the novel he was going to write. During the winter of 1962 he got enough done to send to the Stanford writing program about 30 pages: the first two chapters of the novel, which introduce the two most important characters, Rheinhardt and Geraldine, and some pages dealing with Morgan Rainey, the third principal, who would first appear one-third of the way through the completed novel.

A Bohemian Arcadia

The acceptance to the writing program came in the spring of 1962, and in June the Stones traveled to San Francisco to work at summer jobs—he as a management trainee, she as a keypuncher—until the seminar and the segments of the $2,500 stipend began in September. At that time they moved to an inexpensive apartment in Menlo Park, hard by Perry Lane, the main stem of Stanford's bohemian quarter. In *The*

Electric Kool-Aid Acid Test (1968), Tom Wolfe describes the locale that Ken Kesey had traveled to from Oregon four years earlier:

> As bohemias go, Perry Lane was Arcadia, Arcadia just off the Stanford golf course. It was a cluster of two-room cottages with weathery wood shingles in an oak forest, only not just amid trees and greenery, but among vines, honeysuckle tendrils, all buds and shoots and swooping tendrils and twitterings like the best of Arthur Rackham and *Honey Bear*. Not only that, it had true cultural cachet. Thorstein Veblen had lived there. So had two Nobel Prize winners everybody knew about though the names had escaped them. . . . [T]here was always something of an atmosphere of communal living. Nobody's door was ever shut on Perry Lane, except when they were pissed off. . . . Periodically somebody would suggest an orgy or a three-day wine binge, but the model was always that old Zorba the Greek romanticism of sandals and simplicity and back to first principles. Periodically they would take pilgrimages 40 miles north to North Beach to see how it was actually done. (36)

Things had changed a bit in four years. Life in the Perry Lane section was still sweet: "When I went to California it was like everything turned Technicolor" (Ruas, 273). The flora, great climate, weekend parties, and a fair number of cottages inhabited by stimulating young artists still prevailed. But more powerful drugs than marijuana had come to Perry Lane, and the pilgrimages away were not north to San Francisco but about 15 miles south to the town of La Honda. There Kesey, flush from the great success of *One Flew over the Cuckoo's Nest* (1962), published eight months earlier, had just purchased "his Low Rent Versailles, over the mountain and through the woods" (Wolfe, 55)—a house and a fair amount of movie and sound equipment—and was dispersing equally substantial amounts of LSD to his revelers. By January one of the visitors was Bob Stone, who said almost 20 years later, "Sometimes I feel like I went to a party one day in 1963 and the party spilled out and rolled down the street until it covered the whole country and changed the world."[17] Stone would later argue for the possibility of raising the world's consciousness through moral, carefully crafted art. At Kesey's place he sought to raise it less laboriously: according to Hugh O'Haire, Stone experimented there with "Human Jazz": improvising stories to a background of improvised sounds.[18]

Whether or not the ferment around Perry Lane and in La Honda changed the world, it certainly helped to change Stone and the book that he was writing. To his experiments with LSD he has attributed both his renunciation of conventional realism—a rejection that arguably turned his first novel into a much richer, more various work—and the return of the religious concerns he thought he had permanently put behind him when he was 17. I will consider the pervasiveness and duration of Stone's rejection of realistic representation in the next two chapters and will say here only that in terms of his life and work, the effects of the religious experience he had on LSD were far more significant. Stone told Steve Chapple that,

> What I witnessed or thought I witnessed in my stoned state was an enormously powerful, resolving presence within which all phenomenology was contained. It wasn't a God that said you're good and you're bad. It wasn't a God that said you're going to heaven and you're going to hell. It was more Tibetan, more an Indian conception of God than God as a moral arbitrator. But there was a suggestion that everything was all right. In spite of all the horrors, way down deep, everything was all right. . . . I don't know if that dimension really exists. I suspect so. . . . Agnosticism is literally true in my case: *I don't know*. But I'm not going to say no. The experience was too intense. . . . I'm temperamentally inclined to religion. I do not have faith. I don't. I lack it. I feel it as a lack. (Chapple, 39)[19]

A few months earlier, Stone put it this way: "I feel a very deep connection to the existential tradition of God as an absence—not a meaningless void, but a negative presence we live in terms of. I do have the sense of a transcendent plane from which I'm barred and I want to play off of it" (Woods, 48). God's presence as a form of absence is to varying degrees inscribed into each of Stone's five novels.

There were important but less transcendent benefactions of the California experience. When I asked Stone about the musical background that made possible the relatively erudite discussion of the Mozart Clarinet Quintet in *Hall*, he spoke of his near giddiness at having access to all the resources of Stanford and of his particular love for the music library. As for the writing workshop that brought him to Palo Alto, it must have been extremely supportive, for its other members "listened to the successive chapters with an enthusiasm that grew by the week and that was curiously untouched by envy. They looked upon Stone himself with a gingerly, oblique deference, as something special, anointed, his lips touched with a hot coal. He was the one who would not only publish his book—they all expected [him] to do that—but publish it big."[20]

And Stone's sense of his creative worth and potential had to be heightened when, toward the end of the school year, he received a Houghton Mifflin Literary Fellowship and signed a contract (including an advance) with the Boston publisher.

These emoluments helped the Stones to get through the next year. The Stegner fellowships were for one year only, but he was named a fellow for 1963–64 through a generous act of Wallace Stegner's. Late in 1963, just before he was to enter Montalvo, a writer's colony in the Bay Area, doctors diagnosed a brain tumor as the cause of a broken blood vessel in one of Stone's eyes. At the least, there were expensive tests; expensive surgery and imminent death seemed more likely. The Stones had no hospitalization insurance, but at this point, though he profoundly disapproved of the lifestyle Stone had adopted, Stegner stepped in and declared Stone a member of the writing program so that the expensive tests and hospitalization would be covered by the Stanford medical plan. The two holes that were drilled into his head revealed no tumor, just intercranial tension. With shaven skull, two holes in his head, and severe headaches, Stone could return to his novel and the prospect of living for a good while longer than had seemed likely when the original diagnosis had been made.

Earlier in the fall the Stones had decided that he was never going to get his novel done in the perpetual party of northern California; moreover, Janice Stone wanted to return to working on her degree in psychology at CCNY. Long-range economic pressures had been intensified by the birth of their second child, Ian, on 24 May 1963, and a career in social work, which might be both secure and gratifying for Janice, seemed like a good idea. She and the children had left for New York before Stone's neurological difficulties flared up, and after two months of Montalvo, punctuated by weekends in La Honda, Stone moved back to New York in the spring of 1964 with about two-thirds of a first draft of *A Hall of Mirrors* done.

The Securing of Place

To get some sense of just how far Stone had come in the 42 or 43 months since he returned to New York from New Orleans, we might turn for a moment to a memoir by Stone's exact contemporary, Raymond Carver. Like Stone, Carver was in 1964 in his midtwenties, married, and with two children. Since both of his children were born before Carver was 20, the Carver children were four to six years older

than the Stone children. In his memoir "Fires" (1983), Carver remembers a moment at just this time, in the mid-1960s, when he was in a
laundromat in Iowa City; it was already past the time when he should
have left to pick up his children, but he still had not gotten dryers for his
five or six loads of wet clothes: "I remember thinking at that moment,
amid the feelings of helpless frustration that had me close to tears, that
nothing—and, brother, I mean nothing—that ever happened to me on
this earth could come anywhere close, could possibly be as important to
me, could make as much difference, as the fact that I had two children.
And that I would always have them and always find myself in this position of unrelieved responsibility and permanent distraction."[21] Carver
goes on to describe how the ceaseless financial pressure drove him to
"some crap job or another . . . sawmill jobs, janitor jobs, deliveryman
jobs, service station jobs, stockroom boy jobs—name it, I did it" (40).
He did not get his first white-collar job until he was well past 30. Often
Carver could not find an hour or two a day to try to write, and between
the constant financial pressure, the bedrock uncertainty of the future,
the perception that somehow the children had taken over the house and
were running it, he attempted only forms he could finish quickly—
poems and stories. These conditions were to continue until he was close
to 40; he did not receive any meaningful encouragement from an editor
or publisher until he was in his midthirties.

But Stone at 26 had had his worth as a writer affirmed by the Stegner
fellowship, by the support of Wallace Stegner himself, by all the admira-
tion he had received from local writers in and out of the seminar, and by
the imprimaturs, from a prestigious publisher, of a contract, an advance,
and a cash award that was to permit him and his family to travel in
England and France for ten weeks in the summer of 1964. When funds
ran out in Europe, he had the cachet to wire his agent for money. Carver
wrote that "the greatest single influence on my life, and on my writing,
directly and indirectly, has has been my two children. . . . From beginning to end of our habitation under the same roof—some nineteen years
in all—there wasn't any area of my life where their heavy and often bale-
ful influence didn't reach" (37). Most of Stone's postmarital influences
were benign: his sense that he could deal with his internal tensions by
writing; the stability and encouragement and frequent economic support
that Janice gave him; and all that came to him from Palo Alto and
Houghton Mifflin. And his children do not seem to have been any great
hindrance. Looking back on this period, Janice Stone remembers her
husband writing his book on the kitchen table, herself studying in the

living room, and the children playing with each other in the bedroom: "Sometimes I'd have to ask them to be more quiet, but they weren't that much of a problem. They were each other's best buddies; they hung out together, and each was the other's main source of companionship for a number of years" (JBS interview).[22]

All Stone had to do was to finish the book, but this would take a bit more than two years, until the summer of 1966. For one thing, *A Hall of Mirrors* is fairly long, over 400 pages, and even at this stage of his career, Stone was an unusually careful stylist. As he would say to William Crawford Woods, "I use the white space. I'm interested in precise meaning and in reverberation, in associative levels. What you're trying to do when you write is to crowd the reader out of his own space and occupy it with yours, in a good cause." It is only through these reverberations that the relatively suspenseful surfaces of Stone's novels can be related to his underlying concerns: "You choose words that open up deeper and deeper levels of existence by sustaining a sound which perfectly serves the narrative and which at the same time relates through a series of associations to the larger questions" (Woods, 31).[23] Even for a writer with an ear as good as Stone's, this sort of writing is likely to go slowly. Though Stone feels that he works almost all the time, no two of his five novels have been published less than four years apart; the other three intervals between novels are each seven years.

We will shortly be considering what must have been another impediment: the way in which the political vision imbedded in *A Hall of Mirrors* was being challenged by the progress of the civil rights movement, the intensity and pervasiveness of the antiwar protest, and the eruption of a whole new set of cultural and personal possibilities in the counterculture to a degree that was inconceivable when Stone began writing the book in 1961. And as relatively frictionless as his family life was, full-time writing sometimes had to cease and money had to be made. Stone returned to his pre-Stanford mode of working at low-paying jobs just long enough to collect unemployment compensation, but the jobs proved to be better fodder for his fiction than writing copy for low-end furniture. His first two employers, the *National Mirror* and *Inside News*, were the sources for *Nightbeat*, the *National Enquirer*–like tabloid of Stone's second novel, *Dog Soldiers*. Compelled to construct and palm off sensational fictions as true happenings, Stone and his fellow toilers would give each other outlandish titles and then try to meet the challenge of writing the ensuing stories. Pseudo news items catchily titled "Hoarder Crushed by Small Change," "Wedding Night Trick Breaks

Bride's Back" and "Skydiver Devoured by Starving Birds" first appeared in the *National Mirror* or *Inside News* before they became part of the seedy past of one of the principals in *Dog Soldiers*.

His own mood swings also delayed completion. Stone has frequently admitted that he has periods when he is too depressed to write, and some who knew him even during the high years in California have spoken of the darkness of his moods.[24] But Stone finally did finish his novel during the summer of 1966, and then, for the year until it was published, had a pleasant job as an assistant at an art gallery in midtown Manhattan. There were a few negative reviews after *A Hall of Mirrors* was published in August 1967. For example, an anonymous reviewer for *Publisher's Weekly* called the book "a meandering, pretentiously written novel that does achieve a certain nightmare power at times, but never rises to the heights one expects of a winner of a Houghton Mifflin Literary Fellowship, which it attained." But the two other reviews that appeared in the same trade journal were positive,[25] and the reviewers of more widely read or prestigious publications were, as a whole, celebratory. The brilliance and variety of the prose, the palpability of the New Orleans setting, the range and depth of Stone's imagination and his sympathy for America's underclass, the trenchancy of his critique of America, and the solidity of his characterizations were some aspects of the novel that were praised in publications like *Newsweek*, the *New York Times*, *Commonweal* and the *New Republic*. Stone would in 1968 receive the William Faulkner Award for a first novel. In the same year he sold the movie rights, and during 1969 he was paid well for writing and working beyond his first draft of the screenplay. With these earnings, and with an advance on his second novel, Stone and his family could live in England for four years. And when he returned to live in the United States in 1973, he did not have to seek a job on an assembly line or a loading dock or something more genteel in a bookstore or an art gallery: he returned as an instructor of creative writing at Princeton. With the writing of *A Hall of Mirrors*, Stone had conclusively lifted himself out of the kind of marginality for which his origins would seem to have shaped him.

Chapter Two
A Hall of Mirrors

The Dating of the Milieu

A Hall of Mirrors is emphatically punctuated by the boundaries of the New Orleans experience of the protagonist, Rheinhardt. It begins on Mardi Gras, with Rheinhardt on a bus heading toward the city, and would seem to end about eight months later with him walking toward the station to catch a bus that will take him to Kansas City and then to Denver. The terminal date of the novel is difficult to be sure about: the last date given in the text is 1 May, and it seems as if not more than two months of action follow, but the weather has turned autumnal during the book's last dramatized days. The dates of Rheinhardt's stay in the city could correspond with Stone's had not the novel's third most important character, the tormented Morgan Rainey, dated a journal entry 16 April 1963.

This dating creates a good many problems. When Stone moved Geraldine and Rheinhardt into the same apartment on St. Philip Street in the French Quarter where he lived with his wife, he made the Quarter the way it was in 1960, when an address there "still carried with it more than a suggestion of bohemian impropriety" ("KFB," 57),[1] and where there was only one large hotel, instead of the six large hotels of the upscale section that, according to Stone, existed just a few years later. The New Orleans of the novel is in a more important way what New Orleans was between February and October of 1960: a city waiting to explode. Most important, if, as Stone told Charles Ruas in 1981, he could not start a novel until he had gained a coherent sense of "the shape of people's lives," and of the "pattern . . . in things" (Ruas, 269), his projection of the punitive unfairness of the priests at St. Ann's upon the governors and law enforcers of New Orleans is a large component of the pattern that he saw. The political vision that emerges from *Hall* is, in its simplest terms, a heightened version of that gospel of the 1950s counterculture, Allen Ginsberg's *Howl* (1956). Moloch rules America and maddens, kills, or damages in some other way all decent people; those in political power are pervasively corrupt and power-mad, and only fools believe that they can help to effect a change for the better in the collective order of things. However much John F. Kennedy's luster has dimmed in the past 25 years, it certainly shone in 1963. However cynical such appeals to idealism as the New Frontier or the Peace Corps might have been, they are inconceivable in the America of *A Hall of Mirrors*. Moreover, having received the inciting animus of the civil rights movement, many aspects of the American counterculture were by 1963 aflame with the possibilities of individual and social transformation. As Morris Dickstein observed, "[T]he spirit of the sixties witnessed the transformation of utopian religion into the terms of secular humanism . . . the sixties translated the Edenic impulse once again into political terms."[2]

The only transformation anticipated by members of the New Orleans counterculture of *Hall* is just a deepening of the generally hellish social conditions around them. Having just discovered that his census taking is a cover-up for a plot to strike blacks from the welfare rolls, Rainey appeals to Rheinhardt for information about the racists behind the plot and, eventually, for concern. Rheinhardt gives him neither and in this way justifies his job as a disc jockey and newscaster for WUSA, a violently racist radio station: "[T]hings are taking a cold turn. . . . One by one the warm weather creatures will topple dead with frosted eyelids. . . . The creatures of the cold will proliferate. The air will become thin and difficult to breathe. . . . Very shortly it will start to snow."[3] When Rainey argues for innate moral imperatives—"But there is such a thing as a gift of life. Humanness is given. Clay was raised to consciousness. Blood was made warm"—Rheinhardt's vision of the evolution of a new inhumanity receives support from two of his three beatnik neighbors. Bogdanovich counters Rainey with, "All that gift of life and humanness is a trip. Blood, man—blood was made warm to keep a scene circulating . . . that's the only reason blood is warm." Marvin adds that they all know about "warm blood and gifts and humanness. . . . But it don't apply now, you dig?" (*HM*, 255). All of this is reinforced by a fairly sustained pattern of water and fish imagery that fuses the new moral age of ice with what Melville called in *Moby-Dick* "the universal cannibalism of the sea; all whose creatures prey upon each other, carrying on eternal war since the world began."[4] More significantly, Stone structured the incidents of the novel so that the main characters who are capable of love and concern for others, Geraldine and Rainey, are killed off, and

Rheinhardt—who celebrates his ability to survive in the cold new world and claims that he is really "Jack Frost, baby. I'm the original" (*HM*, 253)—lives on. This, the novel's predictive vision, coalesces with the advice Rheinhardt gives to those who cannot adjust to the cold turn: "Despair and die" (*HM*, 256).

Stone conceded in my 1991 interview with him that he was really writing about the New Orleans of 1960 and that he dated Rainey's journal 1963 to "make the book more recent." This attempt to inject contemporaneity only distracts one from the book's almost continual display of merits, as does Rainey's noticing "newspaper headlines proclaiming the national's daily bag of Asiatics" (*HM*, 266), reporting that began only in 1965. I am not nattering over trivialities here. When one interviewer commented that "*A Hall of Mirrors* is a cohesive book, considering the duration of its composition and the conditions under which it was written," Stone responded, "It was necessary that it be cohesive. I was looking for a vision of America, for a statement about the American condition. I was after a book that would be as ambitious as possible. I wanted to be an American Gogol if I could, I wanted to write *Dead Souls*. All of the characters represent ideas about America, about an America in a period of extraordinary, vivid transition" (Woods, 39). Earlier in the interview he had said, "I put everything I knew into that book. It covers the sixties from the Kennedy assassination through the civil rights movement to the beginning of acid, the hippies, the war" (Woods, 28).

A Hall of Mirrors does a good many things, but these are not among them. Only the civil rights movement surfaces in the novel, but it barely breaks water. The emphasis is far more on the racist reaction to the movement, and the terms of the struggle are very much those of 1960: Stone used in the novel the black protesters marching around a department store, the striking of illegitimate children from welfare rolls, and a riot inspired by white demagogues. The title of the novel is a phrase from Robert Lowell's "Children of Light" (1943), and its epigraph is the whole of Lowell's poem, which was written at a time when the poet, in an apocalyptic phase of his newly embraced Catholicism, was predicting imminent, pervasive union with Christ. Rheinhardt's imagery for the coming age of moral paralysis, which will further distance us from Christ, is reminiscent of the agnostic Lowell of a decade later in "Inauguration Day, 1953." After lamenting the triumph of mechanization, the way the dominant movement of the time is of subways and elevated trains, not of General Grant and his "blue immor-

tals,"[5] Lowell confronts in the last five lines the experiential entropy
America has chosen:

> Ice. Ice. Our wheels no longer move.
> Look, the fixed stars, all just alike
> as lack-land atoms, split apart,
> and the Republic summons Ike
> the mausoleum in her heart. (ll. 6–10)

The novel's sense of the future as a deepening of Eisenhower America
is appropriate enough for a work set in the last months of his second
term. But during the time that he wrote more than half of the first draft
of *Hall*, Stone had a good working knowledge of northern
California–style projects to regenerate America: political action, LSD,
and other forms of larky put-ons that were a part of Merry
Pranksterism.[6] He put nothing of what he knew about contemporary
optimism into the finished novel. Had he done so, *that* would have seriously damaged its thematic coherence, and I suspect that his growing
perception that his vision of the future was a thing of the past contributed considerably to his taking five years to complete *Hall*. Put differently, the novel's depiction of the violence, the social injustice, and the
often sick sexuality of American life is not all that unfair to mid-1960s
America, but the hopelessness, the apparent absence of experiential
alternatives, is.

In my opinion, Stone's compromise was to preserve the 1960 mindset
but to inject the 1963 updating and a Vietnam reference, and also to tip
his hat, with the stylistic experiments in the book's last 80 pages, to the
weird eruptions of the later 1960s. I am referring to his forays into
expressionism, as when the black Lester Clotho turns night into morning
and his appearance into that of a white man, or into surrealism, as when
S. B. Prothwaite, a dispossessed and deranged survivor from a 1915
IWW time warp, drives, in a truck loaded with his dishes, rotting furniture, wife's ashes, and a good deal of dynamite, into the racist rally that
culminates the novel. Even before these turns, Stone undermined the
danger of the right through a presentation of right-wing zealots that is
far more parodic than anything in the preceding two-thirds of the novel.
How seriously can we fear the triumph of zanies with mindsets like that
of "Brigadier General Justin Jurgen Truckee, U.S.A., (ret.) a specialist in
Mongolian archery . . . [whose] global strategy was guided by his dis-

covery that the Russo-Chinese monolith planned to follow its siren call for nuclear disarmament by unleashing hundreds of millions of mounted bowmen over an unsuspecting earth" (*HM*, 286)?

Stone's Narrative Strategies

In their simplest terms, Stone's narrative practices are unusually consistent for a first-rate fictioneer concerned with capturing extremes of experience. All of the five novels and four short stories he has so far published are written in the third person, and since Stone writes within the impressionist tradition, the reader experiences the great majority of the works' locales and happenings through the sensibilities of the principal characters. Stone tries to drive the reader as far into these increasingly taxed sensibilities as possible, and his narrators rarely offer information or observations about a character that are beyond the character's competence.[7] There is only one center of consciousness in each of the stories, and four of the five novels have three principals: two male and one female.[8] Between two and four times in each novel, to advance the plot or reveal how other characters regard one of the principals, Stone either presents brief scenes in which the principals are absent or briefly enters the mind of someone talking with a principal.[9] Stone introduces his main characters into the narrative at different points and then brings them into contact, which always proves to be painful, sometimes fatal. All of this holds even more schematically true in the fifth novel, *Children of Light*, which has two instead of three principals: some of the novel's other characters expend a fair amount of effort to prevent the man and the woman from the interaction that kills one of them. Appropriately, this author who says his sensibility was in good part shaped by radio programs explains his technique by saying, "I was always attracted to the idea of bringing different elements together. One of my favorite radio programs was 'Tell Me a Story,' in which people were presented with three things to weave into one" (Woods, 46).

The Structure of the Novel

A Hall of Mirrors is a tightly structured work of 38 unnumbered parts spread fairly evenly over three books of almost exactly equal length: the first two are 135 pages long, the third 130. Rheinhardt's angle of vision dominates in half of the sections, Geraldine's in nine, and Rainey's in ten. Geraldine and Rheinhardt meet two-thirds of the way through book 1 and begin cohabiting perhaps six hours and ten pages later when, appropriately enough, the alcoholic Rheinhardt passes out in her room. A week later, with some of the advance from his new job with the radio station, he rents the apartment on St. Philip Street in the French Quarter. On the next-to-last page of book 1, as Rheinhardt is taking Geraldine up the stairs to show her the apartment, they are struck by the gawky, embarrassed style of Morgan Rainey, walking down.

The point of view, which had resided with Rheinhardt and Geraldine in book 1, passes to Rainey with the first sentence of book 2 as he receives instructions for his new job in the black slums. Though told that his temporary job of interviewing welfare clients involves neither counseling nor evaluation nor analysis, just discerning income, he hopes to use the job to end somehow the painful isolation in which he has been living. One of the two main lines of action in book 2 consists of Rainey's painful collisions with all the damaged blacks he sees, until he finds, with his discovery of and determination to expose the welfare scam, the cause that might again bind him to humankind. The other main line of action is the collapse of the relationship between Rheinhardt and Geraldine. Rainey wants to ease the suffering of others, but between the cynicism of the welfare system and the limits of his own damaged self, he cannot. Rheinhardt could provide the badly bruised Geraldine with the sanctuary from the world she desperately needs, but he refuses to. As with an electrical system, the touching of Rainey's line of action to that of Geraldine and Rheinhardt results in a sudden flare-up: Rheinhardt's abusive response to Rainey's appeal for support earns Geraldine's criticism, which precipitates so cruel a response from Rheinhardt that Geraldine can only move out. Before she does, she and Rainey briefly draw close, but his need is so immense, with such a strong pathological component, that finally she is repulsed. She realizes at the end of book 2 how badly she needs Rheinhardt, but still she moves out.

When we next see Geraldine, in book 3, she has deteriorated badly; she is seeking Rheinhardt out at the rally, toward which all of the preceding pages of the section move, and at which Stone brings the three principals together for the last time. Rheinhardt talks briefly to the dying Rainey, who has been blown up by Prothwaite's dynamite, in their attempt to stop the rally. As he flees the stadium, he hears Geraldine calling his name from a distance but cannot find her, and so, with only a respite at a playground, where the police pick her up, Geraldine goes from the stadium to her death in a jail cell. At novel's end, we leave Rheinhardt heading toward the bus station, degrading with histrionic protestations the regret he feels about Geraldine's death.

Rheinhardt as the Primary Reflector

As for *Hall* as an American *Dead Souls*, if Stone's novel is much more highly structured and lacks the range of characters and locales of Gogol's, both authors attempted to make major statements about the rot in their national cultures, in large part through the attempts of rogue protagonists to better their conditions. But what a different book would Stone have written had he placed at its center an American version of Tchitchikov, some perversely energetic, relentless pursuer of social advancement for whom the destructive underside of experience holds no fascination, who lacks a sense of irony, a discerning eye into himself and others, playfulness, and culture. Instead we have Rheinhardt, who has all of these attributes to a degree that makes him a most appropriate conduit for the majority of imaginative assertions coming from a creator who was recently a beatnik poet and would always be a tenacious survivor, who would later say that "irony is my friend and brother" (Woods, 52). For example, lines from Shakespeare, Dante, Donne, and Hopkins flow easily from Rheinhardt, but they are always used with conscious self-irony. Twice in the course of the novel Rheinhardt says, "Defend me friends, I am but hurt" (*HM*, 24, 181), a wonderful line and an appropriate one, for he is in real trouble when he utters it. But, as Rheinhardt surely knows, the line belongs not to the protagonist of the play Stone most likes to quote, but to Hamlet's Uncle Claudius. (Three times in the novel Rheinhardt also quotes the protagonist of Shakespeare's *Richard III*.) Toward the end of *Hall*, when he learns that Geraldine has hanged herself, Rheinhardt pleads for sympathy from Bogdanovich, claiming that he is dying, that he is hurt. Before he leaves for the bus station, he cannot resist saying, "I am but hurt" (*HM*, 398). Now the line is even more undercut than before, this time by Rheinhardt's self-loathing: he knows both how hateful it is that he protests his suffering when Geraldine has died in good part because of his treatment of her, and how likely it is that, however hurt he is, he will survive, and on terms he considers loathsome.

At one point in book 2 Geraldine lists Rheinhardt's vices: "You're sick, you're nervous, you're a drunk, you're cowardly, you're a mouthoff" (*HM*, 226). To these we could add that he is on occasion manipulative, sadistic, ungenerous, and amoral. I could go on, but Rheinhardt has enough patches of endearing behavior to remind one of the moment when, after listing all his flaws, "satisfied with his own severity, positively enjoying the hardness and factual rigor of his judgment," Saul Bellow's *Herzog* cannot resist reflecting, "*But how charming we remain notwithstanding.*"[10] Rheinhardt gets off dozens of endearing gestures: sportively waving a wrench to show that he is a willing worker on an assembly line; lustily joining in a song at a mission; telling a greedy young Bible salesman that he will "return to Wisconsin like a merchant prince" (*HM*, 3). Until he hears of Geraldine's death, he never shows self-pity; in particular, he contemplates the deepening of his alcoholic pathology as casually as if he were trimming his nails. What most interestingly complicates the reader's response to Stone's protagonist is the way some of his most hateful performances are transformed by zany humor that I, for one, find irresistible. For example, after he gets his job at WUSA by putting together a five-minute newscast that appeals to some of the most vile racist prejudices, Rheinhardt repairs with the $100 advance on his salary to a seafood restaurant to celebrate with a plate of shrimp and, in keeping with the self-destructiveness always hard by his ambition, beer and bourbon. In the first of the internal colloquies with which most Stone male protagonists justify their immoral or otherwise unsound behavior, the self-admitted son of a bitch in Rheinhardt so trenchantly justifies his newscast to what he calls his "whining fat boy of a soul" that the fat boy surrenders: "All right. Hold! Enough! If you stop, I'll buy you a drink!" Readers of a psychoanalytic bent might pounce at this point: "So that's the way it works with Rheinhardt: it's the familiar suicidal pattern in which the forces of what superego he has combine with the forces of the id to move him further toward destruction."

But what follows has a way of making the insight a little irrelevant. Rheinhardt defends his ability to combine the shrimp and booze in the sudden early spring heat by launching into a very funny account of how, prior to his recent return to Christendom, he had lived for seven years in San Fernando Poo on the west coast of Africa. There, "in the hottest part of the day . . . the splendid Ashanti oarsmen would beach their dugout canoes and hail us with cries of 'Jambo! Jambo!' . . . which means 'Peace' in their melodic language . . . the Ashanti would haul out great masses of shrimp which we would boil in merry wrought-iron cauldrons and eat in dozens with Cayenne pepper in the manner of Paul du Chaillu. And that done we would lie back on the burning sand, our swollen bellies heaving in the merciless sun and each drink a quart of bourbon." After turning to the staring oyster opener and pleasantly hailing him with "Jambo" (*HM*, 119–20). Rheinhardt careens into a farrago, with himself as a committed, deranged liberal, that is even funnier, but it is terminated by his being struck and thrown out.

But all of this is dank humorlessness compared to his antics at the rally. His role as the master of ceremonies seems to offer the long-awaited chance to rise in the hierarchy of Matthew T. Bingamon, the radical right-wing tycoon who owns WUSA, the soap factory in which Rheinhardt met Geraldine, and a good deal more. Rheinhardt's primary preparation for this, the main chance, is to get high on marijuana with his three beatnik neighbors and to call negative attention to himself by arriving with them an hour late. Once arrived, he greets the most substantial political figure there, Senator Archie Rice, by blurting out the name of the diner where he thinks he might have met the senator, who immediately perceives that Rheinhardt is riding some form of inebriation. Deprived of a liquor chaser by the musicians, who stole the old-fashioned mix in the performers' tent, Rheinhardt fortifies his powers by smoking more marijuana cigarettes. By the time Rice correctly accuses the rally organizers of trying to foment a riot, Rheinhardt is a good many tokes over the line:

> "What nonsense," Farley said. "That's nonsense isn't it Rheinhardt?"
> "It is nonsense, Farley," Rheinhardt said. "I mean look at the mind-body problem—there's nonsense for you."
> "Why he's crazy as a loon," Senator Rice cried, staring at Rheinhardt. "Look at his eyes."
> "He gets attacks," Farley said. (*HM*, 357)

But our hero has a chance to redeem himself when he is told to go out and somehow quiet the increasingly maddened audience of 70,000. In *Laughter* (1900), Henri Bergson designates as one of the sources of the comic the interaction of two lines of action that would seem to have no chance of ever colliding.[11] As an example of the comic possibilities of reciprocal interference—Bergson's term for the strategy—Rheinhardt's performance is for me right up there with Harpo Marx's descent upon *Il Trovatore* in *A Night at the Opera* (1935). Having taken to "walking gingerly through red snow" (*HM*, 361) and to seeing hallucinatory rodents

in the shadows, Rheinhardt takes to the microphones narcotically convinced that he can conduct the crowd—70,000 near-maniacs who have
been shrieking crazed threats on their own bullhorns, striking at him
with a string of hot dogs, tossing seatmates out of the stands, and trying
to run down and lynch two black groundskeepers—in the key of his
choice, G minor, with just the right treatment of thirds, sixths, and,
above all, appropriate tempi, about which he reassures himself in gibber-
ish German: "My time *ist bestigge.*" What finally comes out of his mouth
is reminiscent of Thoreau's account of someone who finally has a chance
to shout something into the dowager queen's earhorn and discovers that
he has nothing to say:

> "Why is there all this light?" Rheinhardt asked. "What's the mean-
> ing of all these microphones?"
> He was not prepared to conduct. (*HM*, 363–64)

The narrative line then shifts for two and a half pages to follow
Rainey and Prothwaite making their dash into the stadium. Then we cut
back to Rheinhardt as he gives in to pleas from his terrified confreres to
speak to the mob about God and country. His theme is the power of
American innocence, but, on his wings of cannabis leaves, he soon soars
beyond appeals to recognizable prejudices: "We are not perverts with
rotten brains as the English is. We are not a sordid little turd like the
French. We are not strutting maniacs like the gibroney and the grease-
ball!" (Mr. Rheinhardt, a question from the audience: "What is a
gibroney?") American innocence exported is a terrifying product—a
napalm bomb "with a heart"; its domestic personification is a formidably
empowered "fat old lady on her way to the world's fair. . . . [E]very time
she tells her little daughter that Jesus drank carbonated grape juice—
then, somewhere in the world a Jew raises quivering gray fingers to his
weasely throat and falls dead." But the sweet lady is threatened by a
"gigantic leering coon with a monstrously distended member" waiting
in a watermelon patch. If the rapist succeeds, "it's gonna rain bearded
men. . . . Our boys in uniform all over the world will turn queer and toss
up their hair in sequins and there'll be no more napalm bombs,
Americans" (*HM*, 367–68). And so forth. We never find out how successful Rheinhardt's crazed cadenza might have been because
Prothwaite's truck comes in, is blown up, and turns the pandemonium
of the rally in a new direction.

Wasted Talent

Stone has said that he gave his protagonist no first name because he wanted to emphasize his alienation (Solotaroff 1991), and that the surname came from the Belgian gypsy guitarist Django Reinhardt (Bonetti, 100). We are to feel that the fictional character could also have been a great musician, first as a clarinetist, then as a conductor, but that his "beautiful musical part . . . a thick and highly perishable [*sic*] stuff like cream which, when allowed to settle because you have not the energy and manhood to wrangle it, turns into a deadly and poisonous bile of which one rightly and subsequently dies" (*HM*, 48–49). This is Rheinhardt on himself, and since he's capable of shrewd, often withering self-evaluation, we should not immediately dismiss this as an explanation for why a potential world-class artist becomes a largely conscienceless con man who moves further into alcoholic pathology during the six to eight months of the novel. But his account is so partial. Were alcoholism, beating his wife while he was crazed on marijuana, and leaving his wife and child causes or effects of his inability to manage his talent? We know of the overwhelming experience of the audition that gained him entrance to Juilliard, but what was his experience after he was admitted into this extraordinary concentration of musical talent? Not a word is offered on just how he failed to harness his talent there. When William Crawford Woods commented in 1984 on Rheinhardt's inability "to make America deliver on the American Dream," Stone responded, "What I'm always trying to do is define that process in American life that puts people in a state of anomie, of frustration. The national promise is so great that a tremendous bitterness is evoked by its elusiveness. That was Fitzgerald's subject, and it's mine. So many people go bonkers in this country—I mean, they're doing all the right things and they're still not getting off" (Woods, 49).

This is Stone the determinist speaking, but it was the residual Catholic, with his emphasis upon free will, who a few years earlier used as his point of departure the obvious fact that Rheinhardt does not begin to do all the right things. According to Stone, his character feels "he lacks the energy and manhood" to channel his talent because "he just doesn't have the moral substance to be what he should be—a great musician. In an act of spite, he leaves his family, leaves art, and ultimately, leaves good. He chooses the bad" (Ruas, 276). In his 1987 essay "The Reason for Stories," Stone conceded that artists with very little moral substance can assume an existing ethics and create first-rate, highly moral art. I suspect that he knew this in 1981, as he knew it back in the 1960s when he created Rheinhardt. Of Stone's five novels, *Hall* is the one that argues most schematically that what is worst in America cripples or kills what is best in individuals. But then, there is Rheinhardt, in certain crucial ways the most talented of all of Stone's characters, and we have no clear sense of the workings of the forces that changed him from someone who enables others to transcend pain through his art to someone who collaborates with racists, who chooses as his musical signature "Walk Don't Run" because it is played so often about New Orleans in 1960.

Stone's after-the-fact explanation of "spite" doesn't begin to explain the process by which Rheinhardt turned his back upon the experience of his audition for Juilliard. There, joining the audition quartet in a performance of the whole of Mozart's Clarinet Quintet, "the hungry coiled apparatus in Rheinhardt [hounded down] . . . something of God in this music, a divine thing in it." In one of the novel's loveliest moments, Rheinhardt noticed the blue concentration-camp number, DK 412, on the wrist of the cellist, an old man whose eyes were "bright with love. . . . Just before Rheinhardt picked up his next note the old man had turned expectantly toward him with the rapture and tenderness still shining in his face and Rheinhardt had caught that transfigured look and held it, and begun again." The possibility of transcending suffering through art is a constant in Stone's aesthetic thought; in this case, K. 581—the quintet's catalog number—has replaced DK 412. The 1960 Rheinhardt often hates himself. As "he and the strings came down together in the last lovely *tremolo*," this earlier one had thought, "[H]ow beautiful, how beautiful I am" (*HM*, 46–47). Perhaps his pride was excessive; still, he had served well as an acolyte in an extremely demanding, extremely rewarding ceremony that was simultaneously secular and religious. The 1960 Rheinhardt boasts that his armature is gone, and he takes care of his mouth "by juicing and talking all the time" (*HM*, 146). Though surrounded by the novel's exposé of the malign workings of social determinism, Rheinhardt takes full responsibility for his decline.

In all, we hear very little about Rheinhardt's life before we meet him in the novel's first sentence—all set for the night, for he's squirreled away a pint of whiskey—and some of what we hear is ambiguous or suspect since the information comes from the fanciful character himself. We know that he's from a town in western Pennsylvania called Neckersburg, that he was educated for a while in parochial schools in the next town.

He tells a Greek counterman that he's Serbian and his father was a priest, but is this true or just a number he's trying out with someone whose priests are not celibate? The other detail about a relative comes when Rheinhardt, hallucinating, continually sees the image of his grandfather entering a room with his pajama bottoms soaked in blood. But this comes during a fit of delirium tremens: he will then "begin shaking so hard that his fingers fell off onto the sidewalk and shattered like glass piano keys" (*HM*, 25). He tells Geraldine that, like his creator, he was a radioman in the navy and put in some time in Antarctica (where he perhaps intuited the coming coldness), that he played any kind of instrument but the clarinet best, and that he was at Juilliard for a while. We don't know whether to believe him when he tells Geraldine that he's a college graduate: it's hard to imagine Rheinhardt—who, again like his creator, liked to hang out in coffeehouses in New York—getting through four years of college. That he abused his wife and left her and their child and has come to New Orleans after a sickening procession of jobs in radio stations in the Midwest and the South is incontestable. So is the fact that, in contrast to Geraldine and Rainey, the novel's primary victims, Rheinhardt is relatively unshaped by identifiable events and situations in his past. But Stone's control of his protagonist's musings, assertions, self-castigations, impostures, and hallucinations is so sure, so often surprising and convincing, that we're ready to grant him the freedom that he so badly misuses.

The Diseased City

The New Orleans that he comes to is, as a whole, a terrible place, and from reading the book's epigraph, Lowell's "Children of Light," we are envisioning it as the city of Cain before we read Stone's first sentence. The title refers to Christ's comparison (I Thessalonians 5:5) of the hopelessly misguided "sons of this world" to the Lord's chosen, the sons of light. America's Puritan fathers thought they were building the city of light, the holy city on the hill, but since they had cut themselves off from communion, "[t]hey planted here the Serpent's seeds of light" (5). With the references to the "stocks" in the poem's first line, and their way of fencing "their gardens with the Redman's bones" in the second, Lowell establishes the Puritans' punitive, genocidal ways. By the present time, the religious trappings have fallen away from their emphasis upon worldly success, so that their satanic serpent light now celebrates luxurious display ("pivoting searchlight probe to shock / The riotous glass

houses" [6–7]). The next line—"and candles gutter in a hall of mirrors"—can be interpreted in many ways. Two possibilities are that the
materialists successfully disguise their spiritual poverty (the guttering
votive candles) through illusion, and that the attempt to celebrate the
materialist religion through illusion cannot hide the fact that the votive
candles are guttering, running down.[12] Having completely turned away
from God's light to the dark light of the cash nexus, "the landless blood
of Cain / Is burning, burning the unburied grain" (9–10). The poem's
last lines refer to the practice in the mid-1940s of burning grain to keep
the price up at a time when millions were starving. And like Cain, who,
in addition to committing the first murder, founded the first city, the
contemporary children of the Serpent's light are people of the city,
divorced from the land.

When, in 1988, Stone reminisced about the New Orleans he knew in
1960, he remembered it as "a poor, peculiar, happy place, where the
fateful gaiety of carnival really did last all year long—an antic spirit that
savored very much of mortality and the imperfectness of things"
("KFB," 57). If this was indeed the way the city appeared to Stone at
that time, his treatment in *Hall* was highly selective. Rheinhardt does
experience "ginny exhilaration" (*HM*, 170) at one point and enjoys making love to Geraldine; she's quite moved and happy when she learns that
he and she can move from the furnished room they are in to an apartment. That's about it for happiness in the 409-page novel, save for
moments when one of the novel's lesser or greater monsters is feeling
good about tormenting someone. Brightening weather twice causes
Geraldine to experience a lift, but both times abusive men—an underworld enforcer and a policeman—modulate the lift into terror or
loathing.

What Stone does with the blend of carnival, mortality, and imperfectness is vivid and successful. Though she will not meet Rheinhardt for a
week or so, Geraldine also arrives in New Orleans the day after Mardi
Gras, on Ash Wednesday—a day when traditional Catholics publicly
recognize the death of absolute goodness and when, in New Orleans, the
remainders of carnival gaiety would have taken their annual dramatic
turn to the underside. When the driver opens the door of the truck that
has brought Geraldine from Galveston to the French Market, "[t]he cab
was suddenly cold with rank brown fog." The pavement she steps down
on is "slimy and wet, carpeted with a black scum of crushed leaves and
vegetables. . . . Almost at her feet, a large and unafraid rat wheeled and
darted between two crate fires to disappear into the chute of a dumpster;

its tail writhed in behind it like a ringed gray snake. She could part the mist with her hand—brown, foul, smelling of river water and things rotting; it chilled her insides to breathe" (*HM*, 27–28).

A few pages earlier (but a few days later), Rheinhardt decides that a menacing bellhop whose "uniform was the color of the rugs," whose "face matched the wall," is the "genius" (21) of the cheap hotel in which he has been holed up, boozing. The rat is perhaps the primary genius of outdoors, post–Mardi Gras New Orleans. It would be at home in any slimy, wet terrain, but that festive tail anticipates the detritus of the holiday: the "fouled pastel streamers" hanging from "rusted fancy-work balconies," the "snakehead confetti" in the "gutter stream," and the only customer in the coffee shop Geraldine walks to from the French Market. With his mascaraed eyes, "underlined in sky blue," his hair yellowed with peroxide, "a purple wreath of frosted leaves" on his brow, "trailing a toga-like drape of dye-stained white sheeting and clutching to his breast a bouquet of artificial grapes" (*HM*, 30), he is Celebration Gone Wrong.

The queasy mix of failed celebration and the physically repugnant is reinforced in the next section as Rheinhardt finds that the street he's taking to a charity hostel "had faltered to weeded trunk tracks." He has just been thrown out of the cheap hotel in which he had thrown a two- or three-day binge—given the nature of his blackout, he cannot be sure— and, after buying a pint of muscatel, has only sixty cents left, the price of a wire cubicle at the hostel. The ties over which he drags his suitcase are "rotting," the grass is "foul. . . . All around him hung the square dark shapes of black-windowed warehouses, the butt ends of dead wet streets." After drinking his cheap wine and going on along the track, Rheinhardt becomes frightened by a nearby roaring, but when, in the darkness, he tries to retreat, he touches "moist sponginess that [clings] to his palm . . . his heels sink into yielding slime." Increasingly terrified, "bruised and matted with filth . . . blood on his hands and around him the black evil smelling noise," he finally sees above him "lines of light looping and curving like a sickle-bladed razor across the night; above the roaring, the thousands of headlights stretched to black infinity and reddening sky" (*HM*, 50–51). Rheinhardt has wandered under an elevated highway.

Stone might not have put everything he knew into his first novel, but he loaded a good part of it with such dense symbolic foliage that we would do well to follow some of the tendrils that trail out of such a simple action as Rheinhardt's looking up at a roadway. In book 2, just after

making his way through his usual morning hallucinations to wakefulness, Rheinhardt recites the opening and closing lines from Dante's
Inferno: "In the middle of the journey of our life . . . I found myself in a
dark wood . . . for I had lost the straight way. . . . And at length we
emerge to see again the stars" (*HM*, 181). New Orleans, indeed
America, is the dark wood, hell, but instead of the stars of God overhead
we have—to quote Rainey on his visit to California—only "car headlights going by. Nothing human" (*HM*, 256). The simile of the highway
as a razor recalls "the Great American Razor" Rheinhardt had seen in a
store window perhaps an hour before he wandered along the tracks. The
totem is 12 inches long:

> Its handle was not only set in violet-tinted mother of pearl and delicately
> bordered with eight rhinestones, but imprinted with the picture of a sub-
> limely breasted blond woman, naked but for red garters, whose features
> displayed, on close inspection, an expression of lascivious abandon that
> was reserved for her possessor alone.
>
> The blade itself was music—something forged of a rare transmuted
> ice-like metal, secretly, at night. It was passion and science resolved; it
> burned with a blue light that was not wholly in reflection. (*HM*, 41)

The razor embodies a good deal of the American illness that Stone
located in New Orleans: the harnessing of the immense promise of
America—in this case, passion and science, aesthetic vision and technol-
ogy—for violence or the instruments of violence; the reification of the
instruments of violence; the sick blend of Eros and Thanatos, of sexuality and violence.

To look at a few of the novel's many examples of the last category,
after Rainey confronts Minnow, the district attorney who hopes to add to
his power by striking blacks from the welfare rolls, the latter takes comfort by thinking "that for hundreds of miles around his office there were
muscular and rough handed men with powerful arms and bulging thighs
who would flog and beat, burn and castrate such niggerlovers—who
would pulverize their limbs, smash in their sheep's faces, unmind them
with torture" (*HM*, 265). Clearly, Mr. Minnow, who has displaced some
of his libido upon the pistol he has carried since his undergraduate days,
is aroused by the bulging limbs of his subalterns.

Then there's Philomene, the epitome of the carnival gone wrong, who
seems to be a joint creation of Tennessee Williams and Hubert Selby,
replete with steel braces on her legs, "a delicate, rodent-like face" (*HM*,
198), beer foam on her mustache, and the habits of singing maudlin

Irish songs and dragging herself up to college boys and asking them if they would like to copulate. In book 3 Rheinhardt seeks her out, hoping that she will direct him to Geraldine. Philomene quickly slides her hand down the inside of his thigh, and, looking into her eyes, Rheinhardt sees the blended imagery of cars, razors, stagnant water, and death that Stone establishes early in the novel: "the glint of razors on velvet—headlights in fouled water—the sky above opened graves. . . . Philomene's eyes were blue, blue madness sparkled at their surface, the crusted foam of madness at their rims." Rheinhardt feels "the familiar thrill of yearning and fatigue—rest, rest—the eyes of madness, the doors of tombs" (*HM*, 305–6). As attracted to the perverse as he is, Rheinhardt finds Philomene, a woman with razors in her eyes, a bit too frightening to sample that little death, sex; so he gives her five dollars and leaves. Philomene is delighted with the money, which she will immediately spend at an amusement park where, being a cripple, she can get men to help her onto the rides.

The introduction of the cars overhead, then, helps to develop the America = steel = violence = perversion = death equation that will doom Geraldine. At this point in the novel, though, the dominant imagery is that of the rat, slime, brown land, and garbage, a complex that strikes me as descended from the "Fire Sermon" section of Eliot's *The Waste Land* (1922), in particular:

> A rat crept softly through the vegetation
> Dragging its slimy belly on the bank
> While I was fishing in the dull canal
> On a winter evening round behind the gashouse. (187–91)[13]

Hugh O'Haire has written persuasively of how the imagery Rheinhardt absorbs en route to New Orleans establishes the locale as a spiritual wasteland.[14] Rheinhardt is certainly spiritually sick, as is the Fisher King of the above lines, but he is not at all fishing for rebirth or for a manifestation of the God who is nowhere present in the novel. The rot and slime that symbolize the greater part of New Orleans are also objective correlatives of Rheinhardt's inner life, of what he has turned the perishable cream of his talent into: that "deadly and poisonous bile of which one rightly and subsequently dies." Though Rheinhardt here experiences his inner life as choking terror, he normally takes a good deal of pride in his ability to function in all sorts of morally dubious, slimy situations. When he tells Geraldine that he hates New Orleans because it's dirty and sick, this is just Rheinhardt in one of his moments of self-loathing, talking about himself.

The street trailing out into obvious wasteland is not at all the experiential end of the line for Rheinhardt. Earlier in the evening—just before he passed out on the sidewalk and awoke to troubling hallucinations—he had thought of himself as "the animation . . . out here like Donald Duck walking around technicolored when it's supposed to be black and white" (*HM*, 23). He more resembles Wile E. Coyote or Tom of Tom and Jerry, who get shivered into a thousand pieces and then miraculously reassemble themselves. Within an hour Rheinhardt will have regathered his parts at the hostel, even before he meets his old friend Farley the Sailor, the con man posing as a revival minister, who will soon help plug him into the hot new scam in New Orleans. The amoral survivor in Rheinhardt can prosper here. He was down, unattached, when he first saw the Great American Razor and regarded it as something that would kill him. Once he is the well-paid employee of WUSA, violence does not much bother Rheinhardt. It's all right with him that people like his boss, Bingamon, are "terrible when aroused" (*HM*, 250) because, as Rheinhardt tells his immediate superior at the radio station, "This is my home . . . and [Bingamon's] my daddy" (*HM*, 200).

Unjust Desserts

We get a much more painful sense of what is wrong with New Orleans (and by synecdoche, America) from the experiences of Geraldine and Rainey, the novel's other centers of consciousness. In contrasting the lots of Geraldine and Rheinhardt, Stone doubles the characters to a limited degree. Though Geraldine is from West Virginia and Rheinhardt from Pennsylvania, they are, as he tells her, from the same mountains, and they arrive in New Orleans on the same day. Six pages into the book, Rheinhardt thinks of the depressing row of short-term jobs behind him; five pages later Geraldine thinks, "What a long time ago that road of days and nights began" (*HM*, 14). Both are stopped in the streets of New Orleans by frightening deviants in denim; both are sent to their low-paying jobs at Bingamon's soap factory by corrupt institutions—a religious mission in Rheinhardt's case, the New Orleans penal system in Geraldine's—that, along with the state mental health and penal systems, regularly provide labor at exploitative rates to the ruling capitalists.

The contrasts are, of course, more striking. Though they are from the same mountains, only Rheinhardt can adjust to big-city ways and the nation's descent into the moral ice age. After he hears Geraldine sing, he tells her, "You got some kind of talent. . . . If you weren't such a hick you could be a real American authentic" (*HM*, 224). For once Rheinhardt is mistaken: Geraldine is an American authentic precisely because of a generosity of spirit, an uncalculating directness of speech and action that are, in the terms of this novel, hickish. Most important, we first see Rheinhardt as the victim of his own celebration: the binge that swallows his first two or three days in the city. He is, as Geraldine later observes, his own worst enemy. She is not as fortunate. In Galveston, Woody, her lover, had been for some time delivering to her "lyric recitations" about his own version of oral love: how he was "gonna take that little old gun and stick the ever lovin' barrel right smack up against the top of her mouth and when he pulled the trigger her brains were going to smear the ceiling and so forth" (*HM*, 14). On the night we meet her, Geraldine has somehow angered Woody, and since he seems not to have his gun with him, he completes his celebration of violence by three times slashing open her face with an oyster shucker.

Though only 20 or 21, Geraldine has already put in enough hard time to find Woody's recitation always "a little fascinating to hear" (*HM*, 14). She was married and a mother at 16, when her 18-year-old husband was shot to death in an unsolved murder—"Things like that happened fairly often in Birmingham." Then the baby, who had been sickly in their poorly heated boardinghouse, died. "After that, things were a little blurred. She had moved around a lot. That was most of her life it felt like, the four years since then. It had turned out that there were barmaids and barmaids, and if you stayed at it long enough you just naturally made the second category" (*HM*, 18): barmaid-prostitute. Galveston is, of course, ruined for her when she does get out of the hospital, her parents are dead, there's no work in West Virginia, and so she comes to New Orleans determined to avoid whoredom. Her only job interview is at a nightclub where she is offered work as a prostitute by an underling whose version of encouragement is to tell her that some of her customers might like her better because of her scars, and whose version of realism is to tell her that prostitution is the "one deal" she has. (She had made her way to this interview by climbing "a dusty flight of splintered stairs" [*HM*, 53], an apt symbol for her apparent future.) Geraldine's response—"I don't want your job, mister. I ain't interested in entertainment and I don't work the bug trade" (*HM*, 56)—is as colloquially right as every other line she utters in the novel, indeed, as most of the dialogue save for several of the scenes in which Rainey is involved.

Warned not to try to hustle in the Quarter but hungry and literally down to her last dollar, Geraldine is trying to cadge a meal from (in her internal description) "a big rotten rumbellied hogface bastard" (*HM*, 60) when she is called outside to face an elegantly dressed enforcer who holds his brass knuckles to her lips. The knuckles serve as a transitional symbol between that fascinating pistol of Woody's and the prison bunk chains with which she will hang herself. Six to eight months before she tastes with her tongue the "foul steel . . . the acid surface" (*HM*, 388–89) that will strangle her, she kisses the knuckles and her death: "When she tried to speak the man did not take his thing away. Her tongue brushed it. It was like a kiss. . . . [S]he could taste the sour brass afterward in dreams." What particularly appalls Geraldine is the accompanying command that cinches the enforcer in her mind as Daddy Death, the only capable male to offer her sanctuary:

> "Go ahead little one. . . . Move out."
> He had the gentlest voice she could ever remember hearing. Since her father died no one had called her a name like little one. His voice always came back in the dreams. And the fear. It was worse than with Woody in the White Way. It was worse than anything. (*HM*, 62–63)

Rheinhardt has the intelligence to perceive her long slide into oblivion and the money, toughness, and attractiveness to offer her a desirable alternative refuge. But to give her the reassurance that she will literally die for would be to proclaim a generosity, a worth about himself, that he cannot tolerate. And so, when Geraldine tells him that she likes New Orleans because he is there, Rheinhardt feels "as though someone had savaged him in a particularly brutal and revolting way; he had received her words like a cutting" (*HM*, 148). Better she should be doomed by Woody's cuttings. Or when Geraldine tells him, a few weeks later, that "I want to be with you because you're so groovy, Rheinhardt, and I love you so much. I'm scared that's what I mean." Rheinhardt, who has just said that anyone who needs another's concern should get a dog, responds, "I have this thing . . . about need . . . we have to consider *my* needs. We have to consider them from every possible angle in every minute detail and we have to work tirelessly to gratify them all. That's going to take so much time and we'll be so busy that we won't even have to think about your needs at all" (*HM*, 225–26). In the scene in which they break up, he accuses her of indirectly killing her husband and then, sure that she is going to stab him, hits her. Though he is "numb with regret" (*HM*, 259) as he looks at her huddled in a corner, the son of a bitch in him fights down the regret and he walks out.

By the time he returns, she has gone, and it turns out that the stairs she walked up so hopefully at the end of book 1 were another set of splintered steps that lead her to the bug trade: in book 3 we learn that recently "[s]he had been with a man from Charleston. . . . [H]e was all taken with the marks on her face." On her first day in the city, Geraldine wants only food. By her last day she no longer thinks of food and has not slept or "been straight"—off marijuana or liquor—for three days, appropriate enough behavior for someone who feels that "she had gotten all [Rheinhardt's] dreams and shakings . . . it got at her now *his* way and that was too much" (*HM*, 328). Menace hits at her from every side now. After the man from Charleston, "she had been drunk with one of the boys from the Waterman Line who told her about the time he and his buddy had cut off a man's ears and nailed them to the top of his head." As a kind of sympathetic magic, she now seeks Rheinhardt at the rally, feeling that she could sleep if he were in the same room. As another kind of magic, she has in her purse an eight-dollar pistol she bought to protect her from all the malevolent males she feels are bearing down upon her.

And indeed they are, save that by this time women are joining the men in driving her to her death. The night before, she had walked down the middle of a street "with the cops bopping up one sidewalk and a bulldike following her on the other" (*HM, 329*). At the rally she is routed by her female neighbors before she thinks she sees Woody chasing her; at jail she is slapped by a matron. On her first day in New Orleans she had thought,

> It was natural that the time would come when you could look in a mirror and see where you'd been.
> He had done for her—old Woody and his thing there. (*HM*, 37)

Woody had in fact flamboyantly defined her as a victim; when the police are interrogating her in the playground, she gives her name as "Smith . . . Fort Smith" (*HM*, 385), which is where she met Woody. Stone uses the slashed face as the mark of Cain in two ways in the novel: for victims—like Geraldine and Big Gene, one of the pathetic blacks Rainey meets—and for victimizers, like Mr. Cefalu, who owns the club that offers Geraldine work as a prostitute, and who has three curving scars on his face that are even longer than hers. Geraldine's attempt to transform herself into a victimizer with the gun only pushes her deeper into victimization: that and the marijuana constitute the evidence that would win her a substantial jail term.

Her long plunge toward suicide is so convincing, so fully imagined, that Stone's reaction to what he had written is understandable: "When Geraldine died it was like a death had really occurred. It really upset me, and I stopped writing for over a month while at that scene" (Ruas, 277). But I feel that the delivered effect of her great pathos at the rally—for example, screaming as loud as she can while the audience is singing the national anthem—is vitiated by the degree to which Stone is playing the scenes with Rheinhardt, the right-wing zanies, and Prothwaite for laughs.

The Specter of Goodness

With her tall, large-boned frame, long, strong legs, wide hips, soft skin, lovely eyes over a hard mountain jaw, with her directness and warmth, Geraldine is characterized as an essentially healthy being who is dragged down by the pathology of American life. (She is symbolized by a colt, an animal at Audubon Park to which she feeds branches; she experiences the disappearance of the colt—poisoned, she fears, by the spray that has been put on the leaves there—as a portent of her own annihilation.) There are no prancing colts in Morgan Rainey's constitution. When the angle of vision shifts to him in the opening words of book 2, he shambles "through the rain like an evil tiding; his face suspiciously gray and drawn, his plastic rainhat far too small," his raincoat far too long—a specter who moves schoolgirls to giggling, motorists to fantasies of running him down, and gaping blacks to silent hailings of, "You a fool, white man" (HM, 141). Apparently, his body and mind were bent into anguished shapes by a series of events in his early adolescence, and these deformations were secured by his later experiences. When he was about 13, within a few weeks, his father dropped dead at his side, he came across the body of a black who had been boiled in tar, and he came down with rheumatic fever. The early stages of illness were accompanied by one of those perfect expressions of the terrifying nature of things as they are, a hurricane, and as Rainey lay in fever, "all the visions feared of the day before, the dread procession of God's stricken world broke over him without mercy. In all those days, sights he could not blot away rose again and again before him—voices roared from that wind, and the quiet, joyous voice that for him was the voice of God, had broken, grown distant and fallen away before a terrible maimed chorus, this million-throated howl of a Godless earth, transfixed with note, with death, with darkness" (*HM*, 218–19).

In a very important way, Rainey is the relatively benign ancestor of Weitling, a murdering psychotic in *A Flag For Sunrise* who is, in Father Egan's words, one of the "victims of things as they are. Some chemical in the blood, a shortage of sugar in the brain cells and they get the process whole. What they see is real enough, it's so overwhelming it must seem like God to them. You can't look on what they see and not run mad" (*FS*, 371). The blows Rainey received have been sufficient to knock loose the blinders to suffering and injustice that Stone feels we must employ to live with some contentment in the world. Geraldine's struggle to find a refuge in the world is paralleled by Rainey's struggle to believe that God is somehow immanent, that He "is the power that raised up the muck of the earth to walk and think," and that if we do not recognize the covenant involved in our creation, we will "keep finding out the insect in each other. We tear like insects. Without God" (*HM*, 214).

The auditor to these words is Lester Clotho, the black entrepreneur who has been assigned to keep Rainey in the dark about the pointlessness of his survey by the White Devil. (Rainey's superiors at city hall are the merest appendages of this white collectivity, who run things in the black neighborhoods.) Just about all of the blacks and whites Rainey talks to in the novel are amused or threatened by his attempts to do good; Clotho is the most entertained. Here he argues that, given all of the misery Rainey has seen in the black neighborhood, it would seem that God is in the tearing insect, not in the human. And indeed Stone creates for Rainey enough horrific encounters to try the faith of most do-gooders. An ex-soldier who had his arm blown off by American MPs, a crazy, blind old man who tries to see through a rusted telescope, "a syphilitic middle-aged woman and a freckled idiot child. One of the child's fingers was gangrenous because his sister had tied a piece of string around it" (*HM*, 172). His district is indeed a place that makes it difficult to please God, or even to play Him, as, in a lovely scene, Rainey attempts to in his effort to soothe a dying woman. The most fundamental certainties are in question there: Clotho has possession of a blind male baby whom he says he might bring up as a girl. On his last day on the job, Rainey meets two partial doubles. Upon entering the first room, he looks in the mirror, sees himself, and then, without moving his eyes, sees a black about his age, one who has the facial scars that he finds the most

interesting thing about Geraldine. In the second, he meets a black trans-
vestite con man, also named Rainey, also from his hometown. When
Rainey sees Clotho during the last night of his life, before he goes to his
death at the rally, the black illusionist plunges Rainey further down into
what Jung has called the terrifying ambiguity of immediate experience.
Clotho becomes white, turns night into day, and subjects Rainey to a
hallucinatory review of a panorama of contemporary American experience that narrows down to a reprise of his encounter with the tar baby.

Rainey's painful collisions with immediate experience were not limited to Louisiana. After putting in an unspecified amount of time at
Harvard, he worked as an investigator for the Massachusetts Children's
Bureau. "That year he had collected razor strops and lengths of horse-
whip and nail-ended slats. He had released infants from chain nooses
and inspected the burns that radiators made." All of this had a powerful
effect upon an already vulnerable sensibility: "One night he had awak-
ened with the impression that a child's eyes had been put out in his
room." Because he identified so with the sufferings of his clients, a doctor, "with a reputation for political involvement" yet, told him that he
had become "a natural accuser" with "a very original idea of morality"
(*HM*, 176)—presumably that one should try to ease suffering. Having
entered the novel trying to convalesce from a near-breakdown, he dete-
riorates as book 2 and his position proceed: a recurrent twitch in his
shoulder, trouble with his eyes, increased forgetfulness increasingly
plague him.

Stone's attitude toward his creation is interestingly divided. On the
one hand, Rainey does try to wage the good fight against his own afflictions and overwhelming opposition. But among Stone's many parts is
the street-smart kid from Manhattan who is very suspicious of someone
who makes protestations like, "If they take me to jail, if they put me on
the gang or in the madhouse, if they plunge my legs in pitch, and break
my body with ropes there is nothing they can take from me. . . . Do you
believe that as they have put marks on you they have put marks on me?
When they crush lives, they crush me. Their bombs destroy me. When
men hang, I hang. When they flog women, they flog me." After all,
when Stone participated in a 1985 symposium called "The Writer and
the World," his response to what he apparently regarded as his immure-
ment in A Gathering of the Liberally Right-minded was to keep reminding his auditors of the pervasiveness of human failings and how relatively
little art can do to remedy them. Thus Stone has Rainey protest his
saintliness to Geraldine, who, however drunk and sorrowful she is over

the breakup with Rheinhardt, is still as much of a moral registrar as the novel offers. At first she punctuates Rainey's calls with gospel responses like "Amen . . . Praise God . . . I believe." But finally she is repulsed by the leper-licker in Rainey as he tries to take her scars into himself by looking at them with his "blank eyes," stroking them with hands that are "huge . . . large knuckled, dead white and hairless" (*HM*, 274–75). Geraldine wants a survivor, not someone who is as death-bound in the world of this novel as the meaningfully moral life Rainey tries to embody.

Closing Thoughts

The majority of reviewers felt that *A Hall of Mirrors* was an impressive novel, and they were right. As David Thorburn wrote, "[T]he urban setting is evoked with a brilliant sensory concreteness that is palpably true, and is resonant of the psychic and moral anxieties which press down upon the characters."[15] On the whole, the characters, both major and minor, are arresting, and though the vision of a debased America is much more partial than it claims to be, it is still vividly effective until Stone plays the right wing for laughs in the last 80 pages. But the comedy is so good that one is willing to let the grim social exposé slide away for a while and enjoy the comic novel that is percolating on the page. Stone is fond of saying in interviews that we pay for everything, that the bill always comes due. The reckoning for the distance between Rheinhardt's comic novel and Geraldine's tragic or pathetic one comes due when he learns of her death. The stylistic demands upon Stone are great at this point, and as a whole, he meets them: "Her face, the marks. Her smell. Her anger. All sensations involved in drawing close to her came over him in a wave; warmth, breath, skin, belly, her buttocks in denim or bare, curve of hip, her voice. Soft girl. Soft. Soft. Tough. 'Yet,' she read very slowly in her unearthly mountain speech, 'there is a certain joy in their arrival.' With a chain. Chain on flesh. Stars that are certainly expected. Dead. No more. What? Dead?" (*HM*, 395).

Stone's having his protagonist remember Geraldine's identification with the Ancient Mariner's yearning for the welcome the wandering moon and stars receive is particularly effective and moving. Rheinhardt's last five words are supposed to capture the sudden thrusts of erupting, painful emotions. I find the closing part of the quote a bit forced, unconvincing; this is not at all the case with the majority of the novel's verbal displays. When we first meet Lester Clotho, he asks an employee who is

helping to clean the tables full of catfish, "You goin' to make those catfish whistle and . . . [t]hey goin' to stand up and salute are they?" (*HM*,
161). Quite a few sentences and paragraphs in the novel whistle, dance,
and salute. *Hall* is, as a whole, a very well written book that successfully
employs a wide variety of styles, ranging from the abruptly colloquial to
the highly ornamental. Still, some of the writing along the stylistic spec-
trum strikes us more by its self-consciousness, its preciousness, than by
its bravura success: from Rheinhardt's psychic expostulations above,
through some of Farley the Sailor's Anglo-Canadian locutions, to
Rheinhardt's fleeing the rally: "The sound of one's name as cry of strick-
en grief in a long falling. Lost" (*HM*, 381). Were Stone trying to capture
this note in one of his later fictions, he would likely have found a way to
fortify the words with one of the combinations of tonal correctness,
irony, and declarative force that makes the rightness of the vast majority
of his subsequent fictional sentences seem inevitable. In the same way,
there are passages—like the ones describing the Great American Razor,
or Rheinhardt under the elevated highway—that are written with a certain self-conscious symbolic density that will wholly fall away from the
more austere prose in the later fiction.

Of course, in addition to the comic and pathetic novels of book 3,
there are Rainey's expressionist and surrealist ones. If these also detract
somewhat from Geraldine's pathos, they do contribute to the sense of
social orders breaking open. The problem is more with Rainey himself.
From the moment he assumes the angle of vision in the beginning of
book 2, he makes unusual demands upon the reader's identifications.
When we inhabit Geraldine or Rheinhardt, we are able, with some occasional and interesting exceptions, to sympathize with her and enjoy the
play of his mind and mouth. And Stone proves himself a rhetorical master in later novels with his ability to push the reader into surprising identification with such occasionally or frequently appalling characters as
Raymond Hicks of *Dog Soldiers* and Pablo Tabor of *A Flag for Sunrise*. But
we are from the start on the verge of discounting Rainey as a grotesque,
as, say, we more quickly discount from our sympathies the even more
clumsy Homer Simpson of Nathanael West's *The Day of the Locust*
(1939). But since we are to experience the pain he confronts and experiences as very real, the character always exists in a weirdly lit focus: the
word that best describes my relationship with him at last reading is
queasy. And some of the scenes in which he appears, whether a representational one (a black reporter telling him about the welfare scam) or an
expressionist one (the last scene with Clotho), are unconvincing.

Interestingly, Rainey and the enveloping scenes are in perfect focus when he's in contact with Rheinhardt and/or Geraldine.

On the other hand, Rheinhardt and Geraldine seem to me superbly done, and it is with this novel that Stone begins to create the sharply etched, memorable supporting characters that so enliven his fiction. If Farley's voice is sometimes a bit off-pitch, his antics are most entertaining, and what Stone does with the three beatniks—Bogdanovich, his mad friend Marvin, and the unnamed "dark girl"—catches the fears, whimsies, and sweetnesses of their respective marginalities much better than any of the other dozen or so representations of beatnik experience I've seen in fiction of the 1950s and 1960s. In particular, when Bogdanovich and Rheinhardt begin interacting, the rightness of the improvisational fit is reminiscent of two strangers perfectly meshing in a two-on-two basketball game.

Chapter Three
Dog Soldiers

The Road to Vietnam

Stone did not get a great deal written in the half-decade after he completed *A Hall of Mirrors*, and dissatisfaction attended most of what he did finish. First was "The Man Who Turned on the Here," an amusing piece on Ken Kesey in Mexico, in flight from American law enforcement agents, that Stone wrote late in 1966. But the editor at *Esquire* who had commissioned the piece did not like the insider's point of view, and so Stone published it in a short-lived counterculture effort, *Free You*. During his first winter in England he wrote "We Couldn't Swing with It," about four young Americans in the U.S. Navy who had deserted while on liberty in Japan rather than continue collaborating with the American war effort in Vietnam. Stone's later appraisal of this nonfiction piece for the *Atlantic Monthly* was, "It is me trying to be a good supporter of the movement. It's boring and it's pretentious and (in my opinion) it's essentially false" (Schroeder, 152). What I take to be the falseness of the piece—his attempt to celebrate the four, instead of subjecting them to the corrosive irony he would normally drop upon decent but limited idealists—brings considerable interest, not boredom, to the reader who perceives how stiff Stone's writing can be when he denies any of his subjects whatever shadings of irony or allusiveness they might deserve: "Like most of the subsequent media interviews given out by the four, it was not counted impressive. They have tended to 'freeze' decidedly when faced with cameras and microphones."[1]

The irony was back in "Porque No Tiene, Porque Le Falta" (1968), a sharply written story about an American writer in Mexico whose paranoia brings him cuckoldry. Published in the prestigious *New American Review*, "Porque" was the one unmitigated triumph of the new work Stone did between August 1966 and the early summer of 1971, when he wrote about a recent visit to Vietnam. Stone devoted the greater part of 1969 to an extended stay in California as a screenwriter increasingly appalled by what was being done to his first novel. In 1970 he wrote but never sold a screenplay about Californians vacationing in Mexico, and by the spring of the next year he still did not feel sure enough about what he wanted to do with his second novel to start writing it. Janice Stone has said that, in these pre–word processor days, "Bob did not want to write anything until he felt he was ready, so he wouldn't have to spend a long time at a typewriter rewriting" (JBS interview). As Stone later put it, "It seemed to me that these people—my characters—must have been in Vietnam, even though I didn't know quite who they were. I thought, 'What is their relationship to this Vietnam situation that is filling every-body's life now, that is so much on everybody's mind?' It's all anybody would talk about when I was with other Americans. It was so present, looming large in everybody's consciousness. And I began to wonder sud-denly if I couldn't get some work over there, go and have a look first-hand at what was going on, because it was such an abstraction—the idea of Vietnam as a place and as more than a place" (Schroeder, 151).

Stone got himself accredited by *Ink*, a new "London imitation of the *Village Voice*," and in May, with stops in Kuala Lumpur and Bangkok, flew to Saigon. "It was the time of Vietnamization, and American troops were being taken out of Vietnam. The ARVNs [soldiers of the Army of the Republic of (South) Vietnam] were still fighting and dying, to speak of the allied side, and certainly the other side was" (Ruas, 277–78). As a matter of conscience, Stone did go out to a battle line north of Saigon on the back of a motorcycle, but he spent most of his stay in Saigon, for the capital was "a real carnival." Press accreditation was easy to come by: "[T]here was even a high school paper represented. It was not particu-larly difficult for all sorts of adventurers and wanderers and hippies and whatnot of all sorts to blow into town, coming from Katmandu or from India. It wasn't that difficult to get in." Appropriately enough, the mar-ginal people had marginal accreditations: some were "stringers from quasi-papers"; others had "forged accreditation letters that they had written for themselves." A number of them dealt in dope or gold or cin-namon. But, of course, there were a good many other contributors to Stone's designation of 1971 as "the baroque period of Saigon. You could run into anybody on the streets. . . . There was a whole antiwar contin-gent of people. . . . Saigon was just full of Americans and Europeans of any possible description" (Schroeder, 153).[2]

Saigon also contained a good deal more that fired Stone's urge to get back to his desk in England and start writing. His piece for the *Guardian* (*Ink* having folded) detailed bizarre acts of past violence—for instance, the exaltation of helicopter pilots descending to destroy herds of ele-

phants supposedly smuggling in supplies to the Vietcong: "what might
have been a scene from the Ramayana." There were more recent, mind-
teasing acts of violence: why did the previous inhabitant of Stone's hotel
room crush into the walls and floor about a dozen cute, insectivore house
lizards? And was there any particular reason for his doing so with "a
framed tintype of Our Lady of Lourdes"? And was it the Vietcong, the
ARVN, or an angry taxpayer who, during one of Stone's nights there,
blew up the tax office, killing six, three of them children? Stone's conclusion: "There isn't any moral; it makes no sense at all. It reminds me
of the lizards smashed on the hotel wall." So many of the effects of the
American presence make no positive moral sense either: the way one of
the 20 lovely prostitutes at a bar bursts into tears because the only way
she can get at the money in Stone's pockets is to turn him upside down
and shake it loose; the coming of gang rape; eight-year-old boys waiting
outside to try to snatch one's wristwatch. The response of the average
American to the absurdity, the radical uncertainty that extends in so
many directions—who blew up the tax office? how can we be saving the
country when we are destroying it? can the blind beggar in the ARVN
uniform see?—is the title of the piece: "There It Is." Note the phenone-
na; don't try to organize them into experientially meaningful patterns.

Stone noted much of the material and human phenomena of Saigon
so precisely in "There It Is" that he was able to incorporate from it 10
snapshots—of individuals, actions, and objects—into the splendidly
written 41 opening pages of *Dog Soldiers* set in Saigon, sometimes without having to change a word. Random notation is Stone's narrative pose
in the piece, a mode that takes in both a morally neutral vignette—a
Saigon rock festival—and a positive ethical force like the Committee of
Responsibility: "a handful of young Americans who work with concerned organizations in the U.S. to provide rehabilitation for Vietnamese
victims of the war." But a disturbingly negative sense of life in Saigon
does emerge; it justifies and fleshes out "the abstract outrage"[3] that
Stone brought to Vietnam, though he ironically undercuts that outrage
as futile or self-regarding.

The Apparent Absence of the War in *Dog Soldiers*

One would assume that a fair amount of the outrage was a response
to the ignorance that helped to bring American troops to Vietnam: ignorance of the corruption of the Saigon government and its alienation from
the peasants in the countryside; of the force of the country's nationalism;

of its 1,500-year enmity with China, mistakenly designated by Americans as the real force behind the resistance of North Vietnam and the Vietcong. But in *Dog Soldiers*, the novel that he began writing when he returned to England, Stone offers nothing comparable to the discussions that provide political background and explanation in *A Flag for Sunrise*. His closest approach to either occurs late in the novel, when John Converse tells his wife Marge that we cannot ever understand the motivations or even the meanings of the actions of ourselves or others: "'Nobody knows,' Converse told her confidently. 'That's the principle we were defending over there. That's why we fought the war.'"[4] As Frank Shelton has observed, the novel "assumes the war as a given and traces its effects on the noncombatants both in Vietnam and the United States."[5] One of its effects is an acceleration of the "there it is" response. One way or another, assertions of moral discernment or judgment dissolve quickly; Converse's "explanation" comes a few hours after he is both comforted and terrified by the thought that the immediate death he faces is the just payment for his betrayal in print of Grimes, the novel's ethical exemplar. That Grimes—a noncombatant who "carried candy to give people when his morphine ran out" and whose motto is Lear's "man must endure his going hence even as his coming hither" (*DS*, 261)—surfaces for a page and a half in the last quarter of the novel hints at how glancing is the impact made by traditional ethics upon the world Stone gives us.

Shelton's observation would seem to be a bit off, for the novel's most compelling character, Raymond Hicks, was a marine who saw combat in Vietnam and, after being wounded when he and the men under him were punished by being sent on a very dangerous detail, left the service as soon as he could. But this is not at all a Johnny-comes-marching-home novel in which the damaged hero struggles to deal with guilt, crippling combat trauma, drug addiction, what have you. Hick's character is not much changed by combat. Shelton's perception works best if we understand "noncombatants" to refer to as diffuse an assortment as "Americans." Beneath the nearly perfect representationalism of its narrative and dialogue, *Dog Soldiers* aspires to the condition of allegory—on the purported effects of the Vietnam involvement upon the American psyche. As we will see, Stone does not employ the parallel developing lines of action—literal and symbolic—that to varying degrees characterize allegory but instead offers up a broadside of correspondences to assert that the United States is becoming, in its own way, as much of an amoral combat zone as Vietnam.

An Unsettling Thriller

The result is a fast-paced, violent mix that led Joan Joffe Hall to write that, "despite my profound moral disgust at this novel, my utter inability to sympathize with the characters, and my suspicion that my good liberal notion that the Vietnam war is as American as apple pie is cheaply manipulated, I have to admit I read the book straight through, addictively flipping the pages."[6] To consider here only the way that the plotting most obviously contributes to the novel's suspense, if *Dog Soldiers* does not quite belong to the adventure novel genre, in which the reader knows that the imperiled hero will win out in the end, it is a grim descendant of the Deerslayer capture-escape-pursuit affairs that helped to shape the European conception of the American. D. H. Lawrence found in the five-volume saga of Natty Bumppo "the myth of the essential white America. . . . The essential American soul is hard, isolate, stoic, a killer."[7] The description captures some of the ideals and some of the realities of the psyche of Hicks, the ex-marine now working in the merchant marine who, for $2,500, agrees to smuggle three kilos of high-grade heroin from Vietnam to California. Hicks gets the heroin from Converse, a former marine buddy who has been a correspondent in Vietnam for the past 18 months. Charmian, a Saigon friend and former lover of Converse's, brings him into the deal with unknown partners, promising him that he will collect four times his investment of $10,000 when the heroin is picked up in Berkeley and that "there would be no risk of misunderstanding because everybody was friends" (*DS*, 25). But the supposedly genial collaboration is as much of a scam as the welfare survey in *Hall*. The primary "friend" is Antheil, a corrupt employee of an unnamed regulatory agency (obviously the Federal Narcotics Bureau) and Charmian's long-standing lover, who has no intention of paying the $40,000 to Marge Converse, who is to surrender the heroin for the money. But Hicks, still at Marge's when Antheil's two hirelings (Smitty and Danskin) arrive, bests them and, with several adventures along the way, takes the heroin and Marge east, to a former counterculture commune on a sort of dream terrain that, as Stone has said, is northern New Mexico lifted up and placed on the Rio Grande (Solotaroff 1991). Now the mountaintop property is inhabited only by its owner, Dieter Bechstein, Hicks's former roshi (spiritual teacher), and his son. Antheil and his underlings pursue them to "New Mexico" with Converse, returned from Vietnam and taken prisoner, for the shootout that culminates the novel.

This sketch of the broadest workings of the suspense offers no sense of the novel's singular texture: The extremely suggestive, ominous language is almost always drawn as tight as a Cézanne still life. From *Dog Soldiers'* opening page (with Converse worrying about "the progress of his fever" as he sits across the street from reptilian Vietnamese who lounge "sleepy-eyed, rousing themselves now and then to hiss after the passing of a sweating American" [*DS*, 1]) to its last (on which Antheil, having been left the heroin by the fleeing Converses, must continue to deal with the possibility that his Mexican assistant might murder him), very believable vulnerability and menace exude from its actions, descriptions, and a species of dialogue that William Pritchard analogized with the workings of a switchblade: "the flick and spring of exchange—hardly conversation."[8]

Sometimes, when a character feels safe enough to sink into repose, the reader knows better: serene from a recent heroin injection, Marge plays with fish while she bathes in a stream at Dieter's place; we know the pursuers are almost upon them. It's much more often the case that a character cannot avoid registering immediate menace, hostility, or alienation, even when the encounter has nothing to do with the smuggled heroin. A few examples from dozens of possibilities: conversation with the *patronesse* of Converse's Saigon hotel is "a series of small unpleasant surprises" because she regards him with loathing and suspicion. When, after "staring at him with an incomprehension that bordered on horror," she does deign to return Converse's greeting, she speaks "as though his mouthings were human speech" (*DS*, 20–21). With some time to kill before he drops off the heroin at Marge's, Hicks goes to a bar that once offered "good cheap Italian food" and pool tables. Now, instead of the kitchen and the pool tables, there are topless dancers and a new clientele that occasionally includes "escaped lunatics up from Agnew," there "to engage the suburbanites who came to engage rough trade." Hicks misses the lunatics and has to make do with taking in the "shark-eyed barmaids," the bartender—an informant beneath his entertaining, obscene veneer—and blacks who send off hostile, cocaine vibrations and watch Hicks "like medical students regarding a charity patient with a curious low disease" (*DS*, 78–79). When Hicks and Marge flee to his house in a canyon outside of Los Angeles, it is occupied by five counterculture types: three adult predators who are about to do unspecified terrible things to the two teenagers they've just picked up.

We remember one of Stone's articulated goals as a novelist: to "choose words that open up deeper and deeper levels of existence by sustaining a sound which perfectly serves the narrative and which at the same time relates through a series of associations to the larger questions" (Woods, 31). There are several reasons why *Dog Soldiers* comes much closer to fulfilling this goal than *A Hall of Mirrors:* Stone's control of his craft, his ability to fit sound to sense (or the demands of character and plot) has grown; the later novel does not have a character like Geraldine, who deserves so much more than the fate the author deals her that she escapes the kind of caustic irony that helps to unify *Dog Soldiers*; his return to what he can do best—a sustained version of representational realism—after the expressionist and surrealist flights in the last third of *Hall.* That return also helps to make possible the tonal unity of the novel.

There are for me a few instances when the dialogue does not seem pitch-perfect. When Hicks shows off his street-smart toughness by telling Marge, "You're a mark, Stuff" (*DS*, 95), the put-down does not have the characteristic tonal precision, the sour rightness of his response to Marge's news that she does not have his $2,500 because she went to the aquarium: "I hope you got off on the fish. . . . You're not getting shit until I get paid" (*DS*, 93). In the latter part of the twelfth of the novel's 20 unmarked sections, when Converse and Antheil discuss the former's joining the pursuit to "New Mexico," the dialogue is a bit flat, but perhaps it is that we have here a rare example of the gears of plotting necessity grinding enough to poke through our absorption. We became aware of Stone straining to somehow get Converse to Dieter's place for the finale.

Some Ironic Strategies

The precision of the dialogue and the frequently colloquial diction and cadences of the narrative are crucial aspects of what is perhaps the characteristic note in Stone's voice. William Crawford Woods made a helpful start when he spoke of "the shifting levels of [Stone's rhetoric] which plays the colloquial against high ornamentation. The effect is a constant tone of irony" (32). There are a good many examples of the ornamental and the colloquial in the same sentence— "Holy-o oversaw their going hence with his truncheon stuck in his breast pocket like a cigar" (*DS*, 61); "He was a museum of yardbird reflexes" (*DS*, 87)—but it is much more often the case that the narrative draws its irony from the distance between decorous narrative and the proximate dialogue:

The ethnic reference sounded a ghostly alarm from some dark place in the ruins of Marge's progressive conditioning.

"Sure," she said. "Chinese are just as horny as anybody else." (*DS*, 61)

But for me, the most effective and complex ironic undermining, the one that captures the way apelike humankind tends to explode antecedent forms (which the novel is in fair part "about"), follows from the frequent distance between the mock-genteel pitch of the language and the obdurate reality of what the language describes. For example, consider the first part of a paragraph that explains why Mr. Roche, the owner of the Berkeley building in which the Converses have their apartment, had become particularly wary: "Mr. Roche was a member of the parish Holy Name Society and of the American Party. He had once owned a dog named MacDuff. One evening while Mr. Roche was walking MacDuff on Ponderosa Street, a column of Gypsy Jokers had rounded the corner and the point rider's machine had struck MacDuff and crushed his spine. The rider was overthrown. When Mr. Roche, in his bereavement, had remonstrated with the group, the thrown Gypsy Joker had seized him and battered his small head against the curb until he was unconscious." We have already learned a few paragraphs earlier that "Mr. Roche stood slightly over five feet and had fine womanly features," and that "it pleased him to pretend to be the manager. In that capacity he could refer to himself reverentially as 'The Boss' " (*DS*, 116–17). Our sense of Mr. Roche's amourpropre is heightened by learning the name of his dog. Then come upsetting details: the dog's spine is crushed, and so, nearly, is Mr. Roche's head. Our normal sympathy has been compromised in advance by the landlord's hateful enjoyment of Converse's bewilderment: the latter has flown in from Vietnam to find his wife and daughter gone, rotten food in the refrigerator, and a terrifying, obscene drawing on the wall above his daughter's crib. It's further compromised by the way the diction and syntax capture Mr. Roche's inappropriate formality and punish him for it. Put differently, to have Mr. Roche remonstrate, in his bereavement, to some equivalent of the Hell's Angels is to further distance the reader's identification and thus make him more an object of derision than of pity. His present, contemptible behavior toward Converse seems a part of the prissy formality of the diction and might help some readers to experience the very smallness of that head against the curb as a delicious detail.

In a great essay about Chicago, Isaac Rosenfeld described his fearful fantasy of the coming of the Neanderthal types who live west of the

veneer of civilization along the city's eastern edge to crush with their
hobnail boots the Danish modern furniture in the smart shops. A passage like this, or one that has us identifying with Danskin right up to
the moment he describes crushing a skull with a tire iron, has a way of
placing some readers, however temporarily, on the side of the brutes.
When Converse wrote a feature story about Grime's death, he conveyed
not the compound of "love, self-pity, even pride in humanity" that he
was experiencing, but "grief and rage . . . so that Grimes's moral explo-
rations in the face of mass murder and young oblivion had served him
for a moment's satisfying warmth, like a hot towel in a barbershop"(DS,
261–62). Stone would not permit himself the hot towel of an easy moral
refuge in "There It Is," and, with a cleverness that borders on the
fiendish, he refuses to offer one to the reader in *Dog Soldiers*. This helps to
account for the disgust experienced by Joan Joffe Hall and about half the
students to whom I have taught the book.

More often, the ironic distance encourages a mere loss of sympathy,
not a sadistic identification. For example, here is Converse's deranged
mother imitating a black clerk at her hotel:

> She commenced an impersonation of Hodges, piping inaudible
> words in effete falsetto, rolling her eyes like a stage Othello.
> Converse drank deeply of his martini. (*DS*, 152)

Whether or not it conveys mocking echoes of drinking deeply of the
Pierian spring, the stately description (instead of, say, "Converse gulped
down his martini") captures both the inadequacy of the gesture as a way
of dealing with his mother and the inadequacy of the lunch with his
mother as a respite from his pursuers: Smitty and Danskin will soon sit
near them and pick up Converse in the street a few minutes after that.

I might add that a large part of the narrative is not at all ironic but
appears to be merely a taut recording of fact. But as Paul Gray observed,
Stone's spare language "constantly [earns] maximum effects with all but
invisible efforts. A military career is summed up as years 'of shining
shoes and saluting automobiles' " (111). But sometimes the principals'
exacerbated subjectivities justify extremely rhythmic, suggestive prose:
"Hicks drove on speed. His fatigue hung the desert grass with hallucinatory blossoms, filled ravines with luminous coral and phantoms. The
land was flat and the roads dead straight; at night, headlights swung for
hours in space, steady as a landfall—and then rushed past in streaks of
color, explosions of engine roar and hot wind. Every passing truck left in

its screaming wake the specter of a desert head-on—mammoth tires spinning in the air, dead truck drivers burning in ditches until dawn" (*DS*, 215). This is still highly restrained compared with the baroque descriptions of Rheinhardt's hallucinations. Although several critics disagree, I find no part of *Dog Soldiers* overwritten.

Heroin as God

Unlike, say, *The Last of the Mohicans*, the chasers seek an object, not humans: the heroin is both the gravitational center of the novel and the most effective symbol Stone has ever created. Chuckling sports announcers like to observe that a fumbled football "always draws a crowd," and so does the heroin. But much more is involved than the cash value of three kilos of heroin so pure (in Hicks's words) "it can be cut to infinity" (*DS*, 144). When Charmian first displays the heroin to Converse, "the bleached white jellaba she [wears], with her straight blond hair hanging back over the cowl, [makes] her look like a figure of ceremony, as though she were there to be sacrificed or baptized." She also looks like an acolyte worshiping at the altar of a god who is enclosed in three different kinds of wrappings, whose manifestation is accompanied by her adoring "look at it down there . . . burning with an evil glow" (*DS*, 10–11). Her name (the same as that of the attendant of that incomparable object of desire, Shakespeare's Cleopatra), the fact that one of the wrappings is a Catholic newspaper, and her admission to taking "a little Sunday sniff" (*DS*, 12) also hint at the deification of the heroin.

While on the run from Berkeley to Dieter's, Hicks shows the heroin to three Hollywood types who are about to try it: "[E]veryone regarded it with silent respect" (*DS*, 195). Earlier in the day Hicks dipped into the heroin as a way of dealing with Marge's painful withdrawal from addiction to Dilaudid, an opium derivative only slightly less powerful than heroin. They do not yet have the drug paraphernalia to inject the heroin, to be what Hicks calls "a righteous junkie," and so he has her sniff it. Within a few minutes,

"the tension drained from her in small sobs."
"Better than a week in the country, right?"
. . . .
"It's a lot better than a week in the country," she said. She began to laugh. "It's better than dilaudid. It's good."
She rolled over and hugged herself.

"Right in the head!" She made her hand into a pistol and fired into her temple. "Right in the head."

He sat down on the bed with her. The glow had come back to her skin, the grace and suppleness of her body flowed again. The light came back, her eyes' fire. Hicks marveled. It made him happy.

"It does funny little things inside you. It floats inside you. It's incredible."

"People use it instead of sex."

"But it's just gross how nice it is," Marge said happily.

Hicks touched her breast.

"Walking with the King. Big H. If God made anything better he never let on. I know all those songs, my sweet." (*DS*, 170–71)

In a few moments Marge stares at the ceiling "with an expression like reverence" and then quotes, "Where springs fail not." When Hicks tells her that the phrase is from a poem, not a Polish toast, as she thought, she corrects herself: "Yes . . . it's a smack poem" (*DS*, 173–74). How appalled Gerard Manley Hopkins would have been had he known that "Heaven-Haven: A Nun Takes the Veil" would be appropriated by heroin, the prevailing god of *Dog Soldiers*.

The drug has already made sex irrelevant. Hicks took partial possession of Marge perhaps a week earlier, when he fondled her just before Smitty and Danskin appeared, and solidified his hold upon her when he protected her, helped to get her three-year-old daughter to her father, and, above all, had sex with her in his house. Although both found the sex satisfying, they apparently have not again slept together: their union is about control (from Hicks's point of view) and protection (from Marge's). Earlier in the day, while she was suffering, Hicks reflected that "[t]he pain in her eyes gave him pleasure. If he could make the pain leave her, he thought, and bring her edge and life back, that would give him pleasure too. The notion came to him that he had been waiting years and years for her to come under his power" (*DS*, 167). Which is what the heroin apparently makes possible: it would seem that as the new keeper of the holy fire, the man who will literally be carrying the heroin until he dies beneath it, Hicks either needs unusual powers to be worthy of the burden or gains unusual powers from the heroin, or both. But even at this relatively benign stage of his involvement with the heroin, the god's offerings are mixed, as Hicks suffers from the god's way of excluding lesser deities, like an unsublimated form of Eros. After he brings Marge's physical tone and wish to live back with the heroin, Hicks reminds her of their sexual encounter. Marge then turns "her lofty empty smile" on Hicks, who, ignored, experiences "a dart of loneliness" (*DS*, 172). The way in which Marge, oblivious to his desire, begins celebrating her ability to notice and remember everything is one of the book's many nice ironies.

A student of Zen, Hicks likes to think of himself "as a kind of a samurai" (*DS*, 75). But the narrator's valediction to Hicks, bleeding to death as he attempts to traverse a salt waste, is:

> . . . So much for the pain carrier.
> So much for the lover, the samurai, the Zen walker. The Nietzschean. (*DS*, 330)

Although Hicks's aspirations to Zen correctness and his frequent failures to achieve it have occasioned a fair amount of critical response, a crucial aspect of Nietzsche really has the last word with him, as it does with the world of the novel. In *The Gay Science* (1882) a madman in the marketplace announces that we have killed God and wiped away the whole horizon (or a subject's sense of the boundary between the historical and nonhistorical). Because we have discovered that man made God and not vice versa, the Bible, which asserts the opposite, has become myth, not history. The good news, according to Nietzsche, is that man is now free to re-create himself heroically. The bad news, according to *Dog Soldiers*, is the variety of uses to which this newly conscious ethical freedom is put by people unmoored from a belief in God and the Judeo-Christian system of ethics that depends upon Him.

Only one professing Christian appears in the novel: a middle-aged female missionary, 14 years in Vietnam, who tries to accept with her usual adoration of God's will the recent killing of her husband by the Vietcong. She also brings to the bad news her version of good news: we are into the last days predicted in the Book of Revelation. The missionary is significant enough to be referred to in the first sentence of the novel. But since she rejects Converse's sexual overture, he and the reader walk away from her forever on the book's ninth page to meet Charmian and the heroin—a movement that relates to the way we create new values to replace discarded ones. As the primary source of value in the novel, the heroin has a way of laying bare the deepest yearnings of those associated with it: for Converse, it is a chance to strengthen his battered self-esteem; for Marge, an escape from the pain of her body, and of her conscience for abandoning her daughter; for the deluded Smitty, a chance to rise in Antheil's regulatory agency; for Danskin, sadistic enter-

tainment; for Antheil, money and a chance for self-congratulation.
Hicks's relations with the novel's prime mover are more complex, but
we should realize here that, despite his confusion and contradictions, he,
of all the novel's characters, embodies the most conscious and most
evolved version of the monism to which Nietzsche reduced all motivation: the will to power. As he tells Marge after the first leg of their
escape, "It [the heroin] belongs to whoever controls it" (*DS*, 111).

The Energy of Evil

As with *Hall*, there is a problem with the dating of the dramatized
present of *Dog Soldiers*, though this one can be easily resolved. The narrator tells us that, eight years earlier, Marge had participated in the
Vietnam Day March that was met by the Oakland police. Since the
march occurred on 16 October 1965, it would set the novel in 1973—a
considerable problem, since all American troops had left Vietnam by
March of that year. Stone resolved the problem by conceding that the
eight-year hiatus was a slip; he meant the novel to take place in 1971
(Solotaroff 1991). Since one of the novel's dominant themes is the perversion or exhaustion of counterculture ideals, this dating works well.
The utopian hopes of the 1960s had soured by 1971 and, for most
Americans, the war in Vietnam seemed to have been going on for
decades, with no end in sight. That the war is several times considered as
an event that encourages heroin smuggling, not as a national crisis that
might or might not ever end, typifies Stone's severe focus.

In 1971 a majority of Americans professed belief in a personal God,
and—to refer to conspicuous absences in the world of *Dog Soldiers*—
surely some government employees were free from corruption, insanity,
sadism, and drug addiction; surely a fair number of Americans lived
loving and productive lives. But given the way Stone selected and structured his characters and locales, we have no hint of their existence. The
prospect of addressing a medium range of experience, or even extreme
conflicts in fundamentally healthy organisms, does not normally (as
Rheinhardt might say) set Stone's creative toes to tippy-tapping. He
meshed his fascination for (and his extraordinary ability to represent)
some of the nether reaches of experience with his continuing desire to
make a large statement about life in America by implicitly claiming
that the world of his novel expresses in extreme forms some negative
growths in our culture that have been intensified by our Vietnam
involvement.

One of these, and one that has always fascinated Stone, is the energy of evil. The missionary brings Converse other bulletins from the fundamentalist front besides the imminent apocalypse: the natives in her province worship Satan, who "is very powerful here" (*DS*, 9). If God is largely absent from Stone's world, some malign deity hovers over the majority of his novels, whether Krishna in his war chariot in *A Hall of Mirrors*, Satan in *Dog Soldiers*, the Demiurge of the Gnostic gospels in *A Flag for Sunrise*, or Juggernaut in *Children of Light*. A few hours after meeting the missionary, Converse repeats the news of Satan's local strength to the Percys, the Australian couple with whom he is dining. "Check it out," Ian Percy tells him. "Don't dismiss anything you hear out of hand" (*DS*, 32). Back in his hotel is evidence of Converse's Satanic reconnoiterings: in a rented safe, the heroin; in his room, a thermos that has "[p]rinted across it in bright colors . . . the picture of a wide-winged bat; on the bat's breast was its brand name—LUCKY." Regarding the thermos as "an actual Vietnamese artifact" (*DS*, 22), Converse plans to bring it back to the United States but apparently forgets to, since we do not hear about the thermos again. What we hear of, and what confirms the suspicion that the bat symbolizes a malign deity, is the original American artifact that Converse discovers when he returns to his abandoned Berkeley apartment: the devil with "horns and bat wings and a huge erect phallus" (*DS*, 116) that Smitty had drawn above his daughter's crib. "Lucky" is the devil to be so well equipped in the world of this novel; unlucky is any child who seems to be connected with the course our country has taken. The Percys, the most moral characters that we meet, have been discouraged from having children by what they've seen in Vietnam. In America we see Janie Converse (mildly autistic even before Smitty and Danskin descend), a persistently screaming baby in Beverly Hills, and Dieter's son Kjell, who has his horse killed by Smitty, his father by Hicks. The only intact children belong to a group so marginal they make the principals seem like mainstream Rotarians: the transient Mexican cultist community worshiping at the base of Dieter's mountain.

The presence of the devil image, the endangerment of children, and the residency of the heroin in both Saigon and the United States are but three of the novel's correspondences that assert a moral equivalency of the two locales. A few others: Ngon Loc, the province inhabited by the supposed worshipers of Satan, is said to look much like northern California; Charmian likes Saigon because it reminds her so much of Washington; *True Grit* with John Wayne is playing in My Lat, where

Converse transfers the heroin to Hicks, and *The Searchers* with John
Wayne was playing in Brooklyn when Danskin caved in the head of a
high school rival with a tire iron; the victims of the tax office explosion
are put in body bags, and campers are found dead in their sleeping bags
in the California canyon where Hicks has his house; the proprietor of
Converse's Saigon hotel watches "Bonanza" on television (as Americans
watch the violence in Vietnam on their televisions) and announces,
"Everywhere it's the same now . . . Everywhere it's Chicago" (*DS*, 38); as
Hicks walks from the shootout toward the salt flat on which he will die,
"the track ahead led downward into a canyon that was crowned with
tortured rock spires like the towers of the pagodas along the Cambodian
Mekong" (*DS*, 316); in the first paperback edition of the novel, only an
inch of space marks the movement of the novel from Vietnam to San
Francisco, from the base enclosed by barbed wire in My Lat, where the
resident army journalist has a "pornography collection and the movie
film can that was loaded with Laotian Red" (*DS*, 45), to the porno theater run by a manager who carries a truncheon to protect his help from
local degenerates and himself from attack by American Indians, and who
sells Dilaudid at an inflated price to one of those employees, Marge
Converse.[9] Reading the hardcover edition, one must turn the page.

A Child of Advance

In the novel's morphology of soured idealists, Marge most obviously
models the failure of the traditional left. Once arrived at Dieter's, she
identifies with his son as "a child of Advance . . . born to Solution at the
dawn of the New Age" (*DS*, 228). The terms of the solution would seem
to have been offered by Marxism, which, as a part of its grand, synthetic
resolution of all conflicts, was to triumph over the ethnic differences
between her Jewish father, who wrote for *The New Masses* and fought in
the Abraham Lincoln Brigade in the Spanish Civil War, and her Irish
Catholic mother, who embraced vegetarianism and lesbianism along
with Marxism. But the father advanced into publishing degraded versions of already degraded publications like *Collier's* and the *National
Inquirer*, the mother into suicide, and Marge into working as a cashier in
a porno theater and experimenting with Dilaudid as, in her words, "a
matter of principle" (*DS*, 67).

I suspect that the principle is her assertion of the right to seek the
most exquisite pleasures she might experience. Her first Dilaudid tablets

bring her a good deal that arouses delight: sensations of being beyond quotidian noise, space, and time, experiencing the external world as a series of enclosures—windowed rooms, or vaults within the sea—that she could move through if she wished, conquering if she needed to, communicating with like creatures if she desired. All of this is soon ironically exploded. This pleasure does not compare to what she experiences when an even stronger drug, heroin, with stronger negative consequences, releases her from the torment of Dilaudid craving. When she comments on the ugliness of a Beverly Hills room, Hicks tells her, "We're making all the rooms . . . [c]hecking them out" (*DS*, 136). In the course of *A Hall of Mirrors*, Geraldine Crosby moves from the enclosure of the lavatory in which she hides from the man with the oyster shucker to that of the cell in which she hangs herself. The drugs she takes quickly move Marge from imaginary limitless vaults beneath the sea to more and more ugly physical and psychic enclosures. Correspondingly, the image of herself as a conquering warrior—one who actually writes to her husband, "Re Cosa Nostra—why the hell not? I'm prepared to take chances at this point" (*DS*, 39), or who feels during her first Dilaudid trip that it is "[u]s against them . . . [m]e against them. Not unlike sexual desire" (*DS*, 71)—will not survive her rapid addiction to the drug, let alone the arrival of Hicks, Danskin, and Smitty.

Marge's bravado is an attempt to escape the fatalism that caused her mother, with whom many compare her, to become "a suicide with her lover during the McCarthy days." The same suicidal passivity caused Marge to "sullenly [agree]" to her husband's departure to Vietnam, because she "loved all that was fateful" (*DS*, 24), and enabled her to replace the murdered cashier at the porno theater. With her Dilaudid-fed sense of herself as an independent, powerfully assertive person, she feels a more satisfying commitment to the smuggling of the heroin than to anything else she has experienced "since she was much younger" (*DS*, 71). That the drug caper is not a blow against her death wish but a plunge toward its consummation is made clear when, having perceived Hicks as the incarnation, the terrifying embodiment of "the whole terrifying enterprise," she responds to his sexual advances, gives herself to "the stale mouth . . . the beak across her belly . . . the danger, the death. The thing itself" (*DS*, 96). The need to get Hicks's money and the sudden arrival of Danskin and Smitty interrupt their 'lovemaking,' but that night she bends to "his penis, a resolute harakiri, self-avenging; he could feel the abnegation, the death" (*DS*, 114).

I Fear: Therefore I Am

Toward the end of the novel, both Converses admit that, at some level, they knew they would be tricked by their accomplices in the drug caper. But self-destructiveness played a much smaller part in the complex that drove John Converse toward accepting Charmian's offer. Though he had ten years earlier written a play about the Marine Corps that was performed, praised, and sold to the movies, Converse had for seven of those years, as a writer for *Nightbeat*, been helping to populate the American psyche with lesbian motorcyclists, spanking judges, rapist skydivers, and mad dentists. At the end of this time, the capacity for fantasy that should have gone into honest fiction or drama—but did not— leaked into his life: after assuming the persona of a Latin showgirl who criticizes in *Nightbeat* the performance in bed of Porfirio Rubirosa, Converse began to fear sensational and violent retaliation from the playboy's admirers. His perception of his rampant irrationality fed his sense of the need for a radical change in his life, and so he turned up in Vietnam as a correspondent, planning to mine at least a novel or a play from the adventure. One of Converse's reasons, so he told himself, for getting involved in the heroin smuggling was that "it had become apparent that there would be no book, no play. It seemed necessary that there be something" (*DS*, 25).

But there was already "something." Through the mixed blessings of war, he had been able to replace his neurotic or paranoid anxiety with a realistic anxiety that reached all the way to primal terror. One hot May day Converse was accompanying a native infantry company on patrol in Cambodia when they were fragmentation-bombed by their supposed allies, the South Vietnamese Air Force. As the men around him were cut to shreds—one was "nailed Christlike to a tree beside the road, a shrine"—Converse, "clinging to earth and life," weeping in terror, learned that "the ordinary physical world . . . was capable of composing itself, at any time and without notice, into a massive instrument of agonizing death" (*DS*, 185). For many, the consequent perception would be that there are no innate moral structures in the world. But Converse is, as his wife ambiguously defends him, "a subtle fella . . . a can of worms" (*DS*, 172). Consistent with the Nietzschean world of the novel, he granted moral right to superior force and denied it to himself. So overwhelming are his perceptions of the extent of his vulnerability, of the silliness and pointlessness of his past struttings and frettings across the stage of life, that, "[f]rom the bottom of his heart, he concurred in the moral necessity of his annihilation" (*DS*, 185–86). But if, in this situation, what he called his "heart" responded to moral dictates, a deeper entity—what the slippery Converse calls his soul—had a different, overriding response to surrendering to annihilation. Beneath his sense that he did not have a right to live was a desire to live so great that he vastly preferred being the living dog who will do *anything* to survive to being a dead lion. Of course, the more one wants to preserve a possession, the more fearful one is likely to be of losing it, a truism that helps to explain the workings of the following: "Fear was extremely important to Converse; morally speaking it was the basis of his life. It was the medium through which he perceived his own soul, the formula through which he could confirm his own existence. I am afraid, Converse reasoned, therefore I am" (*DS*, 42).

The Aesthetic Versus the Ethical

But having returned alive to Saigon, Converse was not content simply to survive. He is, after all, a man who sometimes whistled "Non, j'ne regret rien" as he left the hole that served as a toilet, because the song, like the use of the toilet, made him feel connected with the hard-bitten warriors of the romance of French imperialism. He is a man whose briefcase contained only a "Zap" comic and the collected works of Saint-Exupéry when it was snatched by a Korean passing in a jeep. Converse wants to survive with witty, ironic style, with panache. In Saigon he badly wanted to impress Charmian, who "had taken leave of life [fear] in a way he found irresistible" (*DS*, 26). After he turns the heroin over to Hicks, Converse says, "I feel like this is the first real thing I ever did in my life" (*DS*, 56). More than the financial profit from the drug deal, he hopes to bring home from Vietnam the sense that he has extended himself by taking on the dangerous, the illicit, by acting the way he fancies "grown-ups" might. Sharon Lee Ladin has observed that Hicks "is still so much the little boy who *does* need other people to see and commend his exploits like parents," and the same can be said of what Converse wants from Charmian.[10] He's a sort of Walter Mitty playing the jaded heroin connoisseur as he says, before sniffing the heroin, "Now let's see if it's really shit," and, "Christ, it's merry little shit" (*DS*, 11–12) after he is rocked by his inhalations. His final gesture toward her is to avoid receiving a maternal good-bye kiss, a pathetic assertion of adult independence. Of course, Charmian has had her eye on the adolescent-as-mark all along: after they've been together less than a minute, she tells Converse that he's the most frightened man she's ever seen.

Largely for the sake of style—his own as well as Charmian's, with her overpowering flair—this man who had written a good protest play agreed to smuggle heroin. We do not know whether ethical commitment or a desire for sensation led Marge Converse to participate in the 1965 Vietnam Day March turned back by the Oakland police, though the former motivation would better fit in with the decline that Stone quietly traces. What the mid-1960s now means to Marge is a fashion statement: she is very fond of her yellow 1964 Ford "because of the way it suited her. Marge on wheels knew herself to be a thoroughly respectable sight—she and the car together projected an autumnal academic dash that might even evoke nostalgia if one had enjoyed 1964" (*DS*, 67). If the Converses (as protest playwright and protest marcher) had at least at times in the 1960s acted in response to what seemed to them undeniable moral imperatives, the Kierkegaard who wrote *Stages on Life's Way* (1845) might have said that, with these actions, they flirted with the ethical stage. But by 1971 they have, at best, fallen back into a middling level of the aesthetic stage, of living in a world wholly composed of sense perceptions and sensuous gratifications.[11]

After the missionary's disappearance, meaningful religious structures are strangely distanced or hinted at in the novel: the Mexican ritualists at the foot of Dieter's mountain; the fact that the name of the town where Marge and Hicks, on the run, briefly stop is Moroni—a Mormon angel; the way in which A.M.D.G. (for the greater glory of God) is carved above the doorway leading to Dieter's house. The most ethical secular structure hinted at in *Dog Soldiers* is the Committee of Responsibility, and Stone emphasizes its distance from the world of the novel by mentioning it only in the book's outer reaches: in the dedication. Once we enter the novel proper, Grimes is its ethical exemplar because he provided Converse "with an attitude which he [Converse] had publicly pretended to share—but which he had not experienced for years and never thoroughly understood. It was the attitude in which people acted on coherent ethical apprehensions that seemed real to them." Even though "people in the grip of this attitude did things which were quite as confused and ultimately ineffectual as the things other people did," Converse "held them in a certain—perhaps merely superstitious—esteem" (*DS*, 261). But when he is the prisoner of Danskin and Smitty, a few minutes from likely death, the realm of the ethical swells enough into reality for Converse to feel both comforted and terrified by the possibility that he is being punished for betraying Grimes. As I suggested earlier, his apprehensions of the ethical quickly dissolve into his denial of almost any kind of understanding of human behavior. Correspondingly, he argues that he and Marge should not try to pick up the wounded Hicks on the salt flat, even though his old marine buddy would never have gotten wounded had he not tried to save the Converses. But Marge prevails, and when they find Hicks dead on the railroad tracks that run across the desolate waste, the best that Converse can do is to rise to a level of the aesthetic, which Stone renders with particular irony: he is the jaded collector of those beautiful moments that alone are "real." Taking in how lovely his wife looks as she bends, weeping, over her lover, Converse thinks that "[h]e might . . . if things were different, have fallen in love with her again right there. He was not without emotions and it was very moving. Real. Maybe even worth coming out for" (*DS*, 335).[12]

After observing that the would-be exotics of the late 1960s on the Upper West Side of Manhattan might imitate buffalo hunters or desperadoes or troubadours, but not "the businessman, the soldier, the priest, and the square," Saul Bellow's Artur Sammler reflects, "The standard is aesthetic."[13] In his biopsy of American life a few years later, Stone offers up representative traffickers in sensation who occupy considerably lower plateaus of the aesthetic stage than does Converse on the salt waste. The first three words we read when the novel moves to the United States are "The last man"—a reference to the final ticket buyer of the night at the Odeon. The sad masturbator's fingers seek the ticket "like blind predatory worms" (*DS*, 58). Later in the night, on Dilaudid, Marge visualizes the workings of all the hands in the theater (with imagery that could have come from William Burroughs's descriptions of the monsters and grotesques who populate *Naked Lunch* [1959]): "laboring over damp half-erections, burrowing in the moldy subsoil of their trousers like arachnids on a decomposing log" (*DS*, 71). Of course, those first three words place in northern California the blinking drone, the leveling mass man, the Last Man of Nietzsche's *Thus Spoke Zarathustra* (1883). Eddie Peace, Hicks's hustler acquaintance in the movie industry, posits in his colloquial way extended infantilism as the cause of the totality of the culture of sensation in southern California: "The fuckin' people make me sick. . . . The Spock generation. Everything's a tit. I wannit, I wannit." For all their affluence, his New Consumers belong to a lower subspecies of existence than the Last Men to the north: "The people out here, man—they're so rotten they get this shit growing on them. . . . Fungus. You go into a room full of these people and you look around and some of them have it all over them. Every inch of skin, covered with this green

fungus" (*DS*, 146–47). The perverse but perceptive Danskin also attributes an "everything's a tit" mindset to the militants in the antiwar movement: "You're an American college kid—that means you get anything
you want. You get the best of everything that's in—think it up, you got
it. So revolution is in—boots and cartridge belts and Chinese shit. . . .
The richest fuckin' people in the richest country in the world—you
gonna tell them some little guy in a hole in South America can have
something they can't?" (*DS*, 251–52).

The American Samurai

If we could take Hicks at his word and thought, he would serve as an
alternative to the self-indulgence and other forms of moral sloth that
pervade *Dog Soldiers*. To Converse, he protests his honesty and self-discipline; to Danskin and Smitty, who try to lure him into a trap by propos-
ing that he help to beat and rob a homosexual, Hicks is comically
indignant: "You guys are something else. Did you really think I'd lay my
good down and go queer-stomping?" (*DS*, 99). For some time Hicks has
regarded himself as a close student of Japanese culture, and of Zen in
particular, as someone who felt that "he was at home in the world of
objects" and that he could "manipulate matter in a simple disciplined
manner . . . [and] move things correctly. He believed it was all in your
head." Since, as a Zen adept, he can live fully in the moment, his endeav-
or "to maintain a spiritual life" (*DS*, 75–76) can succeed even when he is
dealing in drugs. And, in fact, what he thinks of as his spiritual life helps
him bring the heroin a long step closer to those teenyboppers OD-ing
on rooftops. As Hicks moves his weight—the word the narrator and the
characters frequently use for the heroin—from the carrier on which he
brought it from Vietnam through the heavy security at the naval base in
Oakland, he reassures himself by reflecting that "right thoughts and
right actions enabled one to move discreetly" (*DS*, 77).

The vividness of Hicks's thoughts, acts, and speech encourages one to
take seriously his assertions of his spirituality. But to be a Zen adept, to
be fully awake and live only in the present, is to avoid confusion and
unnecessary conflict. For example, in the *Hagakure*, a seventeenth-centu-
ry "compilation of various notes, anecdotes and moral sayings" concerning the presence of Zen in the life of the samurai, there is the story of
Tsukahara Bokuden's response to an aggressive samurai who is boasting
to his fellow passengers on a boat crossing a lake that he is "the foremost

man in the art." Angered that Bokuden was dozing during his tirade, the braggart

approached Bokuden and shook him, saying, "You also carry a pair of swords, why not say a word?" Answered Bokuden quietly, "My art is different from yours; it consists not in defeating others, but in not being defeated." This incensed the fellow immensely.

"What is your school then?"

"Mine is known as the *mutekatsu* school" (which means to defeat the enemy "without hands," that is, without using a sword).

"Why, then, do you yourself carry a sword?"

"This is meant to do away with selfish motives, and not to kill others."

The man's anger now knew no bounds, and he exclaimed in a most impassioned manner, "Do you really mean to fight me with no swords?"

"Why not?" was Bokuden's answer.

At which point Bokuden directed the boat to an island, and when the braggart jumped ashore, Bokuden, whom Daisetz Suziki calls "one of those swordsmen who really understood the mission of the sword, not as a weapon of murder but as an instrument of spirituality," seized an oar and pushed the boat back into the lake, abandoning the braggart on the island. Then "Bokuden smilingly remarked, 'This is my "no-sword" school.' "[14]

Obviously, this is not Hicks's way of dealing with an adversary. To take only the example of the heroin smuggling, it is not possible for Hicks to avoid conflict as he moves a commodity that attracts so much threatening interest. Marge is fairly deep into Dilaudid withdrawal when Hicks arrives with the drug, but as strung out as she is, she cannot miss the fear of this man who stands before her, nervously chewing his lips. Hicks is a whirlwind of physical efficiency, the samurai he likes to regard himself as, when he overpowers Smitty and Danskin. (I for one find the ease with which he handcuffs Danskin's powerful arms to a toilet bowl improbable.) But why does he not accept Danskin's offer to double the Converses' payment if he turns over the heroin? Of course Stone could not have had Hicks act reasonably about this and still write the novel he wanted to. But the reason Hicks gives Marge is uncontestably within his non-Zen character: "If I hadn't been so hung over and pissed off this morning this shit wouldn't ever have come about" (*DS*, 112). And why this way? Because, with the heroin safely hidden for the night at the base and some time to kill, "self-discipline permitted, or required, light uncomplicated diversion" (*DG*, 78). Which self-discipline requires Hicks's attendance at the bar where he misses the escaped lunatics (but not the hostile blacks and shark-eyed barmaids), his getting very drunk, his going to another bar where, drunk to the verge of defenselessness, he very nearly punches a young man who not only turns out to have a bayonet strapped to his leg but happens to be Smitty, there to lure Hicks into a beating and robbing.

At the first bar, Hicks cannot remember deciding to call his ex-wife: "It was just happening" (*DS*, 81), and he takes out and washes his false tooth "because it seemed like a good idea" (*DS*, 79). An innocuous enough explanation were he not to offer later, as one of his reasons for seeming to kill, with a heroin overdose, a naive, patronizing screenwriter: "I was drunk. It seemed like a good idea" (*DS*, 202).[15] Hicks's impulsivity may be amusing or dashing or horrifying—depending upon its consequences—but it is not Zen.

One unnecessary conflict leads to the next, and within a week he is on the run from his home with heroin worth several million dollars in street value and a friend's wife steadily sinking into withdrawal symptoms. In one of the novel's climactic moments, Hicks stands in the cold wind coming off the high, brilliant ocean and feels, rising in his throat, the urge to jump in his jeep and flee the nearby motel, which houses Marge, painfully huddled in bed. (The scene is a bit confused, since Hicks would also have to abandon the heroin and his M-16 rifle—with, of course, the M-70 launcher attachment—which seem to be in the motel room along with Marge and his clothes.) Hicks recognizes Marge as "some junkie's nod, a snare, a fool catcher." To stay with her "was folly. It was losing." When we first hear of Hicks's involvement with Zen thought, we learn that he has never approached satori, or full wakefulness. First Hicks plays upon his spiritual incompleteness, his still living in the realm of illusion, to justify committing himself to Marge: "In the end there were not many things worth wanting—for the serious man, the samurai. But there were some. In the end, if the serious man is still bound to illusion, he selects the worthiest illusion and takes a stand. The illusion might be of waiting for one woman to come under his hands. Or being with her and shivering in the same moment." But since he still knows how unreasonable this commitment would be, he chucks Zen and its emphasis upon rightness for the dictates of "the blood," a tragic, Dionysian assertion that might have pleased Nietzsche:

If I walk away from this, he thought, I'll be an old man—all ghosts
and hangovers and mellow recollections. Fuck it, he thought, follow the
blood. This is the one. This is the one to ride until it crashes.

He watched the afternoon traffic, southbound.

Go anyway!

Thinking it made him smile. Good Zen. Zen was for old men.

But then, a few minutes later, Hicks tries to use Zen thought to justify
his non-Zen behavior: "The choice was made, and there was nothing to be
had from chickenshit speculation. The roshis were right: the mind is a
monkey" (*DS*, 168–69). But that clamoring, distracting monkey the
roshis are referring to is the ego-mind, which Hicks has not left for a
moment. And so he goes back to the motel room. His feeling bonded to
Marge after the sex a week earlier was merely a preliminary to his breaking out the heroin and wedding her in the church of heightened sensation.

It is the desire for heightened sensation, not money, that propels
Hicks into the drug caper. He has no shortage of reasons to refuse to
carry: Converse is obviously inexperienced and inept; he had recently
decribed Hicks to a mutual friend as a psychopath; he had just told
Hicks that he had designated the latter as a likely drug smuggler to col-
leagues with CIA connections. Small wonder Hicks sourly tells
Converse: "I think this sucks." But then he thinks: "Why not[?] . . .
There was nothing else going down. He felt the necessity of changing
levels, a little adrenalin to clean the blood. It was interesting and kind of
scary. Converse and his old lady would be a scene: he had never seen her"
(*DS*, 54–55).

The impending skirmish with Antheil and his hirelings promises to be
a much more lively scene. It's clear that for some years he has wanted to
be on "[t]he right side for a change," to replace the Vietcong, to be "the
little man in the boonies now" (*DS*, 296), using secrecy and cunning
against superior manpower. But the rightness of the side describes an
ethical dimension as much as a logistical one. As Stone has said, Hicks
"is really extending—he is actually having a shot at greatness, at power,
at true virtue, the old Roman *virtus*. He is really trying for that. He
thinks of it as being a samurai, because that's his Kurosawa-conditioned
Marine Corps orientalism. But he is really after this classic *virtus*, this
classical male virtue[11] (Schroeder, 157–58). *Virtus* is by definition a public thing in a way that *bushido*, the code of the samurai, is not. The first
flicker of virtus Hicks shows in the novel is his commitment to fight it

out so that he has a chance of rescuing Converse. Once reunited with her husband, Marge tells him that they could all have escaped but that Hicks "came down for you" (DS, 306). This assertion is arguable.[16] What is not is Hicks's desire to live within the Marine Corps code of *semper fideles*, of perpetual loyalty, even though he implicitly concedes to Dieter that Converse would never have acted reciprocally.

Dieter earlier described Hicks as being "trapped in a samurai fantasy—an American one. He has to be the Lone Ranger, the great desperado—he has to win all the epic battles single-handed. . . . It may not be a very original conception, but he's quite good at it" (DS, 272). This brings us back to Rheinhardt's speech about the murderous power of American innocence. The distance between the Lone Ranger, that clichéd hero of American preadolescents, and the absolutely mature, illusionless adept of the art of bushido is so great that the superimposition of the two elements has more than a touch of oxymoron to it. It is the preadolescent in Hicks—the one he meets in his delirium on the salt waste—who, as much as any other part of him, opts for the rescue mission.

Whatever the origins of Hicks's attempt to save Converse, it is still a part of his attempt to be the best Raymond Hicks he can be. (Paradoxically, so is the private goal of maintaining possession of the heroin.) The nature of the shootout beautifully articulates the problem of trying to find an appropriate public forum—one that would valorize one's ego thrusts—when communal life is so debased. With Hicks, Stone has the opposition to degraded, murderous authority that the Converses could not provide. But even if Hicks killed all of his four opponents, what effect would it have, what dent would it make in the cultural amorality the novel attacks, and Hicks in part embodies? The battle is simultaneously thrilling and silly; the more one thinks about one of Hicks's prebattle boasts to Dieter—"Watch this . . . this is gonna be the revolution until the revolution comes along" (DS, 292)—the funnier it becomes. Stone moved the light-and-sound show from Kesey's place to Dieter's, and so the former guru can set lights flashing in the forest and mouth into his microphone, "The din of battle . . . bazookas, mortars, rockets, tank guns—it was Dienbienphu, Stalingrad" (DS, 299)—unless you listen closely and hear the breath and spit of the one-man simulator of armies. Hicks is euphoric about blowing up Angel's truck with a grenade launcher. But it's a pickup truck, not a tank. In the midst of what he wants to think is heroic combat, part of his side blown away by Danskin, Hicks explains in the following way how he switched the parcels of sand and heroin: "The pellet with the poison's in the chalice from the palace . . . but the flagon with the dragon has the brew which is true" (*DS*, 303). And indeed, there is a certain Danny Kaye–like giddiness blended into the violence of the shootout.

The Pain Bearer

We can attain satori, full wakefulness, only if we unlearn the false stories about our identity and the identity of the other objects in the world that have been programmed into us by family and culture. Abuse tells one crippling story; privation tells another. When Marge first sees Hicks, he's sufficiently hung over and frightened for some of the stories to show:

> He had a hungry face; in it Marge detected a morphology she recognized. The bones were strong and the features spare but the lips were large and frequently in motion, twisting, pursed, compressing, being gnawed.
> Deprivation—of love, of mother's milk, of calcium, of God knows what. This one was sunburned, usually they were pale. They always had cold eyes. (*DS*, 95)

One of the pleasures that can come with reading novels is learning of a character's appearance long after we've gotten to know him or her well. In *A Flag for Sunrise*, for example, the discovery after 400 pages that Pablo Tabor, whom we've inhabited so intensely, has a hard face and yellow eyes brings with it a small shock of recognition. A much larger one comes with finally seeing Benjy, Jason, and Mrs. Compson in the fourth part of *The Sound and the Fury* (1929). In *Dog Soldiers* Stone gives us Hicks's appearance fairly early on but shrewdly saves until the last section in which he appears alive some explanation of the workings of the abuses that sometimes mark his face and helped to shape him (in Dieter's words) into "the Furor Americansus" (*DS*, 288). The last 12 of the section's 22 pages are dominated by the novel's stylistic tour de force: the overwhelming, increasingly delirious internal monologue that bubbles up in the dying man as he attempts to traverse the salt waste. Or perhaps it's more accurate to say that at a crucial point the monologue splits into a dialogue between the apparent hard case Hicks has turned himself into and the abused, terrified preadolescent he has tried to keep buried inside him: a "turned around kid who made up stories" (*DS*, 324–25), romantic ones he tells the adult Hicks, about being a "part Commanche" from Texas who has shot a 22. Like his creator, he

grew up without a father, was punished for teaching Go Fish to the
other kids at the Booth shelter on the North Side of Chicago, and developed a cringe from abusive institutionalized "care." Stone makes Hicks's
situation—"still pissing his pants at thirteen," and terrified of the beating he'd receive when the disciplinarians at "the Training School" found
his soiled underwear—more desperate than his was at the same age. The
adult Hicks reflects that "nobody can forgive anybody making them *that*
scared" (*DS*, 325–26). As Sharon Lee Ladin has commented, the young
Hicks's "loneliness and resentment lead to the disciplined art of self
defense and he adopts the superiority of style and sensibility of the
samurai to survive his deprivation and emotional vulnerability" (185).
Save that this misses Hicks's inevitable debasement of bushido, as much
as Dieter missed the damage at the center of the acolyte whom he
judged, a few years earlier, to be "your natural man of Zen" (*DS*, 271).

In one of the columns on Jewish culture that Norman Mailer first
published in *Commentary* in the early 1960s, he wrote, "The Jews first
saw God in the desert—that dramatic terrain of the present tense
stripped of the past, blind to the future. The desert is a land where man
may feel insignificant or feel enormous. On the desert can perish the last
of one's sensitivities; one's end can wither in the dwarf law of a bleak
nature. Or to the contrary, left alone and in fever, a solitary witness, no
animal or vegetable close to him, man may come to feel immensely alive,
more portentous in his own psychic presence than any manifest of
nature."[17] What follows—a series of possible responses to the Old
Testament God in such unsupportive terrain—need not concern us: this
deity departed with the missionary on the ninth page of *Dog Soldiers*. The
salt waste is terrifying in its opposition to any familiar human scale. For
John Converse, "[i]t's a lousy place. . . . It's no place to be." His wife,
who perhaps 12 hours earlier walked down a mountain in the dark
toward men who were waiting to kill her, responds, "I haven't been this
scared ever" (*DS*, 334). Converse responds by going into the same kind
of inappropriate palaver about the mind-body problem that Rheinhardt
spews at the rally. What Hicks does with his terror is in striking contrast:

> As he looked out over the salt, it began to glow. For a moment he
> was filled with terror.
> Oh mama. What kind of a place is this?
> He took a deep breath.

> Never mind your mama, never mind the questions. This is home, we walk here. It's built for speed not for comfort.
>
> If you don't like here, then walk away. Nobody gonna do it for you. (*DS*, 323)

This is macho stuff all right, and the last line to describe the living Hicks—"When he had to stop, he leaned his head on his rifle and held to the blazing rail with his strong right hand" (*DS*, 330)—is even more so. But it's great macho stuff. A waiter whom I worked with in the mid-1950s once told me why he could never lose at arm wrestling: "It's just something about my arm; the harder you push on it the more it tightens." This is improbable but memorable. The fight that Hicks puts up against his hopeless situation is a good deal more memorable and, given his lifelong struggle to stiffen himself against that which would make him bend, cringe, is not at all improbable. The insistence upon human assertion in the face of certain annihilation usually finds its way into our masterpieces of the tragic form. I am not trying to compare *Dog Soldiers* with *Hamlet* or *Oedipus the King*, but this is what is convincingly going on with Hicks on the salt waste as much as it conceivably could. Here, he is "immensely alive, more portentous in his own psychic presence than any manifest of nature." Aristotle observed that the tragic hero needs to be better than the average man to fulfill his tragic function: to create pity and fear and to purge those emotions from the play. It is a tribute to Hicks's and to Stone's struggle to transcend that a character who behaved as loathsomely as Hicks sometimes did can generate the tragic frequencies that he does.

Looked at from one point of view, Zen is a sort of instinctual Aristotelianism: the adept automatically blends his own most positive potentials with the most positive potentials in the external situation in which he finds himself. As I argued, perhaps to the point of tedium, Hicks has not been all that much of an adept in the earlier situations in which he found himself. His situation on the salt flat is quite possibly hopeless: the odds are that he will bleed to death before the Converses can get to him—if they even attempt to pick him up. Yet in the desert he is precisely alone; he doesn't have to deal with people who are trying to rob him of his heroin or offering him an insultingly low price for it. There's also a salutary simplicity to his situation: to function well he must contain his pain, keep walking, and keep down the terror that the salt waste encourages. His successful attempt to contain the pain generates one of the most memorable images of the novel. In a Zen exercise, Hicks places the pain in an imagined red circle within a blue triangle against a black background. At one point, he attempts to let his mind merge with the pain, but it's immediately intolerable. In contemporary slang, Hicks is a control freak; more academically, he's a Nietzschean, who functions best when he's wired to his will to power. He reconstructs circle and triangle, and later, as the pain threatens to swim outside the circle, he tries expanding the geometric configuration. He "realizes" that that there was no end to its enlargement; in fact he could contain everyone's pain. In the closest thing to a Whitmanesque moment so far in Stone's fiction, Hicks accepts the pain of all crying women, of children who are whining or shot off water buffaloes, of the napalmed, of older men, of other men.

Hugh O'Haire has concluded from this new capaciousness, from his recitation of the Prajna Paramita Sutra, and from his declared love for both Converses that Hicks undergoes complete enlightenment, so that he experiences "love and compassion for all people and things" (41).[18] But Hicks keeps cutting the sutra off because of its insistence upon transcendence; he feels that he will die on the spot if he doesn't keep intact his embattled relationship to what is around and within him. Finally, Hicks exists more through opposition than through merging. It is not love for the Converses, whom he hopes to meet, that keeps the dying man marching beside the abandoned railroad. It is pride and a sort of contempt for the hopelessness of his situation. Earlier, he had lamented having "nothing to manipulate, nothing to work with but the tracks. What a waste of awareness and coordination" (*DS*, 327). In the last sentences in which we see him alive, he resolves to transcend even this limitation:

> That's enough, he said to himself, I can dig tracks.
>   Out of spite, out of pride, he counted the crossties aloud. He counted hundreds and hundreds of them. When he had to stop, he leaned his head on his rifle and held to the blazing rail with his strong right hand. (*DS*, 330)

And this is not illusion. When the Converses find him dead on the tracks, John Converse can scarcely believe that Hicks walked as many miles from the distant mountains as he did. A good part of the weight he carried was his rifle. Like Natty Bumppo, D. H. Lawrence's quintessentially stoic American killer, he calls it a "creature." Correspondingly, when Hicks is proclaiming his ability to contain everyone's pain, it is the proud assertion of the self-proclaimed master of "the most marvelous and subtle of the *martial* arts" (*DS*, 328; my emphasis). One feels that right up to his collapse, he would have used that rifle on any birds who got too close to him. A key ingredient of the success of the final characterization is the multiplicity of emotions that emerge in his different takes: stoicism, love, aggression, obscenity, pride, spite, irony, humor, the lust for virtus.

Chapter Four
A Flag for Sunrise

The Creation of Tecan

Stone's creative writing post at Princeton in 1971 was followed by one at Amherst, where he taught for the next three years. He took off the 1975–76 academic year to work on the California and Mexico locations where *Who'll Stop the Rain?*, the film version of *Dog Soldiers*, was being shot and to launch another novel. Stone got only about 30 pages into his first short-lived effort. It was about the Munster Anabaptists, "a kind of scatological sect of apocalyptic proto-Mennonites. . . . I just couldn't handle the diction; how was I going to get these sixteenth-century Germans to talk? I had no idea" (Solotaroff 1991). Making little progress and knowing that he had to get away, Stone found himself in March 1976 in Tuscaloosa with $1,000 in his pocket from a reading at the University of Alabama and no immediate responsibilities. What Janice Stone has called the gypsy in her husband took over. From New Orleans, Stone found his way to the scuba diving that was his immediate goal and, more important, to a locale in which his interest in the possible connection between religious fervor and social upheaval could coexist with the kinds of colloquial language over which he had such mastery:

I thought I've got to go somewhere, where shall I go? I found out there was this flight down to San Pedro Sula, Honduras, so I thought what a gas it would be if I got on a plane to San Pedro Sula. I expected a town out of [the film] *The Wages of Fear* [1953], and that's exactly what I got. There it was! I started traveling from there by bus, met some people, and ended up, after some weeks, in Costa Rica. In the course of that trip, just listening to people, keeping my eyes and ears open, I became aware that there was a lot going on down there that was extraordinarily interesting. . . . The situation began to remind me of Vietnam. I was sensing the American presence in the undeveloped world, and I was again seeing

this vaguely irrational sense of mission which Americans are consumed
with when they are about their business in the undeveloped world:
anthropologists, missionaries, deserters, crazies, druggies—various people. (Ruas, 288)

In Stone's six-week ramble he spent a bit more than two weeks in
Honduras, and somewhat less than two in Costa Rica. In between, both
in terms of placement and duration of stay, was Nicaragua, the country
whose repression, intense American presence, and revolutionary potential most anticipated those of Tecan, the Central American hybrid country in which Stone set most of *A Flag for Sunrise*. The earthquake that
rocked Managua in December 1972 had left three-quarters of the city's
400,000 inhabitants homeless and offered great opportunities for
American contractors. Stone took in their wheeling and dealing when he
visited the bar in the Hotel Continental in Managua, and throughout
Nicaragua he picked up a sense of how President Anastasio Somoza's
appetite for profits from the rebuilding was "making it impossible for
everyone, even Americans to make money. He alienated everybody"
(Solotaroff 1991).

Stone returned to pacing his office in Northampton, wondering how
he could get his Anabaptists to talk, and after a few days decided that he
really had gotten into something valuable in Central America. He began
writing what became *Flag* either late in 1976 or early the next year,
before combat broke out in Nicaragua. But the novel was quickly over-
taken by events. One revolutionary group launched a major offensive in
October 1977, and the strength of the opposition to Somoza steadily
grew until the dictator fled the country on 17 July 1979, a bit before
Stone got down, in the last pages of his novel, the flight of the president
from Tecan. With its capital on a huge lake, its eastern and western
coasts, and its ferocious and ubiquitous Guardia Nacional, it is tempting
to regard Tecan as Nicaragua with a different name. But Stone has said
that the relatively underpopulated Honduras—more cheerful, less
impoverished than Nicaragua—was the country that, in 1976 and on his
two returns to Central America in the next four years, "I traveled the
most in, got the closest to the ground, knew what the people were like,
got the feel of the place." Socially, Tecan most resembles Nicaragua
before fighting began, but while writing the novel, Stone was thinking,
"geographically . . . of Honduras in terms of what places looked like"
(Solotaroff 1991).[1]

Tecan and the Revolution

Stone also changed both the incipient cause of revolution and the American response. Though San Ysidro, the capital of Tecan, had been hit by an earthquake perhaps five years earlier, we cannot tell from the novel whether it was as devastating as the 1972 Managua quake. The precipitating factor is not the dictator alienating his former business associates but the discovery of copper in the central highlands of the country and the regime's attempt to drive from these regions the Atapas, so fierce a people that they constitute half of the Guardia. The object of the final loyalty of an army or militia is usually the winner of a revolution. We might assume that a good many of the Guardia's Atapas joined the revolution, since it seems to be successful. But "seems" is the sticking point. On the third-to-last page of the novel, the narrator lets us know, almost as an afterthought, that the president has fled to Miami and that at least one loyal officer of the Guardia is in mufti and on the run. But, says Godoy, an intelligent, native-born priest, "There's nothing but failure here. The country is a failure. A disaster of history" (*FS*, 50). While Nicaragua's economy was progressing nicely until the 1972 earthquake, every morning "Tecan's children were shouldering their daily burdens, prepared to endure with ancient grace the rule of plunder and violence" (*FS*, 375). It would have taken a much different, much more extended book than the one Stone wrote to make believable the bringing of social justice to Tecan. It probably would take a different author, one who is not as temperamentally opposed to optimistic prognoses of human experience as Stone.

Perhaps a dozen reviewers referred in one way or another to the grimness of the vision—both political and individual—that emerges from *Flag*, but none of them mentioned the man who, it would (again) seem, is to assume the presidency of Tecan. Highly cultured but forceful and pragmatic, idealistic but strong, Emilio Ortega Curtis would seem to be the closest thing to a positive wish fulfillment we will ever find in a Robert Stone fiction. He even seems shrewd enough to avoid the intervention of a U.S. government that is far more sympathetic to any corrupt dictator who claims to be anticommunist than was the Carter administration to Somoza. But Ortega surfaces in only one of the novel's 43 sections—at a meeting of revolutionary leaders set around the middle of the novel—after which we do not even hear his name again. So much is made of the misery of the Tecanese people and the unfairness of history, and so impressive is Ortega as a candidate who could do as much as anyone to ease the collective misery, that one wants a bit more on the forces present in the country that might turn Ortega's idealism into something more sinister, or that might depose him. Then again, Ortega's vigor is most evident in his purging of spies from the revolutionary movement, and he dismisses in advance the improbability of success for the insurrection, which will cost Sister Justin great agony and her life, with, "[N]othing is lost if we fail here" (*FS*, 205). If Stone tried to imbed in the novel a prophecy for Tecan that bears out the truth of George Orwell's maxim that the ideals of a Lenin always end up in the cellars of an NKVD—in the torture chambers of the police—he needed to offer this reader a few more hints.[2] Still, though Stone used a cynical paragraph from *Heart of Darkness* as the epigraph for *Dog Soldiers*, and though *Flag*, like *Nostromo*, is a novel about revolution in a two-coasted Central American country, it has none of Conrad's world-weary mockery of the possibilities of revolution.

Welcome to Tecan

The overwhelming first chapter does not encourage the suspicion that any good might ever come to Tecan or to any of its humane inhabitants, native or foreign-born. *Flag*'s principals are four very different American Catholics, one of them a naturalized Canadian. For his first four novels, Stone was not much interested in creating principals who are well qualified to deal with whatever opposes them: three of the four in *Flag* are chemical dependents. In the first sentence of Stone's first novel, Rheinhardt demonstrates unusual restraint by saving the pint he has just purchased so that it will get him through the night on the bus to New Orleans. In the first sentence of *A Flag for Sunrise*, Father Charles Egan, a Canadian-born priest in the Devotionist Order, interrupts his work on the seventh draft of the book he has been writing to make his unsteady way across the room to a bottle of rum. He has two drinks and forgoes a third, but his return to his desk is interrupted by the arrival of Lieutenant Campos, social agent of the Guardia Nacional. Egan's response—he draws in his breath in fear—is unfortunately appropriate: if the cops are robbers in *Dog Soldiers*, they are killers in Tecan. Campos's recognition of the priest's authority—"Holy Father. . . . Bless me, for I have sinned"—is quickly superseded by the assertion of his own: "insane intelligent eyes smoldering in the moonlight" (*FS*, 5), he commands the priest to follow him to his jeep. Later in the novel Sister Justin Feeney, the nursing nun who is Egan's coreligionist at the Devotionist Mission, will reflect that Campos "had a spider's-web aura of schizoid insights around him, an odor of unclean appetites that seemed to concentrate on her" (*FS*, 285). True enough: before leaving the mission with Egan, Campos asks after Justin and observes that her light is still on. Once at the lieutenant's bungalow, Egan receives the benefits of the lieutenant's schizoid prescience. First, Campos parodies hospitality by offering his alcoholic guest one drink, then another: "[A]s he proffered it, Egan had the sense that he might suddenly snatch it away again to torment him. Just as he was imagining the dreadful smile that might appear on Campos' face if he did in fact snatch the glass away—the smile appeared." Then Campos asks Egan if he is a homosexual. At first the priest is outraged, telling himself that no one has ever addressed him that way in his ten years in Tecan. Then he sees himself in town, drunk, a boy scornfully shouting at him that he was a homosexual: "Was it memory? Had such a thing happened? Egan was not clear" (*FS*, 7).

But it turns out that Campos has brought Egan to his bungalow for purposes that are ironically higher than harassment, and that superimpose the horror of surrealist cinema upon such typical and upsetting Tecanese realities as the lieutenant's terrorizing of the priest, or other members of the Guardia feeling up terrified tourists, or children trying to stone to death a trapped cow. The lieutenant leads the priest to a freezer where, among many bottles of beer and a huge, unplucked turkey, Egan finds first a foot, then an eye, finally the frozen body of a Canadian girl killed by Campos and his Guardia companions. In an absolutely convincing demonstration of the way religiosity can coexist with psychopathy, Campos feels no guilt about killing the girl but is drunkenly stricken that he has lived with her corpse for some vague duration. Because "it's the duty of the priests to take the dead," because Campos feels that he's "not an animal," but a human who believes in "spiritual force . . . in life after death," he commands Egan, "for the relief of my heart" (*FS*, 13), to dispose of the frozen body. After stuffing the body into a sleeping bag, Campos deposits the priest and the body at the steps of the mission. Though in poor health and in his sixties, Egan manages to get the bag into the mission's whaler, and after going perhaps a mile out to sea, beyond the inner and the outer reefs, he weights the bag with two anchors and slides it over the side. He is amazed at how easily the bag sinks, at how "the deck of the boat and the ocean's surface held no trace of what they had borne a few seconds before. . . . He [feels] as though he had gained a thoroughly new insight into the processes of the world" (*FS*, 15).

Gnosticism and Egan's Transformation

The mystery here is why a manifestation of the brute indifference of the natural world should come as a surprise to someone who has labored through seven drafts of a book that, to an uncertain degree, endorses standard Gnostic doctrine: God's nature is "alien to that of the universe, which it neither created nor governs."[3] Sophia, or wisdom, foolishly wandered outside the pleroma, or plenitude in which God exists, to create the Demiurge. Ignorant of its origins in some Gnostic teachings, malevolently opposed to all manifestations of divine goodness in others, flawed in all, the Demiurge is the being who created humans and the visible universe. Whether through acts of God or, unsuspected by the Demiurge, through a benign aspect of Sophia's programming of the shaping Demiurge, each human contains a part of the Godhead, and our destiny is somehow to return to and reconstitute Him. This sketch offers no sense of the completeness of the Gnostics' rejection of mundane existence: "[T]he universe . . . is like a vast prison whose innermost dungeon is the earth, the scene of man's life. . . . [I]n gnostic thought the world takes the place of the traditional underworld and is itself already the realm of the dead, that is, of those who have to be raised to life again" (Jonas, 43, 68). One way of describing the dominant thrust of romanticism in the last two centuries is as a series of attempts to humanize the world. If Egan embraced a quintessentially antiromantic vision of terrestrial existence in his writing, he had not done so in his life.

Most of the dramatized action of the novel is set within a closely observed ten days in late January and early February 1976. This period begins in the second of *Flag's* 43 sections, one that covers the drive to, and the overnight stay in, New York by Frank Holliwell, an anthropologist en route to Compostela, Tecan's neighbor to the northwest, to give a lecture. (The date is fixed when Holliwell learns that Paul Robeson, who passed away on 23 January 1976, died in the morning hours of this day.) The burial at sea described in the first section occurred an unspecified number of months earlier—more than one, less than eight, I would say—and Egan has changed in this interval. The Egan of the first section indulges "the notion that his office space suggested the study of some heterodox doctor of the Renaissance, a man condemned by his times but sustained by faith in God and the Spirit in men." He would particularly appreciate this appearance being taken for the reality since he no longer has any flock to minister to, and "the dark of his soul's night was such that he could not bring it to bear. . . . [His] faith seemed moribund" (*FS*,

3–4). But by the ten-day period he seems to have found his faith again, admittedly one that is often as shaky as his initial movement to the rum. In the clearing in back of the mission the whiskey priest preaches night-ly to his drug-addled congregation, perhaps 40 hippies who have inter-rupted their sojourn along the eastern Caribbean shore of Tecan, where the mission is located, to camp out there for a while.

In one account of why Central America seized his creative fancy in the way that it did, Stone wrote, "This band of republics between the Andes and the Grijalva seemed placed by its gods in a very fateful situation. The region seemed to have attracted the most violent conquistadors and the most fanatical inquisitors. When they arrived, the Spaniards found holy wells of human sacrifice. Here, racial and social oppression had always been most severe. The fertile soil of the place seemed to bring forth things to provoke the appetite rather than things to nourish— baubles and rich toys, plantation crops for your sweet tooth or for your head" ("RS," 76). Stone goes to some pains in the novel to make it clear that Tecan is the sinkhole of Central America, but even for Tecan the clearing back of the mission carries an unusually negative charge. On one side is a hill covering a burial pyramid; centrally located are three stelae, whose inscriptions and hieroglyphs tell of the human sacrifice that once occurred in the clearing. To it also come Weitling, a psychotic raised in the country to the south of Tecan, who obeys the dictates of the fertility god he hears by murdering children, and Pablo Tabor, the American deserter from the Coast Guard who arrives a few hours after he has murdered the three other inhabitants of the ship on which he traveled to the Tecanese coast. As Egan tells him, "You understand, Pablo? There's a charge upon the place. It draws people like Weitling and people like you. The field of blood. The place of the skull. They played the ball game here you know. . . . Can that be? A temple? A tem-ple of the demiurge?" (FS, 369).[4]

In this locale, so apparently antipathetic to the possibilities of human transcendence, Egan preaches of the presence of the jewel in the lotus, the shard of the Living, the One, in the putrefaction of our corporeality. He demonstrates considerable eloquence, wit, and unflappability in his sermon to the hippies, one of whom heckles him. He's also appropriate-ly eclectic: he tries to dissuade Weitling, a Mennonite, from the human sacrifice by quoting not Gnostic doctrine but traditional Scripture, which illustrates God's protective love of children. The recent develop-ments in Pablo's strange life have made him a credulous listener, and so to him Egan lays out Gnostic doctrine, "not as he had written about them"—presumably as metaphor—"but as though they were literal, true things, as one might tell a story to a child. Then he thought that perhaps they were true things, real things, as real as the sun which was rising over the clearing" (*FS*, 375).[5]

This is the same sun that is lighting the suffering, stirring children of Tecan, the adolescents in the clearing, and "the depths where a murdered girl lay distantly mourned. Nor would she be alone there. And in the forest, Weitling would be looking at the sunrise and taking fire with fantasies of sacrifice and blood." It is as a part of Egan's attempt to redeem the clearing, the temple of the Demiurge, to make of it an altar from which he broadcasts the eventual return to the "Incomprehensible, Inconceivable One with Whom all things were" that he mourns for the corpse he pusillanimously buried and celebrates the survival of the divine spark in the live body of the Canadian girl once imprisoned. (Stone seems also to be hinting that Egan is recapturing a previously lost, Canadian, feminine aspect of himself.) And it is in the clearing that he tries to replace Weitling's murderous voices with his own. Of course, goodwill and faith have their limits: the paragraph from which I've most recently been quoting ends with Egan contemplating the manhunt for Weitling that he will have to "set afield now, for the saving of other children" (*FS*, 375).

But Egan's finest moment comes in the novel's next-to-last section, which, because of its content and positioning, serves as a yardstick of his growth over the course of the book. Having tortured Sister Justin to death, and having decided that her final words ("Behold the handmaid of the Lord") both "put me in the wrong" and show "that God had played a trick on me," Campos searches out Egan in the clearing. On his knees but pointing his service revolver at the priest, Campos demands penance. Egan—who, in his fear of Campos, collaborated with the official sadism of Tecan perhaps four months earlier—has developed enough inner strength to regard the rapid disintegration of his body as creation's way of bringing him closer to the chaos from which he emerged. Now the priest experiences no flicker of apprehension but plays his own trick on the frantic lieutenant as he tells him that he can find comfort only by imagining a world in which he, Campos, does not exist, that God has no concern for him, and that there is no divine mercy to be found on earth—just "half moments. Glintings. A little rising of the heart, eh? It's dappled" (*FS*, 435): flickering apprehensions of the jewel in the lotus. Though Egan is the only one of the novel's principals who both grows morally and survives, Stone is characteristically ambivalent about the fruits of his amplified insight. Over the course of the novel Egan moves from boozy fantasies of turning to "the Spiritual Church, the masses so hungry for comfort in a violently dying world" (*FS*, 3), to the clearing. He grows by casting his tent in the excrement of life, to blend a line of Yeats that Stone likes with the Gnostic vision of terrestrial existence. Then again, for the one sermon that we hear, "[i]t seemed to him that he had a text." Why? Because "[t]here was a cane fire in his brain" (*FS*, 310). Whatever the heat of his religious fervor, its immediate source is the rum that is animating it. Correspondingly, for all we know at novel's end, the search for Weitling has been forgotten and he's still moving through Tecan, murdering children. And though Egan is freed "from the consuming soreness of heart that had poisoned his life before," the pain his new capacity for sympathy causes him is a nonverbal rejection of the possibility of terrestrial happiness: "it was not easy to watch all the world's deluded wanderings across the battlefield of a long-ago lost war. One had to close the heart to pity—if one could" (*FS*, 437).

Holliwell: The Uses and Abuses of Alcohol

A recurrent metaphor in Gnostic lore is of earthly existence as a drunken whirl. Sects that regard the Demiurge as malevolent argue that he and his archons (or underlings) so tempt and distract us with superficial earthly pleasures that we are as oblivious of the shard of the eternal within us as a careening drunk is of the precise orderings around him. Since "Traveler's Itch" inflames Holliwell's desire for alcohol even more than it does his appetite for sexual adventure, his ten-day immersion in Central American concerns is in large part a quite nonmetaphorical drunken whirl. On the morning of his departure from his home in Delaware, the two Bloody Marys that serve as his breakfast make him high enough to buy his first cigarettes in a month. As he chain-smokes the cigarettes during the drive to New York City, the tall, strongly built, and very intelligent Holliwell responds to a fundamentalist narrative that he picks up on the radio by sobbing. "So much for morning drinking," he concludes. Slipping deeper into the self-indulgence that will poison his travels along with his bloodstream, Holliwell soon decides that "it would be a drinking day—the morning stirrup cup had set off an old mechanism. But his habits had become so generally temperate that it seemed to him he could afford some reasonable indulgence in the field" (*FS*, 18). (We are reminded of Hicks's convincing himself that Zen self-discipline commands the pleasant diversions that cause him to wake up the next morning "wretched and poisoned . . . deeply ashamed" [*DS*, 90]). In spite of the humiliation and terror his drinking brings him in Compostela, Holliwell never expresses any guilt about his consumption or any intention of curbing it. The Brooklyn lunch with his old parochial high school friend, Marty Nolan, for some years an employee of the CIA, is accompanied by two martinis, a shared bottle of wine, two stingers, and a brandy. At night in his hotel room, while he's making his way through almost all of a bottle of scotch, he reflects that "the juice was turning on him altogether, softening him up; it was all catching up with him. His past was dead and his present doing poorly" (*FS*, 30). On the next day, though, Holliwell is obscurely "encouraged" (*FS*, 71) by the steady stream of Bloody Marys he gets down in the Miami airport and on the plane to Compostela; perhaps he was discouraged by whatever he drank between his levee in New York and Miami. So it goes. The path from Compostela to Tecan, and from Tecan to the island to the east that he is approaching in the novel's last pages, is lubricated by the scotch, margaritas, brandy, rum, piña coladas, and beer he consumes en route.

Sometimes he seems unaffected by his consumption, sometimes he gives way to a self-pity and a narrative-clogging, reflective loquaciousness that are quite different from anything Rheinhardt ever shows. Holliwell's self-destructive drinking and the imperatives of the plotting converge during his brief stay (perhaps 22 hours) in Compostela City. At his hotel, perhaps an hour before he is to give his address at the Autonomous University, Holliwell leaves his bottle of scotch and showers "to sober himself and then [drinks] more, as though that would further the process" (*FS*, 103). En route to the lobby he realizes his steps are unsteady and therefore has two more drinks at the hotel bar. Told that the audience at the university would prefer a speech in English, Holliwell casts aside his Spanish-written speech and, emboldened by the alcohol in his bloodsteam, improvises. (Since he had left his reading glasses in the hotel room, "beside the scotch" [*FS*, 106], he could not have used the prepared speech anyway.) The nub of his improvisation is that the United States is exporting to the Third World its debased, popular culture, which is now replacing the equally debased popular culture of countries like Compostela. The first interruption comes from a menacing young Compostelan who accuses Holliwell of "[f]acile nihilism . . . a screen for Communist theory" (*FS*, 109). Holliwell's attempts to defend himself from this and most of the succeeding questions and accusations from the floor largely serve to heighten the audience's animosity and to speed their departure.

Since Compostela is a country with a liberal facade but quite ferocious repressive workings—Stone has said he had in mind the political behavior of Mexico (Solotaroff 1991)—Holliwell receives four telephoned death threats by the next (or Sunday) morning. To bring him to Tecan, Stone adds to his fear for his life and his curiosity about the goings-on at the Devotionist Mission two plot conveniences: the unavailability of space on the Sunday flight out, and the offer of a ride to Tecan by Tom and Marie Zecca, Americans in from San Ysidro for the weekend, who attended the debacle of Holliwell's appearance at the Autonomous University.

The Presence of Vietnam

Holliwell's curiosity is the fruit of Nolan's request back in Brooklyn that Holliwell cross the border into Tecan to observe the activities of two countrymen, Egan and Justin, who are, in Nolan's words, "in a state of social and spiritual crisis" (FS, 22). This would not be spying, runs Nolan's pitch, just Holliwell sharing his concern for, his desire to protect, what he calls his "compatriots and erstwhile co-religionists," whose possible revolutionary sympathies have already made them the objects of the attention of "people who'd love nothing more than to mess with their private parts" (FS, 24).

A crucial component of Holliwell's and Nolan's experience comes from Vietnam, Nolan's more spectacularly: the Vietcong had buried him alive, and, half-conscious, he lay in the earth for six hours before being dug up. Converse posits Vietnam as an experiential litmus test, the place where everyone finds out what they are. Nolan would seem to have discovered there what almost everyone else is, and little in his subsequent experience has qualified his appraisal: "We're at a very primitive stage of mankind," he tells Holliwell. "That's what people don't understand. Just pick up the *Times* on any given day and you've got a catalogue of ape behavior. Strip away the slogans and excuses and verbiage, the so-called ideology, and you're reading about what one pack of chimpanzees did to another." Moreover, historical whirl prevails, for the shape of "history" is determined by whoever is telling the story. Saigon falls, patriotism is discredited, "and the whole card's reversed. Hiss didn't do it, the Rosenbergs didn't do it, nobody fucking did it and Truman started the cold war. Total vindication . . . it's all a movie in this country and if you wait long enough you get your happy ending. Until somebody else's movie starts. In many ways it's a very stupid country" (FS, 25–26).

(Could Stone's vagueness about the future of Tecan follow from his desire to deny the reader his or her usual sense of easy superiority to the kind of confusion and uncertainty Nolan describes?)

As iconoclastic as this CIA employee may seem, Nolan still grounds the need to act, to take sides, on the same old us/them, free world/Communist bloc Manichaeism. Though he implicitly concedes that the characteristically stupid American foreign policy drove dissident elements to the Communist bloc for assistance, he uses this consequence to appeal for Holliwell's aid: "[W]ell, it's them or us, chum. Like always. They make absolute claims, we make relative ones. That's why our side is better in the end" (*FS*, 25). In the kind of passive drift that partly characterizes his behavior throughout the novel, Holliwell responds only by asking, "Is that what *you* believe?" instead of arguing, for example, for the need to support less radical, less dissident groups. (The Carter administration did support dissident Nicaraguan groups that were to the right of the Sandinistas, without ultimate success.) Still, Holliwell's passivity has its limits. He will not go to Tecan for himself—"It's a rathole and it gets on my conscience" (*FS*, 23)—and he certainly will not go for Nolan.

Stone will develop some surprising similarities between Holliwell and Pablo Tabor, apparently so different, whom he will place in an open boat in the Caribbean late in the novel: both men grew up without fathers, feel themselves outsiders to the families they helped to create, drifted into intrigue and danger in Central America, and kill at sea when threatened. Most of Pablo's murderous paranoia follows from his opposition to being "turned around," to being manipulated by others. Holliwell feels that he was turned around, compromised, in Vietnam when, as an anthropologist with AID (Aid for International Development), he did favors for the CIA. Judging from what he tells the Zeccas during his first night in Tecan, the favors seem to have consisted of batting out probably unread anthropological commentary on Vietnamese subcultures for CIA employees who needed to generate some busywork if they were to stay on in the country. But Holliwell must have concluded that the reports somehow contributed to the onslaught on the people; otherwise, he would not so strongly fear being again used by the CIA in Tecan. (Though in favor of his professional association's resolution to refrain from doing work for the CIA, Holliwell abstained in the vote because, as he tells Nolan, "I felt compromised. Because of what I did in Nam. The favors" [*FS*, 22]). Holliwell is equally resolute in resisting the plea of Oscar Ocampo, his old Compostelan friend who was driven by personal difficulties to CIA employment, that he raise his stock with the Agency by turning up in Tecan. Holliwell's clear and accurate sense of the Agency's manipulativeness comes out quite strongly here.

But if Holliwell's Vietnam experience shaped his resistance to CIA involvement, it also contributed to the spiritual aridity that will, by degrees, lead him to do just the work that Nolan wants. At 40, Holliwell seems to have been undergoing an extended *crise de quarantaine* for some time. In his car, between the drinks with Nolan and the bottle in his hotel room, he self-pityingly sees himself as "really without beliefs, without hope—either for himself or for the world. Almost without friends, certainly without allies. Alone" (*FS*, 26). A few hours earlier, with less liquor in him, he tried to play the social scientist and attributed the shakiness that accompanies his despair to "being forty, marriage, soft suburban living." In the next paragraph his getting shaky is "a pattern of class and culture" (*FS*, 18). But once in Tecan, a country whose sounds, sights, and smells, both urban and rural, touch off unwelcome and vivid reexperiencings of Vietnam, Holliwell gives a much more specific explanation for his wintry soul. Over margaritas at the Zeccas, Holliwell includes himself among those survivors of Vietnam who are burnouts, rootless pilgrims. When Marie Zecca challenges this self-description, Holliwell peels back only a little of his negativism: "Maybe just badly seared" (*FS*, 165). It might seem that Tom Zecca is merely playing the good host, smoothing over a guest's social wobble, when he follows with, "Everyone that ever saw that place is a little fucked up" (*FS*, 166–67). His subsequent behavior, however, joins Holliwell's in extending from *Dog Soldiers* Stone's emphasis upon the effect Vietnam has had upon Americans. A captain in the U.S. Army, Zecca has in Tecan been badly compromised by a government policy that has forced him to be a military adviser to a Tecanese administration he detests. But as he, his wife, and Holliwell work their way through a second blender of margaritas and into drunkenness, Zecca's increasingly pathetic protestations of his honor defend his behavior in Vietnam, the locale that still obsesses him.

The American Consumer Abroad

Richard Poirier has observed that "almost any human movement in Stone's novels becomes, whether this is intended or not, a metaphor for intrusion or intervention, and of the suffering that follows from it."[6] While I think this somewhat overstates the case, it certainly describes any imperialist venture, and Stone is, after all, a novelist who has described his career as "the course of wringing a few novels from our *fin-de-siècle*, late imperial scene" ("RS," 75). Holliwell's presence in Tecan is particularly intrusive, and in a way that nicely captures the self-interest and self-indulgence beneath idealistic protests, the dangerous innocence, and the sickness beneath apparent robustness that, at least in Stone's mind, characterize American adventures abroad. As Holliwell sits on his hotel balcony, a few hours before he catches the cab to the Autonomous University, it occurs to him

> that against safety and reason, he felt like going to Tecan after all. The Corazón Islands stood off her Caribbean coast, enemies to winter and the emptiness that awaited him at home. Tecan was what it was, but it was also, like Compostela, the sweet waist of America. A seductress, *la encan-tada*, a place of pleasure for the likes of him.
>   Beyond the snow bird's impulse was his mounting curiosity about the Catholics there. It would be strange to see such Catholics, he thought. It would be strange to see people who believed in things, and acted in the world according to what they believed. It would be different. Like old times. He owed nothing to anyone; he could go or not. What he might do and what he might see there would be no one's business but his own. (*FS*, 101)

Unlike *Dog Soldiers, Flag* contains a principal who is able to exist on levels other than the aesthetic one. Tecan is not primarily a place to seek pleasure for Justin, who struggles to exist on the ethical level, and for Egan, who, in his moments as a believing Gnostic, exists in what Kierkegaard would call Religiousness A.[7] Although Holliwell meets Egan first, he has almost no impact on the priest. But his collisions with Justin and Pablo—his ethical superior and inferior, respectively—are telling for all three characters. Human interactions in Stone's world are largely a reworking of Gresham's Law that bad money drives out good money: morally inferior characters to varying degrees undo superior ones. Rheinhardt helps to drive Geraldine to her death, as, in *Children of Light*, Gordon Walker helps to drive Lu Anne Bourgeois to hers, as Ron Strickland in *Outerbridge Reach*, to a limited degree, corrupts Anne Browne. As I suggested earlier, the relative absence of ethical exemplars in *Dog Soldiers* precludes, for many readers, identification with characters. In *Flag* the intrusive victories of the worse over the better, of Holliwell over Justin and Pablo over Holliwell, are, as we shall see, interestingly qualified.

I mentioned earlier the sexual component of Holliwell's Traveler's
Itch. When, in the evening after his luncheon with Nolan, he calls his
wife from his hotel, he jokingly tells her that he might walk over to
Eighth Avenue "for some twenty-dollar fellatio" (*FS*, 27). A more profound, more veiled suggestion of sexual possibility comes as Holliwell's
longing to go to Tecan rises up in him: he is at that moment watching a
French teenager and her mother playing in the pool beneath him: "The
women were fair; their bodies were tanned and charged with the sunlit
sensuality of fruit in the softening afternoon light," while "two Indians
in braided uniform jackets hosed down the garden, looking neither at
the guests nor at each other" (*FS*, 101). I tend to feel that, at some level
of the text, Holliwell is fantasizing an orgy with mother and daughter in
this (only apparently) permissive locale where the dark-haired natives
will look the other way. The way this theme of sexual intrusion with fair-
haired women permeates the novel is much less arguable. At his debacle
at the university, Holliwell is suddenly infatuated by the beautiful,
honey-haired Minister of Social Services, Mariaclara Obregón. After she
resists his invitation to a liaison and seizes upon an opportunity to leave,
Holliwell melodramatically contemplates what would have happened
had he followed and "insisted. Dramatically. With impetuosity and flair,
like a lover. He felt like a lover" (*FS*, 115). No, Holliwell, just the familiar, half-drunken, middle-aged performer at an academic gathering who
is lusting after a member of the audience. In this case, the academic
turns to cadge what scotch he can before the lone bottle on the table is
taken away. When we learn that Justin's hair is also honey-colored, we
perceive that Holliwell's lurching but mercifully brief advance toward
Obregón was only a prelude to his pursuit of the vastly more vulnerable
Justin.

Although Holliwell and Justin are together for five sections, the angle
of vision is hers for only the first one, when they meet. Holliwell's
despairing way of looking at the world also prevails during the two sections when he is with Pablo, and this dominance, combined with the
facts that he survives and Justin and Pablo do not, helps to make
Holliwell's viewpoint the prevailing vision of the novel. Put differently,
though both the Gnostic viewpoint he comes to and the much more
optimistic Christian one she returns to are in the novel, his dominates.
But we are inside Justin's head when she tends to Holliwell—who, snor-
keling, has just knelt on a sea urchin—and not only perceptively sees his
face as one that "bespoke softness and self-indulgence" but, as he is a few
minutes later mocked by "two young loafers from town," understands

him to be "an absurd and unnecessary person" (*FS*, 234–35). Justin particularly resents what she regards as his intrusion because she has been driven to sleeplessness and almost unendurable anxiety by her commitment to the revolutionaries and the perception that Campos is watching her closely. Still, after Holliwell wittily flirts with her and she decides that he "was impertinent and patronizing, and for all she knew, depraved," she also concedes that "he was sort of nice" (*FS*, 237).

Justin has her anxious watch for news of action from the revolutionaries to return to, but Holliwell repairs to his resort (ironically named Paradise) to stoke with rum the cane fire in *his* head. He picks up on Justin's apparent self-assurance and inflates it until she becomes the embodiment of all female arrogance. After raging against this for a while, he too gives way to concession (he likes her), has some more rum, and then works himself into another emotional crescendo that turns all "positive thinkers" into murderers or approvers of murderers. "The acceptance showed that they were realists which showed that they were real." Then comes a decrescendo into some reasonable reflections— "Despair was also a foolish indulgence, less lethal than vain faith but demeaning. . . . He had no business under the reef. Nor had he any business where he was, under that perfumed sky" (*FS*, 244–45)—followed by a disingenuous justification of himself as husband, father, and teacher. When it behooves Holliwell to reflect that he is honorably bound, he temporarily shelves his stance of owing nothing to anybody.

Then he builds again, in imagery surreal enough to seem like something Rheinhardt in delirium tremens might have come up with: in "suburban shopping centers the first chordates walk the pavement, marvels of mimesis. Their exoskeletons exactly duplicate the dominant species. Behind their soft octopus eyes—rudimentary swim bladders and stiletto teeth" (*FS*, 246). The sense of the imagery fits in well with the kinds of fundamental regressions or atavisms Stone imbedded in *A Hall of Mirrors* and with his attempt to establish, in the opening section of *Flag*, what he has called "the *homine lupus*" (Ruas, 289). But the frequency is so uncharacteristically strident, so unlike any other pitch emanating from Holliwell in the preceding pages, that, even allowing for the new blend of toxin from the sea urchin with the alcohol in Holliwell's blood, it is tempting to charge Stone with losing control of his character. But to do this is to miss the degree to which the novel is shaped by the Adversary, whose force militates against the flag we long to salute at sunrise, against the appeal to the numinous that Stone likes to posit in interviews as the thematic center of the book.

The Thing Itself

During a discussion of the two principals of *Children of Light* playing
out Lear on the heath, Stone said that

> the absolute center of Shakespeare and of the English language comes
> when Edgar, playing Tom, comes up to Lear and Lear says, "Thou art the
> thing itself: unaccommodated man is no more but such a poor, bare,
> forked animal as thou art." That to me is the center of all English litera-
> ture, that confrontation of man with man, the moment when man in his
> self-revelation becomes more tragic and more noble because of that self-
> confrontation and recognition, of men by men. Like a great light, in all of
> literature, stands this electric discovery. (Solotaroff 1991)

But just as Stone might in an interview suggest that the United
States is fundamentally healthy, in a way that he never would in a novel,
his emphasis upon "the thing itself" in his preceding novels has no halo
of transcendent revelation about it, just the revelation of that which is
frighteningly immanent. We remember that these are the words that
Marge uses when she sees Hicks as a freakish death's head. In the open
boat with Pablo, Holliwell correctly appraises his murderousness and
places it in a fearfully pervasive context:

> I know you now, he thought, watching Pablo. Should have known
> you. Know you of old.
> He felt the force he had encountered over the reef.
> The stuff was aqueous, waterborne like cholera or schistosomiasis.
> He had been around; he had seen it many times before. Among swarms
> of quivering fish, in rice paddies, shining in gutters. It was as strong as
> anything in the world. Stronger perhaps, when the illusions were stripped
> away. It glistened in a billion pairs of eyes. Comforting to think of it as
> some aberration, a perversion of nature. But it was the real thing, he
> thought. The thing itself. (*FS*, 428)

A Gnostic might say that the thing itself is everything in the world
we can know through our senses in the light of the totality of its imper-
fection, the brute difference of all the things of this world from God.
Stone (and, through him, Holliwell) is not as inclusive. The evil that
Holliwell sees in Pablo is perhaps stronger than anything else in the
world, but it is not everything in the world: there are four billion more
pairs of eyes. And indeed, in interviews Stone retreats from the sugges-

tion of the innate evil in some humans—which seems to me so obvious a part of the world of *Flag*—and attributes the evil behavior of the homine lupus to "ignorance and greed" (Ruas, 289). But over the course of the novel Holliwell staggers out a retrograde pilgrim's progress toward conversion to a Gnosticism without transcendence, a world that is the embodiment of one of the lines in his mind when we last see him: "Know the one about the Demiurge and the Abridgement of Hope?" (*FS*, 439).

Through the haze of the Bloody Marys, Holliwell recognizes in the terminal of the Miami airport, which handles the flights to Central America, "the gathering of a world far from God" (*FS*, 68). Gnostically God-less terrain becomes more specified as Holliwell travels down the west coast of Tecan with the Zeccas and their other passenger, the reporter Bob Cole. The volcanoes "seemed freakish mountains; only malignant gods could inhabit or inform them. . . . They created the troubling sense of the earth as nothing more than itself, of blind force and mortality" (*FS*, 157). But the prevailing revelation of the horror of the immanent comes when Holliwell is scuba diving at the drop along the outer reef, at the site the locals call Twixt, his first full day on the east coast of Tecan, a few hours before he meets Justin. It takes the dive for Holliwell to rave about chordates in the shopping centers.

The experience of the reef, populated by those fish whose quiverings signal the hand of the Demiurge, is the consequence of his response to the divemaster asking him, on the preceding evening, if he wanted to go diving. The question "aroused in him a thrill of fear and also a longing for the depths, for the concealment and oblivion of blue-gray light at sea level minus seventy" (*FS*, 190). Since the depth at Twixt is 900 meters, the longing for separation from the world above the water (if not from life) is substantially greater. In the dive, Holliwell is so taken with the beauty of the water, the fish, the coral that he realizes "[i]t had been years since he had taken so much pleasure in the living world." This is one part of Holliwell; another is either self-destructiveness or its near-cousin, a secret obsession with evil, which carries him down to 110 feet, far below a depth acceptable to the divemaster. There Holliwell's exhilaration is so great that he is unable "to suppress the impulse to turn a somersault." Close to narcosis, he begins his ascent, but then come what have proven to be the most frequently quoted paragraphs in Stone's oeuvre. The sea seems to tremble with the movement of the fish around him:

[A] terror had struck the sea, an invisible shadow, a silence within a silence. On the edge of vision, he saw a school of redfish whirl left, then right, sound, then reverse, a red and white catherine wheel against the deep blue. . . . Around him the fish held their places, fluttering, coiled for flight.

Then Holliwell thought: It's out there. Fear overcame him; a chemical taste, a cold stone on the heart.

He started up too fast, struggling to check his own panic. Follow the bubbles. Follow the bouncing ball.

As he pedaled up the wall, he was acutely aware of being the only creature on the reef that moved with purpose. The thing out there must be feeling him, he thought, sensing the lateral vibrations of his climb, its dim primal brain registering disorder in his motion and making the calculation. Fear. Prey. (*FS*, 227)

Heath, an English policeman for the developers of the region, had suggested the night before that "this is the eastern Carib, chum. You're likely to see the odd shark out there" (*FS*, 190). Of course, *it* is much more pervasive than a shark. Stone's explanation of what he intended takes us a fair way beyond the obvious:

It's more than a shark, it's more than a killer whale, it's an elemental force. Perhaps the opening to hell. The implication on a realistic level is that there's a shark or killer whale there. But this is where Father Egan dropped the body of the girl. What's down there is evil itself. I was thinking of the speech in *Richard III* where Clarence, just before they drown him in the butt of malmsey, says, "I have passed a miserable night / So full of ugly signs, of ghastly dreams, / That, as I am a Christian faithful man, / I would not spend another such a night, / Though 'twere to buy a world of happy days." And he describes his dream, which is of a thousand men that fishes gnawed upon, and skulls with jewels, and so forth. (Ruas, 292)[8]

Stone weaves a connective web to suggest the pervasiveness of the thing itself, or what he calls the primary process of nature: the fight-or-flight mechanism. A few hours later Holliwell kneels on the sea urchin in the estuary of a river that carries "with it all the refuse and infections of the hillside barrios" (*FS*, 231) and serves as a connective between the evil of the land and Twixt, which it runs toward. The coral of Twixt is called brain coral, as Stone told Charles Ruas, "because brain coral looks like brain tissue when you see it." The sea is then, as Ruas suggested, "the image of the unconscious" and also, in Stone's words, "the undersea reflection of the world. How do the fish live in the sea? As men do on land. So the bottom of the sea, to me, means primary process of nature, nature being most itself. Although it is innocent, it is full of dangers and also frightening" (Ruas, 292–93).[9] From a suicidal Nembutal stupor, the brilliant old gunrunner Naftali tells Pablo that there "are reefs outside . . . [a]nd reefs inside—within the brain of the diver. . . . In the brain coral you see the skull of the earth, the heaping of the dead. You pass it going out . . . you see it in your mind . . . it's your own brain." The fish in the sea live as do the men on land, and so Naftali sinks the murderous ball game of MesoAmerica beneath the depths: "It's your skull down there— white and round. It shines in the clear light . . . eight fathoms under the fan coral. Your skull is the counter . . . it's the only ball in this game, Pablo" (*FS*, 256–57).

Naftali's vision is prophetic: Pablo dies in the ocean, after Holliwell stabs him and throws him from the boat. But far from granting Holliwell the rejoicing of survival, Stone subjects him to a compound identification with Pablo. First comes the recognition of a common, non-murderous side. Looking at Pablo's face just before his victim sinks, Holliwell "was at a loss now to find the shimmering evil he had seen in it before. The stricken features were like a child's, distorted with pain and fear yet still marked with that inexplicable flicker of expectation. It was a brother's face, a son's, one's own. Anybody's face, just another victim of ignorance and fear. Just another one of us, Holliwell thought" (*FS*, 431). Then, during the night, he sees himself and Pablo as two sharks, simply going about and doing their business, as people ashore or at sea do their damaging business. In his troubled half-sleep, a joke comes to Holliwell:

> . . . [A] shark passed near the boat, on his way to a feeding frenzy.
> "What is there?" the shark asked a companion.
> "Just us," the other shark said.
> Holliwell laughed in his thin sleep. (*FS*, 432)

Revolution and Religiosity

Stone has said that he intended with Holliwell's name a "Frank Merriwell gone to seed. . . . I was [also] thinking of holy wells, in the sense of somebody making a pilgrimage to a holy well. There are all kinds of holy wells. There's the kind that he is, in fact, named after, the ones in the British Isles, and there are the holy sacrificial wells, of the

Mayans, which are less attractive in their origins."[10] Holliwell has been a pilgrim to the clearing, to the temple of the Demiurge, and what he eventually sacrifices in the course of the novel is his sense of himself as an essentially good man. The shard that he finds within is not of God but of things themselves, of the fashionings of the Demiurge. And since Holliwell is very much a representative American, it is reasonable enough to move to the macrocosm: the suffering that comes from Americans moving about, doing their business in the world.[11] Holliwell speaks at the Autonomous University of the way America is dying because of the steady demise of "our secret culture" (FS, 110)—by which I think Stone means one informed by unselfish idealism. Thus Holliwell's final, epiphanic thought—"A man has nothing to fear . . . who understands history" (FS, 439)—is both his and his country's surrender to the brute randomness of human behavior, to the rule of the Demiurge. Since, as we shall see, Stone shares Holliwell's vision of history but, at least in interviews, eschews his character's despair, all of this makes for considerable tension, if not confusion, in the deeper workings of the novel.

In contrast, in the epiphanic last moments of her life, Justin finds beneath the electric shock that Campos is administering to her a stronger force:

> You after all? Inside, outside, round and about. Disappearing stranger, trickster. Christ, she thought, so far. Far from where?
> . . . .
> Always so far away. You. Always so hard on the kid here, making me be me right down the line. You old destiny. You of Jacob, you of Isaac, of Esau.
> Let it be you after all. Whose after all I am. For whom I was nailed.
> So she said to Campos: "Behold the handmaid of the Lord."
> (FS, 416)

Richard Poirier has suggested that Justin's announcement to Campos "is meant not as a rediscovery of her faith but as a retaliation on the killer" (39).[12] The desire for retaliation is consistent with her characterization throughout the novel, and Justin had earlier cried out between the shocks, "My dad would fix you, you sucker" (FS, 415). But Stone has, in his comments about Justin, left no doubt about his intention that the reader feel she has found Christ. Still, there are those suggestions of Christ's distance, even as He reveals Himself, and there is Stone's concession, made just after he completed *Flag*, that though he writes about characters' struggles to break out of the box they are in, "[t]hey don't succeed in doing it; I can't have them succeed because I don't know how they'll be able to do it. I just don't know any more than they do" (Bonetti, 95).

Given Stone's prevailing position about the inaccessibility of God, this crucial and climactic scene in Justin's life works best for me if I read it in the light of Holliwell's response, during the debacle at the Autonomous University, to a query about whether there is "a place for God in all this": "There's always a place for God, señora. There is some question as to whether He's in it" (*FS*, 111). Whether Christ is where Justin finds Him is, in the terms of the novel, an unanswered question.

In terms of such conventional virtues as integrity, empathy, insight, intelligence, and emotional health, Justin is easily the most admirable principal in Stone's first four novels. Since at this stage in his career the author's purest note is reserved for the psychologically outré, Pablo remains *Flag*'s most compelling character, but Justin is still very well done. At 20, confronting "the blank soulless world" (*FS*, 131), she decided to serve humankind and traveled from Idaho to Los Angeles to become a student nurse. Still feeling incomplete and questing for God, she was flattered by the Devotionists (so eager to recruit the beautiful, intelligent young woman), took her vows, and came to Tecan when she was 22.

"Justin had soldiered on for six years, cheerful and strong, the wisest of catechists, a cool competent nurse. A little too good to be true in the end" (*FS*, 37). At this moment we are inside the mind of Sister Mary Joseph, a thick-bodied, "good" Catholic—disciplined, obedient, pragmatic—who belongs to a much stronger order than the Devotionists, and who silently speaks well for the Christian alternatives to a Gnostic vision. She has dropped in at their mission to help push Justin and Egan into obeying the demands of their superiors to close up shop and return to the States. In this initial stage of Justin's characterization, Stone departs from his usual practice of limiting interior angles of vision to his protagonists, and uses Mary Joseph's centrality to quickly establish what an improbable nun Justin has become. Moreover, were it not for Mary Joseph's reflection on Justin's beauty, we would get no sense of this crucial fact until Justin, meeting Holliwell, reflects that his flirtatiousness and that of other men has "something to do with the way she looked" (*FS*, 236). Of all Stone's plots, *Flag*'s gets the most suspenseful mileage from our increasing curiosity over what will happen when these four characters we have gotten to know well meet each other. Justin's beauty is a key ingredient in the suspenseful mix.

The opening line of the section that introduces her—Mary Joseph's opposition to what has obviously been Justin's assertion that all life ends in the grave—quickly alerts us to the latter's spiritual crisis. Outraged by what she considers "Mary Joe's Bronxy certainties . . . Justin [frowns] at the sunlit ocean"—a symbol of the God-less emptiness that again pervades the world for her. And, of course, the immediate world is Tecan, a place that seems both literally and figuratively God-forsaken. Or as she will neatly put the question: "Was [Tecan] not all of a piece—Campos on the coast, the President in his mortar-proof palace in the capital, the American interests that kept everything in place?" (FS, 287). She is further embittered by her sense that most of the Catholic powers in the country, domestic and foreign, are in league with the rulers. One example of her outspokenness and overwrought state is her comment to Mary Joseph that another missionary group, the LSAs, "are a bunch of right-wing psalm-singing sons of bitches. They've got a picture of the President on their wall, they suck ass with the Guardia and they fink for the CIA" (FS, 35). The Guardia has judged her instruction of locals to be subversive and has intimidated them into avoiding the mission. Committed to a life of service with no one to serve, with the saints of what she regards as her inner place shrouded, "the tabernacles . . . open and empty" (FS, 55), Justin looks at the sea, a few minutes after Sister Mary Joseph leaves, and experiences the "panicked quickening" of her heart as a signal to the ocean's unanswering void. In her sense of radical isolation, "the desire for death made her dizzy; it almost felt like joy" (FS, 41). Then Weitling walks by, and Stone reasserts Justin's fundamental health with her recognition of the psychotic's hatred for her and of his perversity. The arrival of Godoy, accompanied by some of the boys who join him and Justin at the procession and festival in town, brings her the flag that she has been waiting to follow. Over a modest dinner, Godoy asks her to keep the mission open and to help in other ways the fighters in the insurrection that he expects to erupt in a month or so.

Justin can rake herself and others with considerable shrewdness and wit. For example, she later describes her plight and that of her culturally ambitious sister in this way: "The promising, brainy Feeney sisters—May now called Justin playing Sister of Mercy in the crocodile isles and Veronica playing Carol Kennicott in Arrow, pop. 380" (FS, 131.)[13] Or when, having just met Holliwell, she thinks: "It was as though he was flirting with her. What's the world coming to? . . . And how would I know?" (FS, 236). But Stone skillfully blends an urge for abnegation with her arrogance, a convincing lyricism and forthright innocence with her acerbity. The innocence is dominant when she tries to convince Godoy of her willingness to serve: " 'I have no family,' Justin told him, smiling. 'No special home. Where people need me that's where I go. See, I'm lucky that way' " (*FS*, 52). Holliwell tells Heath that "what's best about my country is not exportable" (*FS*, 267). Stone has identified this superior quality as certain forms of idealism.[14] And, in the person of Justin, he for once does export it. As Stone has said, Justin "despairs of God and turns to man and [then] finds God" (Ruas, 290).

The new religion into which, in her secular swerve, she tries to pour her idealism is, of course, Marxism, but she does so with very little ideological fervor. To be sure, the only book we see her reading is sympathetic to Marxism. But Edmund Wilson's *To the Finland Station: A Study in the Writing and Acting of History* (1940) is a book for someone who is likely to be much more interested in reading wonderfully written accounts of fascinating lives than she is in having the truths of Marxist economics revealed to her. And this woman who so easily quotes Shakespeare and Emily Dickinson cannot keep her mind on Wilson's book. I found only one brief passage in the novel that decisively puts her revolutionary commitment in a Marxist context. The awkward first meeting with Holliwell is followed by one with Godoy, who wants to tell her that he is leaving to fight in the mountains. Afterwards, feeling that her plea to Godoy for a sign of affection was met with condescension, and shamed by her envy of the nuns in the mountains whom Godoy has praised, Justin protests to herself her unworthiness and, with a boppy, ironic lyricism that is one of her most endearing notes, affirms her intention to "struggle unceasingly in the name of history. Gimme a flag, gimme a drum roll, I'm gonna be there on that morning, yes I am. And it won't be the me you think you see. It'll be the worthy revolutionary twice-born me. The objective historical unceasingly struggling me. The good me" (*FS*, 264).

From one important vantage point, Christianity and Marxism are not all that far apart: as Stone has observed, "Whether one is religious or whether one is a Marxist, one is committed to the idea of history as positive. It's Christian dogma that the world is not evil, that the world is good, it's God's creation. The combination of Darwinism and the Christian world view is the essence of Marxism." Stone then added that if some characters "are fighting to maintain their view of history as a positive force . . . I am carrying through my skepticism, not only about religion and humanism but about history as a positive force" (Ruas, 293). Holliwell is the conduit of Stone's skepticism. After taking Justin's virginity, he would seem also to be after her faith in historical process, telling her that "God doesn't work through history. . . . The things people do don't add up to an edifying story. There aren't any morals to this confusion we're living in." (*FS*, 387).

But Holliwell is not quite as rapacious as this. He would not have succeeded in bedding Justin had not a very frightening encounter with Campos two days earlier driven home to her just how closely she was being watched and how suicidal it would be for her to continue in the revolution. By the next day she has dropped out, but after the early morning sex on the following day, a messenger from the revolutionaries approaches. Having climbed out a window "like a man in a bedroom farce" (*FS*, 383), Holliwell wanders to the clearing and returns to find that Justin has agreed to rejoin the insurrection, which is to erupt that night. His recent contacts with local CIA employees have apprised him of just how closely she is being watched, and, in his effort to save her life and get her to leave the country with him, he both reveals his conversation with Nolan and tries to undermine the historical optimism that fuels her hopes for her contribution to the improvement of Tecan. His revelation of his CIA contacts and Justin's consequent punching him are the most dramatic moments of this scene, but what is most germane to Justin's character is her response to Holliwell's comment, "You're just being used." "Damn right," she said. "At last, thank God" (*FS*, 385).

The characterization of Justin is extremely discreet. Save for a reference to the smoothness of her skin, her body is never referred to, and the description of the sex with Holliwell has nothing of the explicitness of the coupling of Pablo and the novel's second most important blonde woman, Deedee Callahan. When I asked Stone about this, he emphatically affirmed that the bloodstained sheet Justin wraps around herself after the sex with Holliwell is her flag only in anticipation of the encounter with Campos:

> I think that the discreetness, my not defining her in immediate sensual terms, was natural and was the result of Catholic conditioning, superstitious dread, regarding the body of a dedicated virgin. But I think it's also appropriate to the book. I think it's important that Holliwell does not succeed in reaching her when they do have that sexual encounter because she isn't really available in temporal terms. She remains a sort of semisacred figure; she belongs to God in a way, as she discovers.
>
> She's really just frightened and confused when she turns to Holliwell. Her renunciation of religion was intellectual and philosophical;

she was not terribly constrained by the physical vows. They were not a big problem with her. She's not exactly brimming with repressed carnal desire, and so her sexuality is really less important. She was kind of in love with Godoy, but what she really misses in terms of physicality is just the opportunity to turn to a person. (Solotaroff 1991)

Holliwell and Justin

And, of course, Holliwell is very much the wrong person. During their second meeting he initiates a political discussion. Fresh from the encounter with Campos and from sending the message warning against the use of the mission during the insurrection, and prodded by Holliwell's questions, the overwrought nun foolishly tells him that "the country is going to be overrun by its inhabitants" (*FS*, 298). Holliwell picks up on her agitation, and from the preceding day's inflated assessment of her confidence, he swerves to a series of steamy, sometimes incoherent orations to himself about the intensity of her feelings, the decency of her desires, and what I take to be his villainous desire to possess her goodness. For example, when Justin says that whether or not history takes care of people, "people take care of themselves," Holliwell takes off:

> Lady of sorrows, he thought, creature of marvel. It was enough for her that people took care of themselves. In the meantime.
> I will show you, he thought, the war for us to die in, lady. Sully your kind suffering child's eyes with it. Live burials beside slow rivers. A pile of ears for a pile of arms. The crisps of Northvietnamese drivers chained to their burned trucks.
> He thought she was a unicorn to be speared, penned and adored. He was a drunk, middle-aged, sentimental. Foolish.
> He wanted her white goodness, wanted a skin of it. He wanted to wash in it, to drink and drink and drink of it, salving the hangover thirst of his life, his war. (*FS*, 299)

Holliwell is certainly right about the sentimentality and his drunkenness, and he wants to possess Justin spiritually considerably more than he wants to sexually. But what are we to make of his desire to rub her face into the horrors of the Vietnam War? A desire to assert the amorality of the past, the randomness of "history"? But why should the war be the one for them both to die in? Is it, in some blurred way, that what idealism either of them has will die in a reexperiencing of Vietnam? Since

a good many of Holliwell's reflections about Justin are on target, the
errors, the sentimentality, the occasional zaniness and incoherence—
above all, the sheer bulk, the size of that cud called thoughts-of-Justin
that he keeps chewing—mars the cleanness and subtlety of her characterization as well as his own. William Pritchard accused Stone of falling
prey to the sentimentality that afflicts Holliwell. I don't feel that this is
the problem so much as Stone's occasional failure to create language that
sufficiently   distances   the   reader   from   Holliwell's   flaws.[15]
Correspondingly, I feel that the issue of Holliwell's final betrayal of
Justin is a bit blurred. Grilled by Soyer—the Cuban exile and CIA
employee who is Justin's case officer—Heath, and Campos, Holliwell
confesses that Justin had conspired against the regime. He confesses not
so much because they will kill him if he refuses to—though this is the
case—but because Heath promises him that he will see to Justin's safety
after the arrest. Stone told me that we are to believe that Heath would
have kept to his promise had he been able to, but "he disappeared in the
confusion" (Solotaroff 1991).

We remember Converse's guilt over lying about his feelings about
Grimes's death so as to serve up a temporary hot towel of pleasure to his
readers. The wrongness of using the struggles or sufferings of others for
an easy social fix figures more importantly in *Flag* than in the preceding
novel. After Holliwell reveals to Justin his conversation with Nolan, she
tells him, "Well . . . you'll have a story to tell, won't you? And a dirty
joke to go with it" (*FS*, 386). From the vantage of his disciplined, conservative clarity, Heath puts his finger on Holliwell's self-indulgence:
"It's like this, Holliwell. . . . While you're observing the situ-a-shon
actu-well and thinking deep thoughts, people are fighting quite desperately over things they believe in. I hope you won't think I'm sentimental. But with you having all these moral adventures you can dine out on
in the States—it's really very difficult to wish you well" (*FS*, 395). The
way in which Holliwell, acting out of self-indulgence, ends up doing just
what Nolan wanted him to do—collaborating with the local agents by
fingering Justin—is shrewdly handled. But his failure to defend himself
fully against Justin's accusations of betrayal by telling her of the promise
he extracted from Heath does not ring true. Moreover, much of the plotting is devoted to this collaboration of Holliwell's self-indulgence and
the CIA's intentions, but his confession in no way affects Justin's brief
future. In this way, one of the novel's major movements is partially
aborted.

Jesus' Self-Designated Sunbeam

No blurrings of focus or temporary failures of voice obscure the very substantial section of the novel that concerns Pablo Tabor; his angle of vision is the dominant one for 15 sections, as many as Holliwell's. From the moment we first see him signing himself off his watch at a Coast Guard station somewhere along the Gulf of Mexico until his head sinks beneath the surface of the Caribbean, Stone's control of Pablo's actions, thought processes, and speech is overwhelming. The idiosyncratic, mean edge of the language with which he usually communicates to others and to himself is particularly welcome in a narrative that is occasionally distended by the verboseness of Holliwell and Egan. Pablo's most inspired verbal display comes during his introductory section. The Dexedrine with which he feeds his amphetamine addiction has turned upon him, and after antagonizing his superior officer and shooting his two dogs, he returns to the trailer where he lives with his wife and nine-year-old son. Enraged by what he feels is her messiness and by the two refrigerator shelves filled with the burgers she brings home from her job, "he delicately [sets] hamburger patties at neat intervals" along the edge of the bed where his wife sleeps, wakes her, tells her that he has killed the dogs, holds his revolver to her head, and asks, "You want to go out on a meat trip, Kathy? Just you and all those ratburgers all over hell?" (*FS*, 68).

This is Pablo, in speech as well as act, at his most bizarrely inventive. But there are a good many other Pablos: the morally indignant one who is "shocked and enraged" when Naftali, whom Pablo has come to rob, tells the American that he's "vicious and stupid" (*FS*, 253), who tells Egan that "you oughta tell someone [about Weitling]. . . ."Or just take him out—bingo" (*FS*, 367); the saddened little boy who complains to the Callahans, "I don't know. . . . Sometimes you get the idea all anybody's interested in down here is money" (*FS*, 100); the overwhelmed-with-gratitude Pablo who, upon being given a diamond by Naftali, says, "Goddamn. . . . You're all right, boss, no shit" (*FS*, 255); the Elected Pablo who informs Holliwell, "You know . . . I'm part of the process and you ain't" (*FS*, 425); the obscenely heroic Pablo who asks McPhail, his superior officer (a head taller than him yet), if he's "combing [his hair] with piss? You didn't wash your hands in there" (*FS*, 60); the keenly intelligent man who sniffs out the Callahans' plans to kill him; the innocent who responds to Holliwell's Gnostic fable of the scorpion and the buffalo with, "It don't have to be like that" (we don't have to hurt or kill others because of our nature), and whose stricken face is "still marked with that inexplicable flicker of expectation" (*FS*, 230–31) before it sinks beneath the sea's surface. The more various the parts of a character, the more effective the character is if the author can somehow make the parts cohere. With Pablo they very convincingly cohere, and the intensity of all the parts and the danger potential of most of them contribute greatly to the character's exciting unpredictability—which itself contributes so much to the whole of the novel.

Flag's title comes from the first lines of an Emily Dickinson Poem ("A Wife—at Daybreak I shall be— / Sunrise—Hast thou a flag for me" [J. 461]), lines that Justin quotes after she perceives that sex will not provide her with the communion she seeks. Dickinson's poem moves toward the assertion of the daybreak wedding with "Sir . . . Savior" in eternity, which is where the most optimistic reading of Justin's progress would place her. Holliwell's sunrise is, as I have suggested, his identification with the sharkish workings of the world, a confirmation of what he earlier described as "his natural, self-appointed place . . . alone and lost, in outer darkness without friend or faction" (*FS*, 405).

A married male's working and domestic lives are the usual nourishing continuities in an enjoyed existence. Holliwell's characterization is weakened by the near-absence of background information on his interactions with his family and with his job (though we do hear that he has obscurely lost his children). In Pablo's opening section, Stone quickly and vividly communicates the character's hatred of what he feels to be the paltriness of the Coast Guard and the mess of his home. In particular, the image of him holding one of the hamburgers until the ice in it melts in his hand wonderfully catches his sense of, and hatred for, the gamy commonness in which he lives his life. (His apparently crazed placing of the patties around his wife's bed is an attempt to define her, not himself, as the primary source of what he will later call "the life of petty day-by-day, McPhail and his like, the crummy trailer, the chickenshit, that bitch and her ratburgers" [*FS*, 238]). At this point in the novel his place of refuge, his sunrise and his Christ, is something as unpredictable and transient as a benign amphetamine surge: "Gimme a rush, Jesus. . . . If you want me for a sunbeam" (*FS*, 60), he says with the strange lyricism he sometimes comes up with as he drives away from the Coast Guard station. Justin responds from her initial despair with assertions of health and purpose. What are the prospects for someone who, at this point in life, feels that his right to live follows from his ability to get high?

> If I were God, Pablo Tabor thought, I wouldn't have mornings like this. The sun up on a swamp, two worthless dogs, a sparky with his blood full of speed and gasoline. No such morning could have a God over it.
>
> If I were God, he thought, if I made mornings I wouldn't have no Pablo Tabor and his dogs in 'em.
>
> "You do this, God?" he asked. "You operate and maintain mornings like this?"

The mean pedantry and colloquial rightness of "operate and maintain" should not obscure the fact that even in his self-hatred Pablo is challenging a force he calls God. Then comes the rush, "speckled, buzzing his brain, old rages in his throat." And so, with "his mind's eye . . . flashing him shit—death's heads, swastikas, the ace of spades. Dumbness. Dime-store badness," Pablo moves away from the sense of himself as a pathetic speed freak to an unrealized identification with the blood-drinking gods in the temple of the Demiurge, to the cool, waiting identity of the empowered killer that is also a part of him: "[H]e felt as though he were a metal image of himself, cool, without much reality" (*FS*, 63–64). His apotheosis leaves the dogs as the only part of the tableau that is unworthy of life, and so he blows them away with his shotgun. But the positive affect is fleeting, and within moments he feels himself a fool for killing his dogs and concedes his own derangement with, "They're fucking with my head this morning" (*FS*, 65).

Stone's 1984 comment about his continued attempts to capture the bitterness, the anomie, of those who have been frustrated by the elusiveness of American promise (Woods, 49) applies more to Pablo Tabor than to any of his other characters. And to compare him with the other three North American principals, the material nature of his score makes him much more characteristically American, just as his behavior, once he feels his interests are threatened, is much more representative of collective American behavior abroad: violence often follows.[16] Usually his goals are clearly shaped by the popular culture. Several times he thinks about the tuxedo he will someday own; at one point, he envisions himself wearing his tux, drinking daiquiris, surrounded by elegant flunkies. In another fantasy a beautiful native woman lives with him in his mountain villa. His whole sense of his life of adventure leading him to the big score seems to be shaped more by *Soldier of Fortune* than by the actual possibilities around him. The distance between his fantasized land of heart's desire and his sense of himself when he's really low is very great. The night before he ships out with the Callahans, he sits in a park in Vizcaya, Compostella, and thinks:

Pablo, son of a whore. *Hijo de puta*. Pablo. Sometimes it seemed that was the world's whole message to him—that was all it ever told him. He could catch in every roll of laughter and see its meaning framed in the mildest eyes.

Let one of these half-nigger *gibrones* try it on me, he thought in a sudden rage. Let one.

Let one and the strange metal figure would form under his hide and death be. (*FS*, 124–25)

But then, after deciding that he has no good qualities that anyone would want, the mixture of stimulant and depressant (Dexedrine and rum) with which he has been dosing himself brings him to a state in which he can dream of a time "when something had come along and the world was different and he was in it after all. There would be a great summoning of powers and dominations; Pablo himself would be a power and a domination, a principality, a mellow dude. Big easy Pablo, the man of power. It was a warm happy vision but it went funny on him as such things often did. For the first time in a while, however, he was not not angry" (*FS*, 126).

After discussing Hicks's quest for virtus with Eric James Schroeder, Stone said: "Pablo is coming from the opposite direction. Pablo is a real little rat who is almost ennobled by his addled mysticism. I want people finally to feel sorry for the guy. Yet I don't want to fudge on how awful he really is. The guy is completely bad news. Ideally, you should be able to understand why Holliwell kills him, to understand and not to condemn Holliwell too much. At the same time, you should feel sorry for Pablo" (Schroeder, 158).

His pathos crests a few minutes after his vision of "big easy Pablo" when he asks Cecil, the impressively centered black bartender, what his, Pablo's, use is. "Same as everybody," Cecil answers. "Put one foot to front of de other. Match de dolluh wif de day." As twisted as Pablo is, his response is one made by the yearning teleologist in all of us: "That's all?" And still he persists, still he asks about the "special purpose [in] everybody," only to be baffled again by Cecil's "Purpose of you and me to be buried in de ground and das hard enough to do. Be buried in de sweet ground and not in dat ocean" (*FS*, 126–27). When his creator denies him this, there's a touch of the exterminating god Pablo fancied in himself. Or perhaps it's more accurate to say that the fated encounter between Pablo and the depths of the sea parallels the one consummated in the preceding section: between Justin and Campos, who has been stalking her for more than 400 pages.

Of course, the shift in point of view makes us much more ready to send Pablo to his watery grave. For his last 15 or so hours, and 15 pages, we see him through Holliwell's hating eyes as "this pill-brained jackdaw, this jabbering shitbird with his pig sticker and his foul little eyes" (*FS*, 425). All things being equal, we identify with the character whose sensibility we occupy. Things are not at all equal in Pablo's electrifying introductory section, where his behavior, both physical and mental, is so extreme that if readerly sympathy is generated, it never lasts too long. But Pablo is really eloquent in his on-the-beach pathos in the next section (Vizcaya), and I found myself becoming his cautious advocate. Once Pablo boards the *Cloud*, the shrimp boat with high-speed engines in which the Callahans are running the arms to Tecan, this marginal partisanship is interestingly tested by the Callahans—elegantly jaded, witty gunrunners who easily quote from *Lear, Hamlet*, and "Under Ben Bulben." A friend of mine complained that the Callahans, delivered to the *Cloud* as recognizable movie types by central casting, are just too smoothly urbane to be true. I find them a good deal more idiosyncratic than that, and the stylistic collisions between their quietly mocking elegance and Pablo's predatory appetites interestingly flesh out the brute, suspenseful questions: Will Deedee Callahan and Pablo have sex? Who will kill whom?

Stone's letting Pablo join the reader, for once, in overhearing the Callahans' plottings turns the suspenseful heat even higher: when Deedee describes him as "one of life's little yo-yos" who "wants to please and will do just fine," Pablo responds by thinking, "I'm gonna fuck her brains out" (*FS*, 219–20). Not that Deedee—whose desire for Pablo is heightened by the fact that she, her husband, and the first mate have decided to kill him the next morning—lacks an illicit edge to her desires. The uncanny frequencies of the long scene between Pablo and the dying Naftali make subsequent, steadily increasing suspense within the Pablo strand of the novel unlikely. But with the different intrigues and collisions of the desires for murder, escape, and sexual triumph— with the *Cloud* all the while approaching Tecan to deliver the arms to the revolutionaries—Stone pulls it off. The great tension of the three sections that culminate with the sex and the shootout is particularly effective since the sections break up the three that cover Egan's sermon in the clearing. Those of the Pablo strand both provide welcome narrative movement and support the darker frequencies of Egan's Gnostic text. Quite appropriately, Pablo identifies with the only benign frequency— the news of the jewel in the lotus, the shard of the Godhead within us—

in that primal way of his that cuts through all sorts of theological and
linguistic niceties:

> Pablo's eyes glazed over. "Holy shit," he said. "Santa Maria." He
> stared at the diamond in his palm with passion.
> "Hey," he said to the priest, "diamonds are forever! You heard of
> that, right? That means something, don't it?" (*FS*, 373)

Usually it means a diamond advertisement. Here it means that Stone
is preparing for his Gnostic agent, Holliwell, to have the final word
about (in Walter Clemons's words) the "murderous innocent."[17] For
Holliwell will toss the no longer talismanic diamond, along with Pablo's
bloodied trousers, into the Caribbean after their suddenly devalued
owner.

Chapter Five
Children of Light

The Uniqueness of the Novel

Two of Stone's responses in my 1991 interview chart, in different ways, the origins of *Children of Light*. When asked about his acting career, he said that in 1983 he accompanied some friends who were traveling to the Santa Cruz Shakespeare Festival to read for parts. The director asked Stone first if he had ever acted, then to read for the part of Kent. After what must have been a successful reading, Stone spent the whole of the summer

> in *Lear*, and of course I was onstage so much since Kent is. That was a very strange production, because it had actors from all over: classically trained actors; soap opera actors from television; people who had to have explained to them what the lines meant. But *Lear* is bottomless, bottomless. To have all these people take on Shakespeare whose educational backgrounds were altogether different, to have everybody subjected to trodding on the edge of the abyss with Lear, was really very interesting. It just subsumes everybody's life; it goes on and on, and the more you do it the more it begins to kind of dwarf you. It becomes your alternative life. This seemed to apply to everybody, no matter how distant their past was from Shakespeare. By the time the show was over nobody knew what to do with themselves at that hour, at eight o'clock at night. People were just gathered together thinking, "What will become of us?" (Solotaroff 1991)

What became of Robert Stone was his return to Connecticut, where he put down the novel, set in New England, that he had been working on and began writing one experienced in good part through the sensibility of a screenwriter and actor who had spent the summer in Seattle, where—though only in his forties—he played the lead in a production of *Lear*. Like his creator, Gordon Walker finds the play "bottomless,"[1] and save for a comment on the weather, his first spoken sentences of the novel are, "Thou art the thing itself. . . . Unaccommodated man is no

more than such a poor bared forked animal as thou art. . . . Pour on. . . .
I will endure." On the one hand, Walker's apostrophe to himself and the
elements has several nice ironies: he's in the shower in an elegant southern California home; when, three days later, he acts out some of the
scene, he will be cast as the Fool, not King Lear. On the other hand, it's
fitting enough speech for someone who is still "chockablock with cheer-
less dark and deadly mutters, little incantations from the text. They
were not inappropriate to his condition; during the run of the show his
wife had left him" (CL, 3, 6).

When I asked Stone earlier in the interview about the origins of
Children of Light, he responded:

> I did a screenplay a long time ago about a bunch of people who went to
> the Baja for a weekend, and I kept thinking about that trip and various
> things, and then of course I'd been down on location a couple times for
> the making of *Who'll Stop the Rain?* and I knew a couple of things about
> the movie business. Above all, I got into the notion of a relationship
> between two people who know that nothing good can happen to them
> from each other and who know that they have nothing but trouble and
> even potential destruction to give to each other but who willfully—and
> one of them more willfully than the other—out of nostalgia, out of weak-
> ness, out of perversity, out of a desire for generalized destruction, for his
> own destruction, out of a combination of self-destructiveness and selfish-
> ness, make this pilgrimage. I thought once of calling this *Death and the
> Lover*. I always felt that this was a knight on a pilgrimage to bring death.
> I had the image of a skeleton in armor, death as a knight errant, going
> after this enchanted princess and bringing her nothing but destruction.
> The fascination between two people who present each other with nothing
> but the abyss. (Solotaroff 1991)

A good deal that distinguishes *Children of Light* from Stone's other
four novels is implied in the above. Most obviously, there are only two
principals, and the central action follows from the decision of one principal, Walker, to seek out the other: the actress Lu Anne Bourgeois, who
acts under the name of Lee Verger. While he was having an affair with
Lu Anne a decade earlier, Walker wrote a screenplay of Kate Chopin's
1899 novel *The Awakening*: his journey is from Los Angeles to Bahía
Honda, in the Baja, where Lu Anne is acting in the filming of his screenplay. His contemplations of the journey south and the journey itself,
interrupted by sections that develop what is waiting for him in Mexico,
occupy more than half of the novel. As a reader watches the principals of

Stone's earlier novels approaching each other, he may feel more or less like a host presiding over the first interaction between two people he has gotten to know (like Rheinhardt and Geraldine, or Hicks and Marge Converse), or between a pair he has gotten to know very well (Holliwell and Justin, Holliwell and Pablo). The detailing of Walker's and Lu Anne's symptoms is so elaborate that, awaiting their collision, he feels more like a member of the audience waiting for the curtain to go up on a play acted at Charenton Asylum.

Although there are no subplots in *Children* to speak of, it is not quite right to say that every scene is ruthlessly subordinated to the central action. A. Alvarez found much in the novel that impressed him, but he complained that "*Children of Light* lacks the narrative denseness and control of the earlier books in which every figure had his own part in the plan and met his own special fate. Each stage of Walker's journey south is rich in wit and detail, but each is complete in itself, a picaresque incident on the road that gives another angle to Walker's depression and destructiveness, but otherwise contributes nothing to the scheme of things" (25). We might quibble with some of this—there are details in two of the episodes that comment significantly on Lu Anne's behavior, and not every figure in the preceding novels meets "his own special fate." But Alvarez is right about the relative narrative thinness: an unusual percentage of the novel is dialogue; the paragraphs tend to be quite short; the characters' ruminations are, as a whole, much briefer than those of characters in the preceding novels. All of this creates a narrative speed unusual in a novel that catalogs so much pain, but the pace is in keeping with Walker and Lu Anne's antic, suffering dance toward the two scenes that culminate the novel: one tears Lu Anne from the constraints of the movie community and casts her, among many other roles, as Lear on the heath; the other is her half-suicidal drowning.

It is not so much that Stone wrote the novel with a weakened narrative imagination as that the ground of the action, far from being a powerfully shaping concatenation of social forces, is something both more literary and more personal. Whether we regard the ground as predominantly literary or personal follows from whether we designate it as an ironic reworking of the medieval trope of the knight setting forth or disregard antecedents like Tristan and Iseult and consider only the psychological imperatives of the *Liebestod*. There is no "larger scheme of things" to which the intentions and afflictions of the principals are subordinated: at bottom, Walker's and, particularly, Lu Anne's intentions and afflictions *are* the scheme of things. (In fact, as Lu Anne's symptoms increas-

ingly erupt, they become the main source of curiosity and energy in
Children of Light.) Correspondingly, no significant plot lines converge
upon the Walker–Lu Anne axis; if what appears to be a subplot surfaces,
it is quickly subordinated to the anticipation, workings, and consequences of the interaction of the two principals. Thus, when a bit of suspense develops from the possible attempts of the writer Dongan
Lowndes to dredge up dirt for a biased article on the making of the
movie, or from the attempt of the unit's publicity flack to blackmail the
production unit, it is quickly dissipated as these plot strands are
absorbed by the main show: Walker and Lu Anne's progression toward
disaster. In his preceding novels Stone created obstacles to block, at least
temporarily, most of what was wanted by all of the principals (save
Rheinhardt). In *Children of Light* the obstacles to the disaster Walker and
Lu Anne in large part seek are removed: Lu Anne could not act well
while on her medication, so she stopped taking it ten days before the
novel begins; her admirable husband and their two children would have
powerfully pulled her away from her dance of death with Walker, so
Stone gets them out of the novel on its second morning; the overconfi-
dent director, Walter Drogue, is not as much of an obstacle as we would
expect, for he thinks it possible that the tension of Walker's presence will
enrich Lu Anne's performance, and "[a]nyway . . . I can swallow that
asshole with a glass of water" (*CL*, 78). Stone completely erases whatever blocking he might have done; there is no shooting the day after
Walker arrives, and he charms the underling appointed to keep an eye
on him into giving him time with Lu Anne so that they are free to give
themselves to sex, mescal, cocaine, and increasingly schizoid eruptions.

Perhaps because the dramatic movement is essentially so simple and
inevitable, Stone offers, in addition to the picaresque episodes Alvarez
referred to, eight scenes in which neither principal appears. (There had
only been one such scene—the meeting of the revolutionaries in *Flag*—
in the preceding three novels.) Walter Drogue is present in each of them.
Though something in each of these scenes can be related in some way to
the principals—for example, Drogue's willingness to work with an
unmedicated Lu Anne because her increasingly severe symptoms film
well, or his consideration of ways to cut Walker out of the production—
they are primarily witty divertissements in which the games that Drogue
and his wife Patty play, and the pronouncements and actions of his
father, offer alternative entertainment. The novel also approaches neo-
classical unities in the brevity of its dramatized present: about 72 hours,
by far the shortest duration of Stone's five novels. (A brief coda, which

occurs two months after the 72-hour stretch, ends the novel.) The narrative speed within the brevity heightens the sense of the gallop toward death.

Children of Light is also unique among Stone's novels for the way the reader confidently expects the disastrous outcome of the central action before he has read 45 pages. Walker, still half-drunk, awakens and greets the novel's first morning, a glorious, early October California one, by vomiting and, in the next few minutes, consuming cocaine, vodka, and Valium. During this time he reflects that his swollen eyes "want pennies" (*CL*, 2), that "he had been poisoning himself for weeks," and that "he had begun to feel as though he might die quite soon" (*CL*, 3–4). In the month since *Lear* closed, the already alcoholic Walker has gotten himself addicted to cocaine. The dying Hicks needed a triangle and a song; Walker this morning decides he needs "a dream . . . [f]ire, motion, risk": new fun and games with Lu Anne. What survival sense he has counsels him to save his own marriage, to "restore his equilibrium. What we need here is less craziness, not more." The same sense reminded him a few moments earlier that, having barely survived their interaction of a decade earlier, "[i]t would not be the same now." Still, he dials Lu Anne, thinking, "Yours in the ranks of death" (*CL*, 15), before he hangs up in terror. In the second of the novel's 32 sections, a few hours and pages later, his agent, Keochakian, warns him of the dangers waiting for him in Mexico and urges him to check into a hospital. In the third section we meet Lu Anne and learn that she is a schizophrenic who has stopped taking her antipsychotic medication, and that the last time she did this, in Vancouver, she ended up in a straitjacket and a padded cell. Toward the end of the section she hallucinates one of her delusional Long Friends.

In the next section, just in case a few readers have not picked up on how doomed Walker's pilgrimage is, Stone has him spend the night with Keochakian's assistant, Shelley Pearce, who tells him to check into a hospital, claims he is a crazy person who likes to make other people crazy, and, the next day, tells Keochakian that Walker is "dying. . . . He's really going to die" (*CL*, 112). When, in a phone call, Keochakian relays Shelley's opinion to him, Walker's response is to fire his agent and pull his car out into oncoming traffic as he resumes the drive down to the Baja. The reader pushes on, as confident of disaster as if he were a fifth-century Greek settling in for a new version of the story of Oedipus or Agamemnon.

In the preceding novels Stone dropped his principals into menacing situations they could not handle: Tecan, the Saigon-Antheil-Smitty-

Danskin nexus of *Dog Soldiers*, and a New Orleans waiting to explode are three sources of opposition that express Stone's sense of the malevolence waiting out there in the world. He seems to be setting up the same sort of ominous destination for Walker when he has Keochakian warn his client, "People are watching you. . . . Always. Evil people who wish you bad things are watching. You're not among friends" (*CL*, 25). Once at Bahía Honda, Walker reminds himself that he's not among friends, but that's not at all the way the location community comes off. Walter Drogue is sometimes a bit of a bully, and always an opportunist, but he does not threaten Walker, even when the latter behaves outrageously. The man with the most institutionalized power on the set is the producer, Charlie Freitag, an extremely kind if sometimes pretentious man. Several critics have made Lowndes out to be the novel's ultimate villain, but only because they accept Lu Anne's psychotic evaluation of the character and pass over what Stone has written into his behavior. Walker is on wittily good terms with the functionary with whom he interacts most—the unit manager Jon Axelrod—and the male romantic lead, Jack Glenn, is bland niceness itself. The only character who hates Walker, the publicity flack Jack Best, is finally a harmless buffoon. Stone does give enough characters mean enough tongues to make for some smashing entertainment, particularly at a party that ends in drunken, brawling slapstick. But the most vicious tongue belongs to Walker; the most abrasive agent is Lu Anne. They are all that is needed for disaster.

Stone's Most Nonpolitical Novel

From his most obviously political novel, Stone moved to his least political one. It is hard to give too much credence to his claim that *Children of Light* "is also political. . . . The process of creating Hollywood movies is loaded with examples of how America works." ("RS," 76). So it might be, but no substantial political animus emerges from Stone's treatment of the filming of *The Awakening*. Of course, with a bit of a struggle, one can translate some acts into generalizations about employment conditions in the United States: a higher-up might try to profit by an underling's infirmity or to amuse himself at the expense of his underlings' discomfort; nourishing solidarity can exist among workers; one individual's collapse can affect many others. But patterns like this are globally pervasive; in the novel their wider, social reverberations are not at all insisted upon. To compare *Children of Light* to the two most famous Hollywood novels, there is no emphasis upon Hollywood—or more accurately, Hollywood-on-location-in-Mexico—as the dream factory for America as there is in *The Last Tycoon*. Correspondingly, though the location at Bahía Honda certainly has its share of deviant behavior, we do not get a sense of the movie community as the center of American grotesqueness as we do in *The Day of the Locust*.

Walker's self-destructive behavior offers more social reverberations. Most obvious in the novel is his steady use of cocaine. By the mid-1980s it had replaced heroin in Stone's mind as the representative drug of "a society based overwhelmingly on appetite and self-regard."[2] To a certain extent, Walker does represent a larger American constituency when he arrives in Bahía Honda, checks into the hotel, reflects that, "on a whim, he had come to a place where he was without friends to see a woman whom he had no business to see," and then hums "an old number" that neatly gathers together several strands of his irresponsibility:

> You take Sally, I'll take Sue.
> Makes no difference what you do.
> Cocaine. (*CL*, 190)

And then there's the Mexican painter, Maldonado, who tells Walker late in the novel that they are destroying themselves and their societies with cocaine. There are also implicit parallels in the first quarter of *Children* between the process of Walker's self-destruction and references to the ways in which developers continue to savage the once glorious California landscape.

But there is nothing like the large symbolic parallels that follow in *Hall* from Rheinhardt looking at the Great American Razor, or the correspondences between Vietnam and the United States in *Dog Soldiers*, or the evocations of national entropy in *Outerbridge Reach*, or the overt political situation in *Flag*. As for the effects of American imperialism, particularly what Stone feels are the contaminating effects of our popular culture, Maldonado, who has started to market his paintings and prints with "a very prestigious department store," drunkenly and ironically claims that he now looks forward to the day "when my visions will be stamped on every shower curtain in America. In every swimming pool, Jacuzzi and bathtub. On the toilet wallpaper and in the toilet bowl. Wherever sanitation is honored—Maldonados. Standing tall" (*CL*, 293–94). And, toward the end of the book, different members of a Mexican village treat the dissolute behavior of Walker and Lu Anne as an opportunity for financial gain. But since more than three-quarters of the novel deals with the behavior of Americans in Mexico, the scarcity of significant interactions between the visitors and the natives speaks strongly for the essentially nonpolitical character of *Children of Light*.

Secret Eyes, Long Friends, and the Heebiejeebieville Express

We have seen many of the strands of Walker's character in Stone's earlier protagonists. Like Holliwell, he is a meddler and an alcoholic, but the acerbic irony with which he treats himself, his love of verbal play, and his frequent desire to strike romantic postures are much more reminiscent of Converse and Rheinhardt. He shares Rheinhardt's alcoholism, love of creating brawls, and a somewhat different version of a blend that suits both Stone's respect for competence and tendency to imagine disaster: professional ambition and a capacity for survival, both of which are radically undermined by self-destructiveness. If Walker shows, in his interactions with Lu Anne, a capacity for caring and sympathy that exceeds any possessed by Stone's earlier male protagonists, he adds to it a compulsion to feed his drug addiction that comes closest to that of Stone's most brutish principal, Pablo Tabor.

With her schizophrenia, Lu Anne brings something quite new to the bevy of deep-feeling but damaged and/or unhappy female principals before Anne Browne of *Outerbridge Reach*. We can perhaps most easily understand schizophrenia as a leaking of separate images and more continuous structures from the unconscious into waking life. The antipsychotic medication Lu Anne has stopped taking blocked the leakage; alcohol and, in particular, cocaine encourage eruptions that terrify Lu Anne. Thus, between the time she stopped taking her medication and the moment when, frightened first by Dongan Lowndes's attentions and then by an anxiety seizure in her trailer, she drinks perhaps eight ounces of scotch, she hallucinates only the Long Friends, who are more bothersome than threatening. But having drunk the scotch while she sits in her trailer, prepping for the scene she is to play, she sees in the mirror

> her own secret eyes. No other person except her children and the Long Friends had ever seen them. She had used them for Rosalind, but so disguised that no one looking, however closely, could know what it was they were seeing in her face. None of her children had secret eyes.

> She got to her feet, transfixed by what she saw in the mirror. The shock made her see stars as though she had been struck in the face. She watched the secret-eyed image in the glass open its mouth; she tried to look away.
>
> Clusters of hallucination lilacs sprang up everywhere, making a second frame for the mirror, sprouting from between her legs. In her terror she called on God. (*CL*, 168–69)

Lu Anne heroically pulls herself together, and she moves from the trailer to the set down by the water, where, as Edna Pontellier, the protagonist of *The Awakening*, she goes through three takes of stripping off her bathing suit and swimming out to her death. That night she hopes to find religious consolation by having her friend, the homosexual stunt-man Bill Bly, take her to the church in the village of Bahía Honda. Here Stone uses the possibilities of her psychosis to bring new terror to his familiar motif of the unavailability of God. After praying to "You who are more real than I am. My only One, my Reality," she sees on the crucifix not the darkened image of Christ but a "cat . . . burned black as the figure had been, its fur turned to ash, its face burned away to show the grinning fanged teeth" (*CL*, 202). She tries once again to pull herself together, this time in the hotel bar, but the presence of the continually terrifying Lowndes at her table drives her to seek sanctuary in Bly's room, where her old friend helps her to get through the night with Quaaludes and Hollywood location stories. We do not know if the Quaaludes accelerate the terrifying eruptions, but the cocaine she consumes with Walker the next day certainly does. Er Siriwai, the former drug dispenser to the stars, whom Walker visited en route to Lu Anne, had warned him, "No coke for her. You want to see fair Heebiejeebieville, my lad, give one of them cocaine. . . . Hide it. Throw it away before you let her have any" (*CL*, 141). This proves to be as heavily portentous as all of the warnings to Walker about the damage he will do if he goes to Mexico, or the storm that is threatening all of the second day of the novel and explodes on the third.

During the first few hours alone with Walker, Lu Anne consumes only mescal, and though the Long Friends are present in her bungalow, her speech is fairly reasonable as she slips in and out of some elegant roles: the all-passion-spent autumnal beauty who touches her ex-lover's face with "an infinite weariness"; the practical romantic who invokes Titania to tell Walker, "We'll have to be spirits of another sort" (*CL*, 241–42). They make love; she sleeps, wakes, and surprises him sniffing cocaine in the bathroom. Walker, who can refuse Lu Anne nothing, shares it with her, and, to borrow the title of Jean Strouse's review, the Heebiejeebieville Express is on the rails, to roll with increasing force toward the destination of her death.[3]

The first sign that the Express is in motion comes perhaps an hour after Lu Anne first takes cocaine. Walker thinks of her as having two speeds: "Bad Lu Anne and Saint Lu Anne." Lu Anne is wrong about having kept her secret eyes from all but her children and the Long Friends: a familiar and frightening change in her eyes signals to Walker the shift into Bad Lu Anne, "not in fact malign, but formidable and sometimes terrifying." A decade earlier they must have worked out a sort of drill, for in an attempt to contain her heaving body, he immediately embraces her and hangs on until the unidentified eruption that is causing her "unvoiced scream," her "grief and rage" (CL, 270–71), subsides. The secret eyes can indeed signal the malign. When, later in the novel, they blaze amethyst against a background of lightning, Walker understandably fears for his life. When I asked Stone if her secret eyes are "an aspect of her as sacrificing priestess, some aspect of the White Goddess," he agreed that this murderous aspect is there but added that the secret eyes are "also something that she as an actress would do. Actors sometimes try to use this; it's a kind of prepping device, to look a whole lot of different ways. Kind of like, 'I'm going to show my glossies, my eight-by-ten glossies.' It is her secret power" (Solotaroff 1991). And Stone then assumed a glittering look and executed five or six rapid-fire takes as he moved his head about.

There are delusions within the different delusional systems. Lu Anne likes to think that she can harness the secret eyes vocationally, as when she used them in a disguised form for her great triumph at the Yale Drama School: her performance of Rosalind, the luminous heroine of *As You Like It*. Hugely healthy, high-spirited, strong—above all, a successful master of disguise—Rosalind serves as an exemplar for Lu Anne, and her successful habitation of the character seems to have been the high point of her life: "Gone that young Queen of the New Haven night. Sometimes it seemed to Lu Anne that she missed Rosalind the way she missed her children" (CL, 109). (The great difference between the psychological health of Lu Anne and the character she most happily inhabited in the past—even the distance between the health of Lu Anne and Edna, the woman moving toward suicide she is presently portraying—powerfully adds to the actress's pathos.) We do not know if she thinks she can manifest the secret eyes at will or if they simply appear and sometimes she can harness them—whether in her acting or when she uses them to terrorize Walker. Certainly there are times—in the mirror when lilacs sprout not from Whitmanesque dooryards but from her groin, while she is in bed with Walker—when they emerge enclosed by her own helplessness and terror.

Things are much more negotiable with the Long Friends, whom Lu Anne sometimes caresses while they "chew the tips of her fingers with their soft infants' teeth" (*CL*, 154). She can scold them when they become too bothersome, and sometimes she orders one of them away. Still, Lu Anne sees herself as their victim. Though she did not begin to see and hear the Friends until she was sixteen, she sees them as "a sickness [she] breathed in from a graveyard" (*CL*, 166) she played in when she was six or seven. Surely she is here trying to give an experiential explanation for a genetic condition, but Stone has suggested that, as a child, she might indeed have played with the bones of skeletons in a graveyard.[4] As a whole, though, they are domesticated if meddlesome companions who "were always there when it was dark and reality in question" (*CL*, 166). Although they sometimes inquire sympathetically about the state of Lu Anne's health, they mostly serve as a sort of uncanny superego: as conservative, inhibiting forces that, for example, chide her for experiencing a ripple of physical desire for Lowndes when she first meets him, or for not having more children, or for talking to Walter Drogue instead of to them. Since Lu Anne mistakenly traces her psychosis to her childhood contact with them, it is appropriate that they should be continually associated with the old: sometimes they speak to her "in the old language" (*CL*, 185), which I take to be the Creole Lu Anne employs at one point when she curses at one of them; they always have

> bags with them that they [keep] out of sight, tucked under their wings or beneath the nunnish homespun. The bags were like translucent sacs, filled with old things. Asked what the things were, their answer was always the same.
> *Les Choses démodées*. (*CL*, 154)

But as the later Freud observed, nothing is more conservative than death. The "nunnish homespun" is black and obviously a sort of shroud that speaks of the Friends' supposed place of origin: a well-stocked mausoleum. The description of one of the Friends—with its "venous, blue-baby-colored forehead . . . [the] skull shaved like a long-ago nun's," and "frail dragonfly wings [that] rested against its sides" (*CL*, 154)—speaks of a horror movie degree of ugliness blended right in with their solicitude for Lu Anne and for her dead son. She feels that he is still in a way living, since she left him in their care, just as she feels that she is in part dead because she is also in their care. (As she puts it to Walker, she counts her dead child among the living because "that's the custom in Louisiana . . . where the living and the dead are involved in mixed entertainments" [*CL*, 268]). When she tells her husband, a physician whose specialty is the treatment of schizophrenics, that she has a name that will neutralize them, he warns her—as did another specialist—never to utter it. Is it that they feel she will be agreeing to her literal or psychic death if she does? At one point, Lu Anne addresses one of the Friends by her name, Marie Ange, without any discernible negative effect. Sometimes it seems that the games she plays with them open her to frightening eruptions. For example, the terror that leads her to seek first a sedating drug and then the liquor occurs after she lies down in her dressing room, crosses her forearms over her breasts, and responds to the motherly Friend who whispers, *"Tu tombes malade"*:

> "No, I'm dead. . . . Mourn me."
> In the next moment she found herself fighting for breath, as though an invisible bar were being pressed down against her. (*CL*, 155)

Did her paroxysm follow from her playing at completely giving herself to their care—as she had given up her son—in death? Or might her terror be independent of the nearby Friend and follow from moving more deeply than she so far has into the persona of a character who commits suicide? Or might it simply be an unattributable terror erupting in her? It is impossible to be sure.

Although the Friends chide Lu Anne for her initial attraction to Lowndes, "[t]hey were attracted to him. . . . He had power over her. The aura that drew the Long Friends gave him great strength" (*CL*, 106). When it was put to Stone that these creatures of the crypt are drawn to Lowndes (whose work has languished since he wrote a very good novel some years earlier) because he is someone who, like Rheinhardt, could not wrangle his talent and is exhibiting a kind of living death, the author agreed, adding that Lu Anne, who says that Lowndes is "one of what I am" (*CL*, 342), sees him "as connected with the cemetery, as part skeleton, whether it's a bone god or a knuckle deity [both of which she calls Lowndes], a thing of death and corruption. Everything about him is awful to her: she calls him the shit between her toes, calls his eyes fecal. She is subjecting him to the most dreadful psychological terrorism. . . . I meant him to be just a poor guy; he's having a miserable time. . . . Her savagery toward him is so demented that if he feels half of what's in her mind it's terrible for him" (Solotaroff 1991).

The Geisha and the Samurai, the Fool and Lear

Lu Anne—intelligent, often witty and lyrical—is a good deal more than a collection of schizophrenic symptoms, and there is also a certain vocational typicality built into her uncertainty about her own identity. During her husband's last night on the continent, as Lu Anne plays for him the dutiful, concerned wife, she reflects, "Well . . . I am acting for him now. Perhaps she always was, day in, day out. Perhaps away from the shadows and the Long Friends it was all acting" (*CL*, 39). As Donald Spoto wrote in his biography of Lawrence Olivier, "Actors often wonder, as they assume one personality after another, just which might be their own; library shelves groan under the weight of theatrical autobiographies redolent of self-doubt, of performers confused about their identities."[5] Still, it is one thing to be afflicted by doubt and confusion about which nonpsychotic identity is most yours; it is another to feel that one's most undeniable bonds are to creatures of the crypt, and—as serial killers sometimes do—to hallucinate ferocious cats. The convergence of Lu Anne's symptoms (particularly her liaison with the Friends), of Walker and his cocaine, and of the role she is playing shapes a death trap for her.

There is a good deal of disagreement over what we are to make of Kate Chopin's version of Edna Pontellier and her suicide. One critic sees the act as the appropriate defiance of a repressive society by a strong woman;[6] another sees it as "originating in a sense of inner emptiness," committed by a woman damaged by schizophrenic and narcissistic symptoms;[7] a third sees the suicide as being made possible by the author's sudden and unconvincing diminishment of her protagonist—by making Edna a much weaker and less resilient character than she has been throughout the whole of the novel.[8] I tend to see the suicide as an attempt to merge with nature in the tradition of nineteenth-century American romanticism. This is roughly Walker's approach to the ending, save that, with his characteristic kinkiness, his notes in the screenplay have Edna as a fin de siècle epicurean who dies "for life more abundant. All suicides died for life more abundant, Walker's notes said" (*CL*, 134).

For Edna's final walk into the Gulf of Mexico, the accompanying notes read, *"She moves like Cleopatra . . . as though impelled by immortal longings. . . . She senses a freedom the scope of which she has never known. She has come beyond despair to a kind of exaltation"* (CL, 164).

Rightly or wrongly, Lu Anne feels that this is "the spirit of the book and its ending. But exaltation beyond despair? She had never found anything beyond despair except more despair" (CL, 164). Given the pull of the Friends and the suffering she often endures, Lu Anne is at least half in love with easeful death. But—unlike Edna—she is a committed artist who badly wants to excel in her métier, and a mother who is frantic not to lose contact with her children. (She feels that her husband has left her and will gain custody of their two children.) Thus, on this second day of the novel, she counts out her prescription pills, sees that she has enough to kill herself, but reasonably concludes that there will always be enough and pours them back into their container. Correspondingly, she regards Walker's treatment of Edna's suicide as a "mean trick . . . a pretty tough one to lay on your own pal. He had rewritten the ending over the past year, not the action but the emotional tone in his descriptions. It occurred to her that he might think he was about to die. Or be wishing himself dead, or her" (CL, 165).

Lu Anne's characterization is rich and complex. Blended into the self-destructive schizophrenic—the woman whom Siriwai calls "that schizophrenic poppet . . . [t]hat little southern creature with the booby eyes" (CL, 140)—is a toughened survivor who often expresses herself in endearingly gritty ways. For example, in her trailer as she recites her part, Lu Anne begins with what I take to be Walker's sententious words ("If I must choose between nothingness and grief") and then segues into something very different: "I'll have the biscuits and gravy. I'll have the jambalaya and oyster stew" (CL, 133). Or she can display ironic assertion even when she's putting herself down:

> Edna knew what living was worth to her and the terms on which she would accept it. She knew the difference between living and not living and what happiness was.
>
>   It occurred to Lu Anne that she knew none of these things. Too bad, she thought, because I'm the one that's real, not her. It's me out here. (CL, 135)

Still, as Walker thinks, "the philosophy whose comforts she represents was Juggernaut" (CL, 318): an aspect of Krishna, whose idol is drawn in an annual procession on a huge cart or wagon. The fanciful might regard the vehicle as an overblown anticipation of the Heebiejeebieville Express since, in earlier times, worshipers are said to have thrown themselves beneath the wheels to be crushed. Walker's observation puts in proper perspective his witty greeting to Jack Glenn, made a day and a half earlier: "I am death . . . destroyer of worlds. I've come to write people out of the script" (*CL*, 230). The novel implicitly asserts that Lu Anne would have finished making the movie and lived on, at least for a while, had Walker not arrived with his cocaine. But she takes over as the primary Krishna figure in the novel's crucial later stages. The victim that dies with her is the raison d'être of the Bahía Honda location: the movie of *The Awakening*, which, as Shelley Pearce puts it in the coda, is "on the bottom of the Pacific . . . with the late Lee V" (*CL*, 351).

Her destruction of the movie is signaled by her effect upon Charlie Freitag's cast party, which the perambulating folie à deux attend after their day of mescal, sex, cocaine, word games, and hallucinations. The producer sees the party as an appropriate celebration of all the fine work the unit has gotten done. "You lovely girl . . . [y]ou champion" is his greeting to Lu Anne. "Here's to all of you . . . [a]rtists of the possible" (*CL*, 278) his toast to the assembled principals. But Lu Anne and her stand-in, a drunken, profane Australian named Joy McIntyre, offer up behavioral possibilities Freitag had not contemplated when he planned the party. On the preceding day Joy (as Edna) had gone through trial runs for Lu Anne: several times the Australian had ridden on a trolley and walked into the bay. Now she insults Freitag, seizes the dinner gong from him, and rings it as an accompaniment to her high-volume rendition of the trolley song from "Meet Me in St. Louis." After she's carried off by Bill Bly, whom she flamboyantly and loudly curses, it's time for the main psychotic show, for "[i]n the shadows Lu Anne ruled" (*CL*, 282). ("In the shadows" is the table at which Stone seated, for maximum volatility, Lu Anne, Walker, Lowndes, Axelrod, Freitag, the Drogues, Maldonado, and his companion, the retired comic actress Ann Armitage.) During this splendid comic scene, Axelrod harasses Lowndes, Ann Armitage insults Lu Anne (first as silly, then as crazy) and, sensationally, Walker: "What's he doing here anyway? . . . Why isn't he somewhere chained to a hospital bed?" (*CL*, 292). Walker insults Drogue and Maldonado; much more tellingly, he tries to crush Lowndes for not having "the confidence or the manliness to manage his own talent" (*CL*, 299), and he comes close to topping Armitage with the viciousness and originality of the invective he directs at her.

But Lu Anne is needed to bring to the scene the strain of Jacobean bedlam Stone was after and achieved. In the past the Long Friends had been reclusive, afraid of sound and light, but now, as they murmur encouragement to Lu Anne, it seems to her that they are "almost ready . . . to join her in her greater world and make the two worlds one" (*CL*, 283). It is easy to discuss the Friends as if they have a fictional existence independent of Lu Anne's hallucinations. Now, as a part of her deepening madness, she seeks to make her two worlds one, using the decorous diction she sometimes affects to tell Ann Armitage and Maldonado that they "have the good opinion of my friends," that they are "admired in secret places. . . . In quarters that you mustn't imagine, they think well of you and they give good report" (*CL*, 283). All decorousness has fallen away, perhaps a half hour later, when she apologizes to the gathering for, as a girl, playing with bones in the broken crypts where, she explains— pointing at the Long Friends she sees trying to touch Lowndes and to wrap him in their diaphanous wings—she "breathed them inside me from a cemetery wall. Playing with the bones. Them, there."

Though Lowndes has already suffered several bizarre accusations and insults from Lu Anne, and though her flirtatiousness has dragged him from a two-year abstinence into a two-day drunk, he responds with considerable lyric sympathy ("Little sister . . . [y]ou're a long way from home"), which modulates into his bewildered response to all the abuse he has been receiving ("You're a sweet woman. . . . You don't belong with this pack of dogs"). Since Lu Anne believes that he is one of the living dead who has found her out as a fellow zombie, his expressions of concern earn only her full fury; she sees him as a hideously degraded form of what she is and denounces him as such to her already embattled companions: "The shit between my toes has stood up to address me. . . . He's all filth inside. . . . Look at his eyes." These "pale brown myopic eyes, tearful and angry like a child's [dart] from side to side, trying to focus on the enemy center." Where will the next attack come from? But eventually Lowndes recognizes the ultimate enemy: he calls Lu Anne a crazy bitch and reasonably tells her to get away from him. At which point Walker, drunk and stoned as usual, leaps into parodic chivalry and—"making fierce faces" at Lowndes, "his right hand floating somewhere back of beyond in the ever-receding future"—is decked by Lowndes's "bone-ended ham fist [thrown] all the way from Escambia County" (*CL*, 300–301). Walker amusingly comes to his version of his senses: when he reaches into his pocket for a handkerchief to wipe the blood off his face, his hand comes out "glistening with coke crystals" (*CL*, 302), which he immediately licks up.

Now Lu Anne must somehow cleanse from her what she sees as Lowndes's polluting effect, and so, Walker in tow, she hires a private plane and flies perhaps a hundred miles to "holy ground . . . [because] [t]he earth is bleeding here" (*CL*, 320). That the psychotically sanctified earth is the peak of a hill called Monte Carmel permits fine ironic vibrations. I take the choice of the name to be an allusion not so much to the ridge in what is now northern Israel as to the most famous member of the order that was founded there in the twelfth century: the sixteenth-century reformer of Spanish monasticism and the preeminent poet of the Spanish mystical tradition, St. John of the Cross. In his most famous poem, "The Dark Night of the Soul," St. John describes the process by which the soul first detaches itself from everything in the immediate world and eventually passes through a reexperiencing of Christ's crucifixion to His glory. Stone brought a hard-earned respect for the severity of schizophrenic symptoms to Lu Anne's characterization, and her quest for spiritual illumination is, among other things, a painful parody of St. John's. When, in a 1987 interview, the author compared the heroines of his third and fourth novels, he observed that "Justin is really whole; she's not a broken person the way Lu Anne is. . . . Lu Anne's plight is much worse" (*Contemporary Authors*, 403). Stone was not about to grant to so damaged a person any version of the end-of-the-book spiritual illumination he gave to the nun.

Lu Anne does not fall short of transcendence for lack of effort. As she and Walker approach the peak of Monte Carmel, she cuts short their word games and traverses the last yards on her knees because, as she informs Walker, "this is how the Bretons pray. . . . The Bretons pray like crazy" (*CL*, 319). Her religious gestures seem more reminiscent of the style of André Breton, one of the fathers of surrealism. Once at the summit, and having discovered that the "church" of Lu Anne's holy place is a ten-year-old location police post—which was thrown up in a day or two for the filming of a B. Traven novel and is now being used as a corncrib for pigs—Walker laughs a bit, then dozes a bit more. He awakens to find standing over him a naked Lu Anne, who, in her apparent attempt to add to the fancied blood in the ground, is bleeding from the wounds she has cut into her hands, feet, and left side with sharp stones. So much for a contemplative experiencing of the crucifixion. Stone had earlier made clear the ludicrousness of her Christian gestures: during the walk up the hill, the promiscuous actress had paused to kneel in the dust, "her eyes upturned in absurd rapture, doing the virgin's prayer. Walker was appalled" (*CL*, 317). Or, in Lu Anne's later attempt to strip away from Walker mundane trivialities, she throws his cocaine and Quaaludes into the bushes but a few minutes later drinks some scotch from what is perhaps the novel's closest approach to the miraculous: the bottle she had Lowndes buy for her two days earlier that never seems to get emptied.

But the Lu Anne standing naked and bleeding over the terrified Walker is only in part an improbable Christ; she is also a pagan priestess or an enraged goddess who seems ready to take life. Here Stone makes his closest approach to the spectacular melodrama of the third act of *Lear*, with the corn crib transformed into the hovel on the heath and Walker as the Fool cowering, as a storm rages, before Lear's emerging madness and Edgar's feigned madness. Save that the maddened Lu Anne does little feigning:

> He turned to her about to speak and saw the lightning flash behind her. The earth shook under him like a scaffold. He saw her raised up, as though she hung suspended between the trembling earth and the storm. Her hair was wild, her body sheathed in light. Her eyes blazed amethyst.
>
> "Forgive me," Walker said.
>
> She stretched forth her bloody hand on an arm that was serpentine and unnatural. She smeared his face with blood.
>
> "I was your sister Eve," Lu Anne said. "I was your actress. I lived and breathed you. I enacted forms. Whatever was thought right, however I was counseled. In my secret life I was your secret lover."

Several elements converge here. We remember how Lu Anne resented Walker's screenplay emphasizing the deliciousness of death for a character she had felt herself become, however temporarily. In aesthetic matters she seems to have believed that Walker was always right. (As Eve, she was made from his body, imprisoned by his sense of things.) But now, with her secret eyes, in her holy place, roles are reversed: "I own the ground you stand on. This is the place I want you" (*CL*, 321–22). For the second time in perhaps 12 hours, Lu Anne is trying to expand her secret, schizophrenic world, this time by welcoming into it Walker, who, in one of her delusory systems, has always been her secret lover, chosen for this role because his eyes are also her secret eyes.

This breakdown of logical self-other distinctions, this assertion of magical combinations, is also behind Lu Anne's appeal to the animism of

Louisiana folklore: "Down home they say you shoot a deer you see your love in his eyes. A bear the same, they say. It's a little like that, eh? Hunting and recognition. A light in the eyes and you're caught. So I was. So I remain." She and Walker can be each other's mirrors not because they are playing with cocaine images (as Walker suggests) but because "[i]t's the end of the road. It's through the looking glass. Because there's only one love, my love. It's all the same one" (*CL*, 323–24). When I told Stone that Lu Anne's "one love" assertion baffled me, he responded, "By that she means a sort of space; what I'm thinking of is a great space to fall through. What's on her mind is the phrase 'to *fall* in love,' which is an abyss, which is that one kind of space of love and destruction, Eros and Thanatos. There's just one love; it's close to saying it's death, it's destruction, it's darkness, it's just one big void. There aren't all these individual things, these individual emotional attachments, that's just an illusion" (Solotaroff 1991).[9]

Whatever Walker's problems, he is not her schizophrenic semblable but a very intelligent, very self-indulgent man who is trying to keep this suddenly dangerous woman from injuring him while he ministers to her as best he can. (After Lu Anne sees the Long Friends seeking to fondle Lowndes, the reader is denied direct access to her mind and so is put in something of Walker's difficult position as he tries to puzzle out the implications of her erupting symptoms.) The day before Lu Anne had expressed her desire to play Cordelia or the Fool—whom she interestingly claims is the same as Cordelia—to his Lear. But when on Monte Carmel they play out as much of the storm on the heath as they do, it is Walker who becomes the Fool, jerked into placating gestures by the extremity of Lu Anne's anguish and menace. (One can only guess at how much the Monte Carmel scene was shaped by the author's memories of his hopeless attempts to deal with his mother's schizoid flights.) Lu Anne had accurately predicted Walker's eventual relationship to her when, just after his arrival at Bahía Honda, she compared them to "[t]he geisha and the samurai. . . . You're the geisha. . . . I'm the samurai" (*CL*, 215).

But Lu Anne's most extreme mode (which incorporates into her own delusory systems flickers of the White Goddess, a pagan priestess, the suffering Christ, and Lear on the heath) does not last even as long as the storm, which quickly passes. After she hurls some stones at Walker, he talks her into having a drink with him in the sheltered doorway of the corn crib. Then they sleep through the passing of the storm and awaken to the beauty of a bright rainbow, arching from an adjoining peak. Apparently exhausted emotionally, Lu Anne weeps as she watches the rainbow fade and struggles to interpret it as a positive sign from God: "I know it all must mean something, Gordon, because it hurts so much. . . . Gordon, I think there's a mercy. I think there must be." This is the novel's closest approach to a dialogue over the unavailability of God. Pressed by Lu Anne for his honest opinion of the rainbow as a portent of mercy, Walker replies, "Mercy? In a pig's asshole." At which point, in the author's ironic commentary on the availability of divine mercy or the possibilities of the miraculous, Lu Anne spots a number of huge pigs, feeding on a lower slope. Reaching for transcendence in the most improbable places, she finds it remarkable that they appeared so soon after Walker's invocation of the porcine. Trying to humor her, Walker agrees—"It's a miracle . . . [t]he Gadarene Swine" (CL, 331–32)—but this reference to embodied demons merely reminds Lu Anne of the Long Friends' habitation of herself and triggers screams, howls, and a crazed plea (reminiscent of the sort of thing that Edgar as Tom o' Bedlam came up with) to "the last wisps of rainbow. 'I adjure thee, Son of the Most High God, I adjure thee. Torment me not.' "

Then Lu Anne calms a bit, and perhaps remembering that it is not blood but pig manure that oozes from the ground, modulates into playing a very earthy earth goddess who is resigned to finding not the glory of Christ's ascension but "[t]he pigshit at the end of the rainbow. Didn't you always know it was there?" "Play high; play low," instructed Thoreau in *Walden*. Denied a transcendent high ground, Lu Anne reclines in a pile of pig manure, some of which she rubs, in the shape of a cross, on Walker's forehead, baptizing him "in the name of pigshit and pigshit" (CL, 335–36).[10]

So much for transcendence in the sacred precinct. Then it's time for one last game—a fight with pig manure before police come and arrest them: Lu Anne is wearing only a shirt Walker has thrown over her; all their clothes are covered with her blood. With ugly, ill-fitting clothes purchased for them by the Mexican woman who offered them a shower, and with police and other locals paid off, the principals are flown back to the airfield not far from Bahía Honda. Now Stone uses the clothes to have Walker accede to Lu Anne's wish to leave the car driving them back to the hotel and walk along the shore, though it is unprotected and large rollers are pounding it: "[I]t would be horrible to arrive at the hotel's front door in broad daylight. He decided it would be unthinkable. They could walk slowly . . . watching the sunset colors, and then he would put her to bed." But Lu Anne soon tires of this scenario and, as a part of what Walker earlier thought of as their "relentless

Shakespearianizing," claims that she must wash off "blood and shit" (*CL*, 342) (already showered off) as well as her milk (which she mentions in only one of her Monte Carmel invocations). So much for Lady Macbeth: now it's time for other allusions in this much more conclusive reworking of Rheinhardt's inability to save the drunken Geraldine from Lake Pontchartrain. Once in the ocean, easily evading Walker's attempts to take hold of her so that he might get her back on land, Lu Anne offers up an antic revision of the sententious version of a woman preparing to drown in Walker's screenplay. The Ophelia of act 4 of *Hamlet*, with a bit of Lear on the heath, fades into the fairy tale of the cathedral beneath the sea: "Give me my robe. . . . Put on my crown. . . . Hey, it's Shakespeare, Walker. . . . Immortal longings. . . . Here comes your dog Tray, Gordon, lookit here. . . . Want to marry me, Walker? . . . I see a church."

It's hard to be sure of just how much Lu Anne intends to choreograph her literal drowning. On the one hand, she has in the previous 36 hours undergone considerable pain, terror, religious disappointment, and general degradation. Once in the water, she calls out to Walker, "Come with me, Gordon. This is best. . . . Come or else save me" (*CL*, 344–45). On the other hand, she's having a terrific if maddened time in the water; the shore is nearby, and she's a strong swimmer who is standing in only a few feet of water when she's swept away by a tall wave that has little interest in such subtleties of motivation. Nor does Walker, once he is driven down against the sand by the same wave. Whatever Lu Anne intended, there is no Whitmanesque embrace of nature for her, just being overpowered by immense force.

As for Walker, however much he might have come to Mexico to die, he has been struggling against the pain that has just exploded in his chest, and he fights the riptide back to shore. In the coda, set a few months later in a Hollywood bar where, after a memorial service for Lu Anne, Walker joins Shelley Pearce, Jack Glenn, and a French actor, we learn that the pain was from a hepatitis attack and that Walker would indeed have died in Mexico had he not had a gamma globulin shot. Now he joins the living dogs of the preceding three novels: the self-indulgent men who survive the deaths of more admirable or more powerful characters. Save that, unlike Rheinhardt, Converse, and Holliwell, Walker appears to be cleaning up his self-destructive act: he now drinks Perrier in a bar and tomato juice at home; drugs are out of the question; and his behavior is both dignified and efficient. He puts up with a good deal of abuse from Shelley (who blames him for Lu Anne's death), gets the business done with her that he has to, and leaves. He's writing again, is back together with his wife, and they're relocating on the East Coast. As Walker tersely sums up his situon, "I thought that at my present age I might stop going with the flow" (*CL*, 353). Save that, for reasons I shall shortly consider, his survival seems an irrelevant afterthought.

Closing Thoughts

Two of the comments that Stone made as I peppered him with questions about the workings of Lu Anne's psychosis are relevant here: "I wish others would have read the book as closely as you did," and, "It really floors me to go back through this and to realize, to remember, that I put all that stuff in there, that I actually did it. I don't know why the world didn't beat a path to my door. There's lots of great stuff in there. Just kidding, just kidding" (Solotaroff 1991). Of course, Stone was not kidding at all. As a whole, the critical world did not beat a path to his door: *Children of Light* received a much higher percentage of unfavorable reviews than his other four novels, and a good many reviews were marked by singularly high percentage of factual errors.[11] Admittedly, when I first read the novel, I was a bit dismayed by the immediate and prolonged immersion in accounts of the taking of cocaine and liquor; I felt that Stone had done this and done this and it was time to move on. Eventually, I perceived that, at bottom, the drugs and booze—indeed, the greater part of the novel—primarily serve to further Stone's deepest intention in the novel: to depict not the workings of the film industry in general or the principal's careers in particular, or the reworking of some medieval trope about death as a knight errant, but the release of Lu Anne's schizophrenia at its fullest tilt.

No critic considered Lu Anne's delusory system with even the detail appropriate for a review-length effort. When attention was paid, the tendency was to mention the Long Friends but regret their melodrama.[12] They're melodramatic all right, but compellingly so; one way or another, Lu Anne's world *is* a melodramatic one. And repeatedly, critics took Lu Anne's explanations for the origins of her schizophrenia as Stone's. Thus, one of the novel's best reviewers, Jean Strouse, described the scenes in which Lu Anne "remembers" acquiring the Long Friends by playing in a crypt, as "contrived, called upon to explain too much." If Strouse found the culminating Monte Carmel scene "wildly sad and clever" (24–25), A. Alvarez felt that this scene "is the exact point where the narrative unravels into histrionics, as if Stone had lost patience with the harsh and unsavory world he has so elegantly created and settled for something more stagy but less demanding" (25).

Alvarez's review is, line for line, perhaps the most penetrating criticism written on Stone's oeuvre, but he misses the fact that the Monte Carmel scene is the culmination of the main show of the revelation of Lu Anne's symptoms. Drogue's antics, Walker's mutterings about his wife and children, even his survival, seem unconvincing or irrelevant because, at the deepest level of *Children of Light*, they *are* irrelevant. Everything after Monte Carmel, even Lu Anne's drowning, is anticlimactic in more ways than one. Of Stone's two inciting animi for the novel—Lear, and the death and the lover collision—Lear took over. With Lu Anne's eruption, Stone tried to offer up something of the senseless pain, the histrionic suffering, and the grueling demands upon his readers that the play makes on its audience. And with its cause and center, Lu Anne's schizophrenia, he had a subject that must have obsessed him at many parts of his life. In fact, it seems to me possible that Stone's near compulsion to create characters who are addicted to alcohol or drugs might be the displacement of his earlier concern over the way his mother was overwhelmed by her symptoms. While talking about his mother to Peter Prescott, Stone said, "I knew about the Long Friends."[13] I feel that Lionel, Lu Anne's physician husband, is speaking for the adolescent or preadolescent Stone when he says of schizophrenia, "I've finally come to think of it as evil" (*CL*, 37). If Stone's attempt to give fictional form to his confrontation with and aesthetic mastery over this personal demon drew energy or a density of motivation and convincing detail from some aspects of *Children of Light*, so that its power is fitful, overall it made for what is still an extremely interesting and sometimes very powerful novel.

Chapter Six
Outerbridge Reach

Origins

Late on a November afternoon in 1986, as a part of the preparation for a piece for the *New York Times* on the ports of New York, Stone was motoring south down the Arthur Kill, the channel between Staten Island and New Jersey, when he came to an unusually arresting prospect. To his left, on the Staten Island side,

> was this old yard named Woodie's, filled with all these skeletons of old steam tugs piled on each other so that the proportion was lost, and because of their shape—the old straight stacks, instead of raked ones— they looked like little kids' bathtub toys piled on each other. And on the other side was a tank farm: these oil storage tanks, almost as far as you could see. And then in the middle of the reach were these blue herons that were feeding so that there was at the same time a kind of marine landscape and a blighted landscape. When I looked at the chart and saw Outerbridge Reach, it suggested so many things to me. It suggested a crossing; it suggested extending, stretching, trying for something, trying to get across something. All of the weight of the name came to me; it was coming on that on the chart that made me decide to put down what I was working on and write this. (Benson and Solotaroff)

When Stone described the locale in his fifth and best novel, he vitiated what there was of the pastoral and moved it a bit to the north of the salvage yard, with a single heron taking flight and sailing "over the oil storage tanks on the Jersey side." Further down the channel, the blend of animal and petroleum takes a more sinister turn—rats run "along the oily bank of the Jersey shore"—and the sense of humankind's pervasive, dirtying presence is reinforced by the stench of the garbage from a nearby dump and the way the starless "gathered night" is "soiled by the glow of the harbor." Then one comes to the salvage yard, "ringed with lights like a prison yard," where decay seems formally preserved and imprisoned. All of the boats, half-submerged or stacked, rotting or rusting, are "floodlit and girded round with electrified fence and razor wire"; some have been there for close to a century. Beyond the yard, "the marshes of Outerbridge Reach [receive] the soiled tide." The adjective is a pervasive one; "soiled" turns up seven more times in the novel.

Stone transferred the ownership of the salvage yard from Woodie to Jack Campbell, "the presiding chief of a race of water ruffians—Irish and Newfie by origin—who had lorded it over certain sections of dockland since the last century." Surveying the blighted vista is Owen Browne, Campbell's son-in-law and the novel's protagonist, who remembers "scraps of the place's history. Thousands of immigrants had died there, in shanties, of cholera, in winter far from home. It had been a place of loneliness, violence and terrible labor. It seemed to Browne that there was something about the channel he recognized but could not call to mind"[1]

The recognizable but elusive flicker, the common ground between the experience of Jack Campbell, the immigrants, and himself—the son of English immigrants—is the intensity of the struggle for footing in America. The deterioration that sometimes follows from that struggle is another connecting strand. We remember Stone's 1984 comment to William Crawford Woods: "What I'm always trying to do is define that process in American life that puts people in a state of anomie, of frustration. The national promise is so great that a tremendous bitterness is evoked by its elusiveness. That was Fitzgerald's subject and it's mine" (Woods, 49). Fitzgerald's name fits nicely into considerations of the interrelationships between national aspiration, frustration, deterioration, and the southwest corner of Staten Island. As John Leonard observed, the contemporary Reach is the novel's Valley of Ashes, the ghostly site (in the book that triggered Stone's decision to become a novelist) that symbolizes the apparently inevitable consequences of the struggle to act out one's desires, to bring the ideal to earth.[2] Of course, Fitzgerald's dramatization of this massive theme was not some abstracted allegory: "what preyed on Gatsby, what foul dust floated in the wake of his dreams"[3] was American culture of the first three decades of the century, in particular, brilliantly depicted segments of upper- and lower-class Long Island in the 1920s. Gatsby's quest for romantic consummation ended on "that slender riotous island" (Fitzgerald, 4). Browne's sense of growing up in a world waiting for him to find consummation in it began on Long Island, though his status spoke of the uncertainty of his footing: he grew up on an estate, but as the son of the steward. For all of Browne's relative centrality and his attempts to be a good team player, he was never fully at home in any of the intervening milieus between

Long Island and Outerbridge Reach: the Naval Academy, Vietnam, American society of the 1980s, his home. But questing is still possible, even among the moldering, gutted ferries and tugs, the filthy waters of Outerbridge Reach. There is the bridge arching over the Reach, and more importantly, there is Browne, motoring along in a bare-masted sailboat, which he named Parsifal II. But the ironies are strong here: were there some wounded king to be healed, the United States would still not be healed; though Browne brings some virtues to the novel and develops others during the roughly 16 months that it covers, he is no Parsifal I: "the Deliverer that has been promised—the one who has 'been made wise by pity, the Blameless Fool.' "[4] His experience during this period purges him of the foolish acceptance of some of the large social lies that have in good part shaped his life, but an exacerbated form of the idealism that encouraged his acceptance of the lies combines with a complex of other corrosive sources to drive him to suicide. What limited wisdom Browne is brought to is, from a survivor's point of view, a fool's wisdom.

In the last months of 1987, as Stone sought a way of dramatizing his nautical and terrestrial tale of reaching, vastness, and decay, both social and individual, he remembered the story of Donald Crowhurst, an English electrical engineer and small-time inventor and entrepreneur. In a trimaran in large part of his own design, Crowhurst sailed from Devon on 31 October 1968 as he competed in a single-handed, around-the-world race. Far from circumnavigating the globe in the prescribed easterly direction, Crowhurst never again made it as far east as his point of departure or further south than the Falklands, for he perceived that his unstable boat would capsize in the strong winds and 13,000-mile expanse between the points south of Cape Hope and Cape Horn, where his proper course lay. Between December and June he largely sailed down and then up the coast of South America, but in April, after a radio silence of 11 weeks, he reported that he was approaching Cape Horn from the west (though he was about 3,000 miles northeast of the Cape at the time). On 1 July 1969, as he approached a hero's welcome (and some acute suspicion) in an England about 1,800 miles away, Crowhurst, who had for weeks been moving into deepening insanity, almost certainly jumped off his boat and drowned himself. Ten days later, a British mailship came across the drifting boat with its logs that revealed—as Crowhurst's biographers, Nicholas Tomalin and Ron Hall, have put it in *The Strange Voyage of Donald Crowhurst* (1970)—that he had never left the Atlantic and sailed in the Southern Ocean, that he had started faking his positions less than six weeks into his voyage. The revelation of Crowhurst's attempted hoax, disordered mind, and probable suicide "was the national sensation of the weekend of July 27th. It became the lead front-page news in almost every rival Sunday newspaper. [The story was broken by the *Sunday Times* of London.] It inspired an increasingly demeaning series of speculative follow-up stories."[5]

Stone, who was living in England at the time, told me during a May 1992 radio interview that when he originally read the account in the *Times*, "it seemed like such a wonderful example of the connection between heroism and folly, which are never too far separated, and often the line between them is very fine." I then observed that Crowhurst "was this wildly extroverted life-of-the party type, a kind of roaring boy of the pubs who was reportedly drummed out of the RAF for driving a motor-cycle through his mates' sleeping quarters," and asked Stone to talk for a bit about how and why he created Crowhurst's fictional counterpart in the person of Browne, "whose only public manner is that of the naval officer, who is such an introverted type." Here is Stone's response:

> Well, because I wasn't all that taken with who Crowhurst himself was or Crowhurst's individual circumstances. The human dimension of the story is wonderful, but it was more the universal aspect than the particular world of Crowhurst that interested me, and it seemed to me that the points I wanted to make are not necessarily the same points that are brought to the fore by the people who handled the Crowhurst story. I wanted to illustrate a theme of mine, which is how difficult it is for people to behave well and how even a good person in certain circumstances can trap himself in something like a lie. In a way he ends up being undone by his own honesty, and he makes the discovery, at one point he actually says, "The truth's my bride." Of course he has to find this out the hard way. So I had my own agenda, very much my own agenda, but I really loved the idea of someone reducing their circumstances to the ocean, and the sky and the boat, and of course their own mind, and having to live it out to the most intense degree. (Benson and Solotaroff)

In his prefatory note to the novel Stone wrote that "an episode in the book was suggested by an incident that actually occurred during a circumnavigation race in the mid-1960's. The novel is not a reflection on that incident but a fiction referring to the present day." The Crowhurst affair occurred in the late, not the mid, 1960s, but this slip is characteristic of Stone's frequently casual attitude toward dating.[6] More curious is his reference to Browne's doomed sail as an episode: almost the whole of the book can be described as the causes, workings, and consequences of the voyage. And finally, though Stone's depiction of the doomed voyage, the dramatis personae, and the worlds they live in is quite different from Tomalin and Hall's, there are enough similarities in the two accounts to argue that some of the details of *Outerbridge Reach* would be different if Stone had read only Tomalin and Hall's 1969 newspaper account and not the 300-page book they published the following year.[7] Responding to the frequent queries about why he did not acknowledge the earlier book in his prefatory note, Stone told one interviewer that he had not mentioned Crowhurst's name in the prefatory note "[b]ecause I was afraid that, if I made that connection, the Crowhurst family would feel I was writing about them. That was my anxiety."[8] Obviously, he could not have mentioned Tomalin and Hall's book without using the name Crowhurst.

In response to some accusations that he had "copied" Tomalin and Hall's book, Stone published, in the *Times Literary Supplement*, "The Genesis of *Outerbridge Reach*," an 1,800-word piece in which he defended the originality of the novel and his right to use some of the details of Tomalin and Hall's reporting. Stone claimed that he got all of the information about the Crowhurst incident that he needed for his novel from Tomalin and Hall's 1969 *Sunday Times* reporting. In a letter to the same publication that was published three weeks later, Stone repeated the claim that "my original information came from [Tomalin and Hall's] version in the *Sunday Times*. Their book is the relevant document now. I might add that the Tomalin-Hall account was not the only one I read." Though Stone concluded that "[t]he work Tomalin and Hall did on the Crowhurst story stands as one of the great achievements of contemporary journalism," he never conceded that he read the most significant component of this work—the book. Then again, he never said that he had not read the book. His emphasis upon his use of information offered by the press accounts and not those of *The Strange Voyage* is no small thing, for Stone argued in his letter to the *TLS* editor that "[p]ress accounts exist for the information and use of the public, including novelists. Events do not become the property of the journalists who cover them."[9] But what about using a source and not giving credit? There are incidents in both *The Strange Voyage* and *Outerbridge Reach*—like the mariners' wives' doubts about the voyage, and their varnishing eggs when they should have tended to more pressing needs for the outfitting of the respective boats—that are not in the press accounts. But Stone's use of these facts does not at all constitute plagiarism or even "copying," to use the word his English attackers were fond of. The worlds of the novels are completely different. Above all, Stone's appeal once again to the aesthetic Conrad proposed in his preface to *The Nigger of the "Narcissus"*—that the best books "justify themselves in every line"—is appropriate. *Outerbridge Reach* very much succeeds, in Stone's words, because of "the quality of music I could coax from my ink-stained sensibility" ("Genesis," 14).

Heroic Dreams

In *Children of Light* Stone worked his way free from his habit of casting St. Ann's as some aspect of the social world, one that crushed one or more of his principals. However damaged the social orders of *Outerbridge Reach* might be, they are not particularly malevolent, and with Owen and Anne Browne, Stone brought a good deal of health and social centrality to his existing gallery of self-destructive and/or socially marginal principals: alcoholics, drug addicts, drug smugglers, psychopaths, candidates for martyrdom, a schizophrenic. The Brownes, particularly Anne, do not enter the novel carrying on their backs the kinds of obvious afflictions and deviancies that burden all of Stone's earlier principals save for Justin (who is, of course, terribly isolated and unhappy for most of *Flag*). The third principal, the moviemaker Ron Strickland, whose origins contain interesting similarities to his creator's, is more characteristically twisted. But though he uses liquor and marijuana, he could easily do without them, and his very good documentaries are the product of considerable labor, intelligence, and canny grantsmanship. His origins, tastes, and beliefs may often be marginal, but his mode of functioning is not.

In his review of *A Flag for Sunrise*, Robert Towers wrote that Stone's "hero-adventurers tend to be self-exiled; externally to the farthest reaches of the Euro-American imperium . . . or internally, to the underside of their own cities, where they consort with criminals, spies, psychopaths, and fugitives."[10] This intelligent generalization does not square with Stone's next novel, but between addictions and schizophrenia, Gordon Walker and Lu Anne Bourgeois are very marginal people. But as Leonard has written, only a little erroneously, Owen Browne is "someone new to Stone's fiction: Northeast Middle-Class Normal, Dick Tracy Square, Wonderbread WASPy, as if wandering in from a Cheever or an Updike; monogamous husband, worried father, Navy pilot, sailboat salesman. He seldom drinks, never drugs, and listens to the music of

Russ Columbo" (489). Browne was never a pilot, and associating him with the blandness of Wonder bread overdoes it a bit, but this portrait is largely the man Browne presents to the world, and it describes part of his inner life. After four years at Annapolis and four more in Vietnam, the 42-year-old Browne finds himself 16 years later, in the unseasonably warm winter of 1987–88, living in a large old home "on the edge of a slum in an unprestigious outer suburb" (OR, 12) that feels like Norwalk, Connecticut.[11] There Browne does what Strickland would call postprep-pie work: he brokers—a more genteel word than "sells"—for Altan Marine Corporation; because of his verbal facility, he bats out the com-pany's copy; because of his good looks and confidence in his articulate-ness, he acts in Altan video promotionals, which he also writes.

To many then, and almost always to women, Browne's presentation of self is impressive. But the armature encasing his romantic yearnings is crumbling as the novel opens: Browne will realize during a subsequent upswing that he was in a state of "paralysis and despair" (OR, 124). The vapid weather seems to serve as an objective correlative that dimly alerts some people to the vapidity of their inner lives. And so Browne, "stirred by the weather and some obscure guilt" (OR, 3), visits Buzz Ward and Teddy Federov, two naval buddies in Annapolis. The latter declares that "[t]he heroic age of the bourgeoisie is over." To which Browne adds, "So is the cold war. . . . We're all redundant." On the train back to Penn Station Browne sees himself approaching a diminished kind of life; anx-ious and disappointed, beset by "old rages and regrets," he feels "in rebellion against things, on his own behalf and on behalf of his old friends" (OR, 10–11).

Perhaps four months after his return from Annapolis, Browne tells Duffy, his PR representative, that Vince Lombardi (the football coach who enjoyed great success but crippled some of his players by driving them to perform when injured, and brutally underpaid almost all of them) was "a great coach and a great sportsman. A good example for the kids." Browne might have a good deal more delicacy and depth in some areas—he quickly punctures Duffy's attempts to hype him into some-thing he is not—but in his readings of the workings of American mass culture, Duffy shows himself here to be much closer to the author than to Browne: "He [Lombardi] was a fucking monster. He caused the Vietnam War" (OR, 181). Which is, of course, hyperbole, but Duffy has picked up on a certain gung-ho mindlessness that Stone would see as a common strand in the worldviews of Vince Lombardi and William Westmoreland, the commander-in-chief in southeast Asia who infallibly saw light at the end of the Vietnam tunnel. Leonard captures this in the kind of language that Strickland and the author (who by no accident have the same initials) enjoy: the Brownes "bought a package tour, the Vince Lombardi 'narrative' like one of Owen's videos" (490). And having bought the heroism narrative as a boy, Browne also acquired the Vietnam package tour: as long as he did not allow himself to participate in exceptional atrocities, whatever he did there was justified; he was a soldier in the war against the communist monolith, against what Ronald Reagan, the man who made so much so simple for so many Americans, would later designate as the Evil Empire.

This holy war offered Browne opportunities to fulfill his desires to serve his country and to prove himself in heroic struggle. A few days after Browne's Annapolis comment about his sense of redundancy, he thinks over his situation more cogently. The decisive war against communism "would never be fought because the enemy had proved false. All his fierce alternatives were lies. Surely, Browne thought sleepily, this was a good thing. Yet something was lost. For his own part, he was tired of living [only] for himself and for those who were him by extension. It was impossible, he thought. Empty and impossible" (*OR*, 45). How much simpler it was when Browne could see his country as a fountain of rectitude that he must defend against Marxist defilers. The introverted Browne still yearns, perhaps paradoxically, for heroic collectivity, not easily attainable now that, as he sees it, the presiding national spirit is "No Can Do. It was everywhere lately, poisoning life and the country" (*OR*, 70). (Browne still wears his class ring from Annapolis, whose physical presence speaks to the canny Strickland as "Republican virtue in the water" [*OR*, 236]). An alternative, much more elite lodging place offers itself a few weeks later with the opportunity for the single-handed circumnavigation: it seems a chance to join the invisible brotherhood of disciplined adventurers, some of whom have written the memoirs Browne likes to read.

Within a week of his return from Annapolis, more violent symptoms of his midlife crisis are erupting: troubling dreams, frightening and vivid fantasies, flashbacks of presumably upsetting war experience, insomnia, strange reveries "without much content but vaguely religious and sentimental. Inevitably it ended in anger, sleeplessness and fear" (*OR*, 65). As part of his unconvincing attempt to present a healthy, functional front, Browne speaks of none of this to his wife until the alternative of the voyage presents itself: "Sometimes I feel like I'm in the wrong life. . . . I've never done the things I ought to have done years ago. . . . Sometimes . . .

it's as though whatever I'm feeling is completely artificial. I have these highs and lows and I don't think they attach to me at all. That isn't life" (*OR*, 99).

Mark Edmundson observed in his largely admirable review that "Browne is shallow enough not to recognize that he is going through something of a standard midlife crisis, but he is brave enough to translate his unfocused desperation into something more than a down payment on a Porsche or a fling with a 19-year-old."[12] But someone who speaks of emotional swings not attaching to himself—instead of, say, "being a part of the real me"—is not likely to be pervasively shallow. Browne's wit, aesthetic taste, and perceptiveness have their limits. But they are often fairly impressive aspects of a man who has not learned to integrate the demands of his self and those of his persona, who is ignorant and gullible in some very important experiential areas but whose thoughts are often too subtle, whose feelings are too intense and complex, for him to be described as shallow or—as Robert Adams would have it—hollow.[13] And his yearning is not so much unfocused as generalized: during his winter of discontent Browne longs for "a bright expanse, an effort, a victory . . . a good fight or the right war—something that eased the burden of self and made breath possible. Without it, he felt as though he had been preparing all his life for something he would never see" (*OR*, 45).

The operative phrase here, "the burden of self," is the master theme of the most impressive fictional and poetic achievements of the last half-century of American literature, the most obsessive concern of Saul Bellow's and Robert Lowell's careers. In Bellow's first novel, *Dangling Man* (1944), Joseph, the embittered protagonist, formulates what his author has long felt are the immense personal consequences of the romantic movement:

> Of course, we suffer from bottomless avidity. Our lives are so precious to us, we're so watchful of waste. Or perhaps a better name for it would be the Sense of Personal Destiny. Yes, I think that is better than avidity. Shall my life by one-thousandth of an inch fall short of its ultimate possibility? . . .
>
> Six hundred years ago, a man was what he was born to be. Satan and the Church, representing God, did battle over him. He, by reason of his choice, partially decided the outcome. But whether, after life, he went to hell or to heaven, his place among other men was given. It could not be contested. But, since, the stage has been reset and human beings only walk on it, and under this revision, we have, instead, history to answer to.

We were important enough then for our souls to be fought over. Now, each of us is responsible for his own salvation, which is in his greatness. And that, that greatness, is the rock our hearts are abraded on.[14]

Joseph's claim that none of us will settle for less than greatness reflects Bellow's immense ambition more than it does the imperatives of most contemporary Americans. But the rest of his generalization speaks to the condition of a great many in a country where part of what we are taught is that each of us is "special," where Whitman celebrated "Oneself . . . a simple separate person," where the army's primary appeal for enlistment is "Be all that you can be." It also speaks most pointedly to a man who "had begged all his life for such a chance [as the single-handed circumnavigation] and all his life done what had to be done and never once regretted risk or contest" (*OR*, 167), and who, after a lifetime of conformity to proper forms, strengthens his rebellion with the injunction Melville kept on his writing desk: "Be true to the dreams of your youth." "Gatsby turned out all right in the end" (Fitzgerald, 2) because he was true to his dream of perfect existence. It kills the former James Gatz of North Dakota and West Egg, just as clinging for as long as he does to his dream of asserting his specialness through heroic behavior kills Owen Browne of the North Shore and Fairfield County, Connecticut—save that Browne is far from all right when he jumps from his boat into the South Atlantic.

The Boat

At Altan Marine one of the ways Browne tries to adhere to his straight-arrow conception of himself is by selling himself the product as he tries to sell it to others. Several characters refer to Browne as a salesman, and as one of them also says, "Commercial is a state of mind" (*OR*, 117). Then again, as the same speaker also says, "Hype doesn't float" (*OR*, 120): sometimes the truth rises as surely as the water in an ill-made boat. In the novel's opening episode Browne attempts to sail to Annapolis by delivering a Highlander Forty-five, Altan's 45-foot sloop. But the sail is quickly aborted by a malfunctioning bilge pump. "Some kind of South Korean fuckup. . . . Keep it quiet, will you?" (*OR*, 5) is his branch manager's compromising summary of the situation. At a boat show perhaps a month later, Browne's solution is not to play a tape he had made in which he praised the Highlander forty-five, "which from his own experience [he] knew was badly made," but to play "his pitch for the Altan Forty" (*OR*, 85)—the stock version of the prototype that Matty Hylan, the head of the conglomerate that owns Altan, is to sail in the circumnavigation race. After learning at the show that Hylan—who had, among other swindles, been buying banks "with junk bonds making loans secured by worthless boats" (*OR*, 387)—has disappeared, Browne conceives the idea of volunteering to take his place in the stock boat: "He was sure it was a good boat" (*OR*, 87). Why should he be sure? The stock boat, constructed by unknown builders somewhere in the Far East, is a knockoff: the Finnish boatwright's beautiful design, which Hylan stole, was copied, but there is no evidence that the rigorous specifications of the Finn's prototype and the process by which it was built were followed. Moreover, Browne has recently been burned by the shoddy construction of the Highlander Forty-five. Why not another "South Korean fuckup"? Because this boat from dangerously unknown origins offers him the chance for the heroic testing he has come to feel would always be denied him, and his knowledge of boat-building practices is too limited to counter the opportunity with reasonable caution.

Stone adds to the suspense of the novel by planting a fair number of hints of the boat's inadequacy. One of Browne's competitors ominously says that he "knows all about" (*OR*, 195) the stock boat and, with some derision, praises Browne's courage for sailing it. But only he communicates his doubts to Browne, and these but two hours before the race begins. The captain of the yacht club sponsoring the race questions the wisdom of racing in a stock boat, and Altan's chief architect admits uncertainty about the boat's workmanship. Two workers at an Altan boat yard are convinced that the boat is badly made; put off by Browne's rigid, naval officer demeanor, however, they say nothing to him. For whatever reasons, the captain and the architect are also silent, and Browne's sale of the boat to himself is not significantly challenged.

Stone did a splendid job of creating a character who is enough tweedy, conscientious WASP to represent convincingly that part of American culture, but impulsive enough to set out around the world with very little single-handed sailing experience and in a dangerous boat. Browne's disparities also come through in the way that women are intensely attracted to him, but his parts do not cohere for a good many men. They see inconsonance in his appearance—the rugged jaw and well-muscled body belied by what Strickland calls "the eyes of a poet" (*OR*, 110)—or between the upright competence his persona protests and the uncertainties, the lack of full maturity, that lie beneath the appearance. In spite of Browne's good looks and his attractive wife, he cannot get a good table in a New York restaurant; Jack Campbell tells Anne that her husband has "got it all wrong," (*OR*, 207), he doesn't know how to carry himself; one of the workers at the Altan boat yard sees Browne as "a phoney," "a fuckin' hype artist . . . a pussy . . . a preppy . . . a fuckin' salesman and he's not even a good salesman." Another worker, who is given to more thought and less derision, sees Browne as being "like a bad officer . . . [t]he kind you don't want over you. Gung-ho do-or-die bullshit. Sometimes they do, sometimes they die. Take you with 'em too" (*OR*, 175). But Stone gave Browne enough gung-ho idealism and competence to make his way to what his creator has waiting for him in the southern latitudes, where his realized potentials of emotion and articulation combine with circumstances and his emotional frailty to generate commanding eloquence and pathos. If Browne's *crise de quarantaine* comes more or less on schedule, an atypical man is undergoing it. It takes a singular man, a very unusual collection of parts, to become the man who confronts the devastating Doctrine of Singularities.

Browne's Military Career

No such cynical appeal as "Be all that you can be" pulled Owen Browne to Annapolis; he went to please his father, just as he had gone to a top private school to please his father's employer, the owner of the estate on the North Shore of Long Island. For one of Browne's dominant traits—against which his growing desire for rebellion defines itself—is one we find in no earlier principal: obedience to authority. The mid-1960s rebellion came a little late for Browne, and for Federov and Ward, his two close friends at the Naval Academy. Had they "graduated from high school only a year or two later they might have resisted. He and his friends had been the last good children of their time" (*OR*, 9). Put differently, had they been born a few years later, they might very well have bought the Counterculture Personal and Social Wholeness Package Tour instead of the Red Monolith–Vince Lombardi Package Tour. What rebellion there was at the Naval Academy was mildness itself: the three friends had been "wrongos and secret mockers, subversives, readers of Thomas Wolfe and Hemingway. They had appeared 'grossly poetic,' as Federov liked to say, naively literary in a military engineering school where the only acceptable art forms were band music and the shoe shine" (*OR*, 11). Which did not stop Browne and Ward from being straight enough arrows to conclude their senior years with marriage in the academy chapel. Federov, who was or became gay and then an alcoholic, was a bit more outré, but he, like the other two, did his best to be a team player in Vietnam.

Leaving the academy in 1968 to the jeers and spittle of civilian coevals—peace creeps, as the three thought of them—hardened their conformity. Sixteen years after leaving Vietnam, Browne is still obedient enough to invoke, silently or explicitly, the classified nature of his Vietnam responsibilities, to respond to queries with cursory bits of information: he worked with the Tactical Air Control; he was a public affairs officer for the Naval Advisory Command. In an interview Stone said that with his first assignment Browne coordinated carrier strikes:

> He'd be getting as close as he possibly could to the target and he'd be sort of talking the strikes in, which is dangerous and demanding work. [Later, because Browne was] presentable and well spoken . . . they made him a briefing officer in Saigon. So it became his task to conduct what were called in Saigon the Friday Night Follies, which was the press briefing. . . . And, of course, very often he had to misrepresent things and their attempt to misrepresent things was extremely transparent: they weren't kidding anybody. And very often the officers didn't really know how much truth there was, especially when they got into statistics like body counts, which irritated everyone, because everyone knew that lurking behind the statistics was, first of all, the ineffectiveness of the military effort and then a lot of needless killing of civilians, for you couldn't tell combatants from noncombatants in that situation. So it was a really uncomfortable lie for everyone concerned, but he was drafted into that situation. (Benson and Solotaroff).

Since a good many of those wounded or killed in the air strikes Browne directed were also noncombatants, he was doubly compromised. Browne surely had his bad moments there: we hear once of a dark night in Vietnam when he had been startled and demoralized by the cries of the "well-motivated oriental cavalry" (*OR*, 167); there's the month or so of flashbacks after his return from Annapolis. But Browne never thinks negatively of his Vietnam experience until the last month, particularly the last day, of his life, when all reassuring beliefs have been torn from him. And for all we know, the flashbacks, which seem to cease within a month when he is offered the chance for the sail, might have been of good times, though the context argues otherwise. Even though Stone tells us that Browne's naval career was ruined in Vietnam—without telling us why—the Vietnam period is usually offered as a preferable alternative to his present situation: in Vietnam he had been able to deal better with his fear; there he had been able to read himself out of his threatening milieu; when he was with his wife and they were playing the Dashing Patriot and Woman of the Dashing Patriot, the pleasure they gave each other was intense. Anne tells Strickland that Browne never talked to her about his work with the carrier strikes. Whether his reason was his somewhat silly fear of revealing bad moments or still classified, though obsolete, information is not made clear.

As a whole, Browne's negative stance derives from neither embarrassment nor the sort of pain that forces or prohibits him from talking or thinking about Vietnam, but rather from an annoyance, verging on bitterness, over the inability of others to perceive that he did the best job he could in a difficult situation. It is a sign of his occasional obtuseness that Browne tells Dolvin, a carpenter whose assistance he needs and a man who lost his boat because of his resistance to the war, that he served there for four years. Browne leaves his activities there quite vague, but his attempt to justify himself to his sudden adversary by invoking the Rules of Engagement and denying Dolvin the right to an opinion speaks of his rigidity, and then either of the tenacity of the gullibility with which he accepted his indoctrination over there, or a species of bad faith.

When Bellow's Artur Sammler asks himself whether a doctor with a few days to live knows that he is doomed, his answer is, "Both knowing and not knowing—one of the more frequent human arrangements" (Bellow 1985, 81). Selling himself the Altan Forty is one such arrangement, and since Browne has finally conceded that the Red Menace was a lie, his way of dealing with the moral implications of his Vietnam involvement is another one. A more vivid example comes early in the voyage after a radio reference, from Hebrews 4, to "the dividing of soul and spirit and of the joints and marrow": "Browne found it curious to consider the dividing asunder of soul and spirit. The dividing asunder of joints and marrow was a sight he knew, familiar to him both from the dinner table and the aftermath of tactical air support. One might think of osso buco [cubed veal shanks] but also of someone's arm, impossibly bent, its boiling tubes exposed to flies, its red-mottled white bone to beetles. Hebrews Four, Browne thought, unquestionably had war and sacrifice on its bloody mind" (*OR*, 251). This thought comes to him early on in the voyage, when it's possible to dodge any flicker of guilt, any resentment toward the forces that encouraged him to collaborate with raids that caused such carnage. On the last day of his life he concedes that "[t]he order of battle, the hamlet evaluation reports, the Rules of Engagement, were dreams" (*OR*, 383). At this point, though, the mad-

dened Browne is too obsessed with how he betrayed what he has come
to feel is his true bride, truth, to be concerned with how he may have
betrayed mere humans.

Browne's Marriage and Family

There are no ethical compromises in Browne's marriage, surely the
strongest relationship in Stone's fiction: each member of the union
offers a good deal of tact, passion, support, and humor to the other. We
can believe Anne when she defends Browne against her father's slights
by protesting that, after 20 years of marriage, she has never known her
husband to do a cheap thing; we believe her when, after Browne
responds to questioning by faking some sailing experience, she tells him
that she has never before known him to lie. We see Browne confronting
one fairly open overture from a woman, and we hear of another in the
past that he rejected. As far as we know, he has never in his life slept
with another woman. Certainly he has never been sexually unfaithful
during their marriage, and it takes the unraveling of his psyche in the
latter stages of his voyage for him to experience sexual interest in a
woman besides his wife.

But it is characteristic of this thoroughly meditated novel that neither
spouse now feels wholly fulfilled in the marriage, and that the great
respect Browne has for Anne contributes to his journey to experiential
extremity and death. Warming to what he sees as the demands of a public situation, Browne announces during an interview that "I'm not
ashamed of achievement. I'm not ashamed to prevail" (*OR*, 140). The
statement much better describes Anne: like Browne, she is tall, attractive, and youthful, but unlike her husband, she comes from a family
with a record of hard-earned economic success. She is a better sailor than
Browne, she is more ambitious vocationally, and most important, she
possesses a good deal more of the emotional consistency and strength of
resolution he pretends to than he does. In the last weeks before the sail,
as his fear of what he has taken on deepens, Browne cares much more
about proving that he is not a coward than he does about winning. The
first of the novel's two parts closes, in the chapter after Browne's departure, with Anne reflecting: "Winning was all. . . . It was the only
revenge on life. Other people wanted reassurance in their own misery
and mediocrity. She required victory" (*OR*, 208). And though she has
taken to telling herself, after her husband's death and disgrace, that *she*

must perform the solo circumnavigation to gain expiation for her family, she still seeks personal triumph more than forgiveness. In the same way, the alcoholism that Stone gives her really amounts to little more than a relatively minor annoyance, barely worthy of the control over it she quickly gains.

Anne had told her father she was sure that Browne was undertaking the sail in part to make her and their daughter proud of him, and she's right. But it is this concern for Anne's opinion, this desire to preserve her approval, that prevents Browne the night before the sail from sharing with her what seems an overwhelming insight: "[H]e was not sailor enough to make the trip . . . he lacked the experience, the patience, the temperament" (*OR*, 188). But as he had earlier told Ward, "She doesn't want to hear my chickenshit doubts and ponderings" (*OR*, 155). In fact, chapter 27, which deals with the night before Browne's departure, is the only one in the book in which the Brownes share the angle of vision. Stone wanted to make it clear that Anne cares desperately about her husband's doubts, agrees with him, but does not ask him not to go because he would "regret it forever. She would always have stood between him and the sky-blue world of possibility. She would be responsible for every boring repetitious day as things went on and the two of them grew ever more middle-aged, disappointed and past hope. Their lives would be like everyone else's and it would always be her fault. . . . The weight was more than she dared carry" (*OR*, 190).

The partial fracturing of Browne's sense of identity by the symptoms that emerge in the novel's opening month, and by the fearfulness of the months before the sail, is nicely tested and complemented by his interactions with Maggie, his 15-year-old daughter. Her adolescent developmental strategy of attempting to separate herself from her parents by throwing tantrums when she feels pressured is a difficult test for a man with as strong a sense of propriety as Browne. His sympathy for her is deep enough for him to be incapable of bearing the thought of the pain she might suffer: "[S]he did not, at this point in her life, seem very clever at protecting herself from it" (*OR*, 25). But he also cannot stop nagging her for not calling in when she stays overnight at a friend's, and when he last speaks to her, on the night before he sails, he cannot resist rebuking her for having placed a sandwich (on a plate) on her bed. Stone then has her try to excuse herself from seeing him off. What follows in the next hundred words captures a number of the rigidities and vulnerabilities in each, as well as the baffled communication between them:

The fact was that he preferred her not to come. He knew it would make things easier for both of them. Nevertheless he felt compelled to stand up for convention.

"But you came home to see me off."

She gave him a trapped look.

"You're right," he said. "So be good."

A quick frightened smile crossed her face and she picked up the book, fleeing the moment. He had always found her physical resemblance to him an impenetrable mystery. Someday, he thought, the two of us will be able to speak. He bent to kiss her and she froze as she had done since the age of twelve or so, went rigid in the presence of his affection. Touching her cheek with his lips, he could feel the tremors that beset her. Outside her door, he was struck by a wave of regret. (*OR*, 186–87)

Their physical resemblance is paralleled by an emotional volatility that Browne has learned to conceal but that will increasingly emerge at sea. As Strickland puts it, after meeting Maggie, " 'She's high strung. Like her dad and her mom.' He pronounced the household words with an edge of disgust. 'The Browne Package. It's very fragile' " (*OR*, 136). (The moviemaker will discover that he has underestimated Anne's psychic strength.) Maggie's physical rigidity and a good part of her exacerbated emotions have to be caused by repressed oedipal desires. Correspondingly, Browne is enough of a creature of the superego that he never notices what must be his daughter's beautiful young body.

Social Implications

Of all Stone's novels, *Outerbridge Reach* articulates his negative criticism of America most generally, least obliquely. Browne's own initial malaise is representative: the unseasonable warmth might be the result of the greenhouse effect, to Browne one of the many symptoms of the wrong turn his country has made. The "South Korean fuckup" that aborts Browne's first voyage speaks of the immense amount of manufacturing farmed out by American companies to Third World countries. When, between Cape Hope and Antarctica, Browne perceives some of the inferior construction[15] that offers little resistance to the big winds that prevail at that latitude, a fair part of his condemnation is collective: "*Res sacrum perdita*. He could not remember the origin of the phrase. Sold our pottage, overheated the poles, poisoned the rain, burned the rain, burned away the horizon with acid. Despised our birthright. Forgot everything, destroyed and laughed away our holy things" (*OR*, 301).

With Browne, Stone creates a sympathetic Republican, an elitist who is powerfully offended by the liberal humility and left-wing bias he perceives on PBS, but who longs for the communal vision he also sometimes finds there, for a "homeland that could function as both community and cause. . . . Browne felt that his country had failed him in that regard" (*OR*, 44). That silent *e* gives his name an old-fashioned feeling and suggests his identification with old-fashioned virtues like courage, moral probity, self-reliance, and excellence—identifications that interestingly clash with the demands of his job and his perception of his emotional and moral inadequacies: the terrified child still within him; what he admits to Ward is his sense of how "shitty . . . [h]ow fucking pedestrian and dishonorable" (*OR*, 154) his life has been. They also clash with the banality, antienvironmentalism, and economic voraciousness of so many members and practices of the Reagan administration. Stone dealt with these contradictions by never permitting either Browne or his wife— both so disgusted at the way the country is going—a thought that relates to a specific political action or party commitment. The closest they come to any such position is relayed in a few words about Mary Ward, Buzz's wife: her "politics had sheared leftward. She and the Brownes sometimes found themselves on different sides during the age of Reagan" (*OR*, 151). But the way in which the Brownes' political placement contributes to the tensions that propel the novel is better captured by Strickland's early appreciation for Anne's "big Republican butt" (*OR*, 115), or his later appraisal of the Naval Academy as "Republican virtue in the water" (*OR*, 236).

The conflict between Browne's house and its surroundings captures his anomalousness in late 1980s America. Built in 1780, with shutters, a balcony over the front door, a portico, "[t]he whole front had the charm and incongruousness of ancient, handhewn carpentry." But "between the hill on which they stood and the water's edge lay the rooftops of a city housing project daubed in black graffiti and a few disused skeletal mills" (*OR*, 133). Browne tries to preserve his broad-shouldered, trim body— what Strickland contemptuously sees as "a conscientious preppy's body" (*OR*, 112)—by regularly jogging six miles along Long Island Sound. His turnaround point, the object Browne cannot get beyond, is a huge power plant: "The harsh squares of [its] fence and the ugly metal sheds behind it made him feel vaguely captive and violent." When his run is completed, the litter in the cul-de-sac at the end of his street makes it that much harder to escape the "anguish and disorder" (*OR*, 23) that plague him. In the novel's opening pages the Brownes lose heavily in a

stock market plunge, surely in good part created by the leveraged buyouts and junk bonds that typified the 1980s. Altan, like so many contemporary companies, is a part of an overextended conglomerate, the
head of which mysteriously disappears, à la Robert Maxwell. Matty
Hylan's love of sailing, his "vain and lippy" style—he's "a millionaire
vulgarian in the contemporary mode" (*OR*, 47)—his fortune made in
real estate and entertainment industries, capture varying sides of Ted
Turner and Donald Trump.

But Stone was beyond portraying empowered Americans as
inevitably corrupt or depraved or both. Harry Thorne—intelligent, honest, and toughly idealistic—had been second in command at the Hylan
Corporation and runs things after Matty Hylan's disappearance. The
mechanisms Stone employs to get a relatively inexperienced sailor with
little money into the circumnavigation race show the joints of the plotting, but Stone glues the mortices well with appropriate characterization. Thorne seems always to have appreciated elegance and integrity,
and when he briefly meets Browne, he's impressed by the younger man's
diffident presentation of self and enthusiastic but dignified praise of the
Altan Forty: "It's sound. . . . It's beautiful. . . . It's something to be
proud of. . . . For what that's worth" (*OR*, 68). The unspoken adverb is
"nowadays." As Anne later tells Strickland, her husband "believes in
those things people used to believe in. Before people were like you. Like
us. . . . [v]irtue . . . [n]avies" (*OR*, 138). With his company already fac-
ing criminal investigations and with lawsuits on the way, Thorne, a former navy man, also sees in the apparently assured Annapolis graduate
and Vietnam veteran a possession the company can still be proud of.
When he tells an underling to find a place for Browne if Altan Marine is
disposed of, the employee's response is, "Now you got your eye on this
guy. . . . You're always falling in love." To which Thorne's response is,
"That's me. . . . It's nearly spring. I'm romantic" (*OR*, 68–69).

Once we accept the assumption that the Hylan Corporation will continue to sponsor the race to bolster its corporate image, the rest follows
easily: Thorne knows little about sailing; Browne is a natural media
adornment to the corporation; it's "all systems go" for Browne to have a
free boat and a budget of $80,000 to equip it and himself for the sail.
And Thorne will fall a good deal more in love with the Brownes when he
meets Anne, who was born to charm tough old romantics. As Thorne
tells Duffy and Strickland on the October day the competitors are towed
south toward the Atlantic, "They're deserving people. . . . They're the

kind of people this society doesn't put forward. But it ought to recognize them, don't you think? It might learn something from them" (*OR*, 200).

An Artist of Disease

Strickland's response to Thorne's praise of the Brownes—"There's always something to be learned . . . from people"—reveals a bit more of the Chillingsworth in him than he intended, for Thorne gives him "a long and not altogether respectful look" (*OR*, 200). A bit earlier in the novel, Strickland had wondered if he understood Browne as well "as I think. . . . And if I do, why? It was a question he scarcely dared consider" (*OR*, 184). The normally fearless filmmaker's timidity is understandable. He prides himself on a perceptiveness that ranges from street smarts through aesthetic discernment, and he sees Browne as a pilgrim, someone so enmeshed in his idealizing constructions that he sleepwalks through existence. Yet if Strickland is not depraved enough to be the Kurtz to Browne's Marlow, the Svidrigailov to his Raskolnikov, a certain amount of doubling occurs. For one thing, Strickland is in his own way as rigidly principled as Browne, and both idealisms rest on suspect foundations.

Both proclaim their obsession with truth, though Browne's assertion comes on the last day of his life and he begins to brood over the nature of veracity only during his last month or two. Before that, the most important aspects of truth were integrated into his high-minded value system: a few months before he sailed, the terrifying truth came to him that he was not courageous and disciplined enough to make the voyage; one does not lie because a good man, which he badly wanted to be, does not lie. Almost always, the most important aspect of truth for Strickland is interpersonal, connected with the assertion of his sense of power: "Above all, he thought, you had to stay in charge and ensure that your definitions prevailed" (*OR*, 326). And what he seems continually to be trying to redefine in his documentaries is the worth of his subjects, the validity of their professed ideals: "My problem is the bottom line. . . . The difference between what people say and what's really going on" (*OR*, 19).

This comes from the second section of the novel, which introduces Strickland and characterizes him with considerable economy and force. He is in an unnamed country, surely Nicaragua, where he has just finished shooting for a new documentary, sitting at a table by the side of his hotel's pool with Biaggio, a Swiss correspondent, and two women. One of them is a German, named Charlotte, who wears a red and black rib-

bon around her neck, as does the other woman, an American named
Rachel Miller. The ribbons are of the kind displayed by members of the
national youth movement, and the two foreigners wear them to protest
their solidarity with the movement. In addition, like the other
Americans sitting at the table from which Strickland has just led her,
Rachel wears overalls and metal-rimmed spectacles that, as Stone puts it
with exactly the kind of smugness-puncturing irony Strickland would
employ, serve "to identify them as internationalists." Strickland knows
what neither of the women does: both are the mistresses of the aged
minister who gave them the ribbons. With the mordant version of sympathy he sometimes favors, Strickland shares his knowledge: "Maybe we
shouldn't judge too harshly. The guy was a priest for about seventy
years. He's making up for lost time" (OR, 19). Before Charlotte sat
down, Biaggio had told Strickland he loved her; now he joins the
American in mocking the two women. Though Strickland is usually concerned with his demeaning definitions prevailing in his documentaries,
here in life he cannot resist debunking.

John Leonard has described Strickland as being (like Rheinhardt,
Converse, Holliwell, and Walker) "that self-marginalized, understanding know-it-all who shows up in every Stone novel" (489). This does
describe a common aspect among the five principals, but the differences between Strickland and his four antecedents outweigh what is
similar in the cynical stances they all present. None of the earlier characters would have gone in for this kind of reality instruction. But
Sandor Himmelstein, the demonic lawyer in Herzog, determined to cut
"everybody down to size," who thinks facts are "true because they're
nasty," might have (Bellow 1964, 109). And Strickland has a fact to
impress upon Rachel that is much nastier than the minister's hypocrisy
or her own gullibility: no matter how many appropriate causes she
embraces, she is so fundamentally suspect that she can be seduced by
someone as objectionable as himself. She is so torn by the tension
between her perception of his hatefulness and the knowledge he convincingly offers to give her if she'll sleep with him that she slips into a
near fugue state by the elevator in which he hopes to lead her to his
room. The disappointed Strickland salvages what he can by announc-
ing to the elevator operator that "I work in the service of truth, which
is nowhere welcome" (OR, 22). And he is enough of an ironist to
appreciate the way in which his florid statement is lost on the
Nicaraguan, who does not understand English.

As loathsome as Strickland's behavior in this section is, he is not hyp-ocritically coming on as the last honest man to justify the rock-bottom sadism of his character. He has no end of opportunities to behave sadisti-cally to Pamela Koester, the ex-prostitute he's befriended, whose mind is often so addled by the drugs she takes that it is, as Strickland sweetly puts it, "a fucking omelet" (*OR*, 33). In fact, Strickland usually treats her with surprising kindness, occasionally letting her use his credit card, and offering at one point to support her drug habit for a while. He may nourish her sometimes touching aesthetic aspirations by talking to her about film, but Pamela is so much a creature of the id, she speaks so freely of her sexual appetites, that Strickland has nothing at all to teach her about the secret workings of depravity within her. Perhaps this is why he never attempts to sleep with her. Pamela is bisexual—one feels she would be trisexual if it were possible—and when she first sees pic-tures of the Brownes she moves quickly from ironic comments about Anne's suburban dress to the heart of the matter. Anne is "the handsome prince I've always dreamed of. And the guy is a hunk." *Outerbridge Reach* is not about evil in the way that *A Flag for Sunrise* is, and, with the possi-ble exception of Strickland's attempt to seduce Rachel, the novel's clos-est approach to depravity comes with Pamela's judgment of the immensely vulnerable Maggie: "I love the kid. . . . I'd like to lick her" (*OR*, 115–16). Shadow figures tend to invade the homes of their dou-bles, and if Strickland is several shades darker than Browne, Pamela—for all the good-natured largeness she often expresses toward the Brownes—can be several shades darker than Strickland. She certainly seems that way on Christmas Day when she accompanies Strickland to the Browne home for dinner: her advances to Maggie unsettled me a good deal more than they seem to bother Anne.

Strickland's "unquiet mind and thick tongue had taught him the arts of silence. Untended silence was anarchy, potentially anyone's, an unac-ceptable free-for-all. He knew how to work the silences, the white noise and dark frames" (*OR*, 327). If we apply Mann's famous distinction between artists of health and artists of disease, there is no more question about Strickland's placement than there is about how his documentary of exposure is his revenge upon the world. Shortly before Anne gives herself to him sexually, she thinks of him with accuracy, sympathy, and mockery: "You had to pity the man's early life, she thought. It was all confusion—no religion, no father, a scandalous mother. If he was some-times frightening, it was because he had been so often frightened.

Almost a handicapped p . . . p . . . person" (*OR*, 281), she concludes, mocking the stammer that Strickland often utilizes to have his way with people who have more sympathy than he does.

Strickland can work silence, exercise patient detachment with women as well as with film. In part, he keeps Pamela around because of the interesting spectacle she promises: "Looking into the future, Strickland saw the Tower ahead, blood and flaming curtains, slaughter" (*OR*, 79). This sort of cool distancing seems to characterize his relations with the many women he has bedded: "He had always watched women cure themselves of him with the detachment of a philosopher. All things passed" (*OR*, 337). So does his affair with Anne Browne, though he is anything but detached as he fears and resists its end. Though Strickland "[g]enerally . . . favored the mysterious and perversely turned and, on the face of it, Anne Browne was neither" (*OR*, 174), he's overwhelmed by her beauty, size, intelligence, enthusiasm, psychic health, humor, and lovemaking. When, a third of the way though the novel, he comes to the Browne home for the first time, "[t]he sight of her [rocks] him" (*OR*, 136), and it continues to rock him until their final meeting in Brazil. Then his need to overpower Anne's resistance to his completing the movie of Browne's doomed voyage displaces his concern about resuming the affair, which she had ended a few weeks earlier. Not that he doesn't make an overture along these lines, even though he perceives that she sees him as the enemy who would, if she let him, make the documentary broadcasting Browne's disgrace.

Of course, the more one loves, the more vulnerable one is. When Anne easily repels one of Strickland's attempts to convince her that her marriage is over, Strickland "is suddenly bemused, as though he were just another fellow like his patron and quarry, the average asshole in the street. All at once he was afraid of losing her" (*OR*, 330). His descent into what he feels is the clichéd world of the average insentient lout becomes more precipitous when Anne, believing that her husband is approaching Cape Horn, proclaims their affair "hopeless . . . impossible." He tries to undercut the obviousness of his pleas by prefixing "you can't do this to me" with "To coin a phrase." The ironizing falls away as his desperation increases, and one of his lines, "Do you not see . . . what a great team we could be" (*OR*, 376–77), is just about what the screen-writer of the movie *Trading Places* has Dan Ackroyd say to his fiancée to show how square he was until he got involved with Eddie Murphy. Such banality coming out of the month of a character whose normal dialogue is singularly edgy typifies the obvious care with which every paragraph of the novel was written. Just a few phrases, and Strickland becomes even more pathetic than when he's being cudgeled with a baseball bat in the last dramatized scene in which we see him.

Even his raison d'être—his sense of the frailties of others is right, their sense of their worth is wrong—is challenged by that need for Anne's acceptance, which is a tribute to his sense of her worth. While he is in Cambridge, trying to sell his Central American movie to the PBS station there, he begins what must be a frequently pursued line of self-justification: "No one, he thought, could ever accuse him of trimming. He had never changed a frame to suit a soul. Although gold was honorable he had never whored after money or even purchased a cheap recognition. . . . The trouble was, Strickland decided, that his work was too much like things. People required their illusions. They wanted to be inspired and he had nothing for them. He had only the news they wanted not to hear." But then, his confidence shaken by his need for Anne and his sense that she lives in a world of experiential plenitude he can never fully occupy, he shows an explorer's courage of his own as he confronts a frightening terrain:

> On the other hand, he thought, perhaps that was not the trouble. Perhaps the trouble was that things had some aspect he could not perceive. Sometimes he suspected they must. Sometimes he almost hoped for it. The other aspect of things might be routinely visible to the average asshole in the street, a personage upon whose inner life Strickland had long speculated. Then his own insight might be the result of some minor mutation, like the ability of the color-blind person to see through camouflage. It might be that he perceived in relief and reversed all signifiers. (*OR*, 326)

The cure for the anxiety that comes with this sort of thought is to call Anne in Connecticut and tell her that he will travel through the New England night to be with her as soon as he can. But this is a devil's fix: his implicit assertion of her worth further erodes his sense of the worthlessness of others and his consequent superiority.

It is possible to argue that Owen Browne instructs Strickland in the hidden potential of others at least as much as his wife does, but the evidence argues otherwise. Before he reads the logs he steals from Anne and sees the videotape that Browne made on board, Strickland seems to show as much insight into Browne's hidden strengths as he had into the sailor's weaknesses. In his pleas to Anne to let him go on with the documentary, he argues that Browne "was a true hero . . . [n]ot as some hyped-up overachiever but as an ordinary man. He reduced his problems with life to that diagram—the sky, the ocean." To Anne's lament that her husband "would have lied to us," Strickland responds, "I think he would have told you everything . . . his problem was really his honesty. . . . Some men would have faked it and spent the rest of their lives laughing. Not our Mr. Browne. . . . You should be proud of him. He wasn't a great sailor. But he was an honest man in the end" (*OR*, 391).

Since Strickland has not yet stolen from Anne the logs that reveal Browne's maddened fix on sky and ocean, his insight seems impressive, not simply a product of his willingness to say anything that will keep the documentary alive. But his responses to the logs are surprisingly shallow, and a new sense of Strickland's limitations is only increased by Pamela's banal enthusiasms:

> "The logs are astonishing," Strickland mused. "I have to find a way to get them in. I mean, he quoted Melville. 'Be true to the dreams of your youth.' He wrote that in."
> "Wow," she said. "The dreams of your youth?"
> "Melville!" Strickland exclaimed. "*Moby* fucking *Dick*."
> "Yipes."

Of course, the line was Melville's personal motto and is not included in *Moby-Dick*. Judging from Anne's response to the logs—she refers to them as "mad" and refers to Owen's megalomaniacal image of himself as a sun-fetcher—we are to feel that Browne set down in them the majority of the crazed conclusions of his last months. What Strickland comes up with falls short: the stuffed shirt he had previously taken Browne for could as easily have quoted Melville, and his conclusion about the occasional monologues Browne got on videotape is equally banal: "What little he could make out led him to conclude that Browne had been speculating on weighty matters. The Big Picture" (*OR*, 396–97). Mark Edmundson has interestingly argued that "[b]y putting Strickland in the novel, by showing the limits of his character and suggesting the limits of his art, Stone, it seems to me, is trying to pass beyond whatever there is in himself that would be satisfied with Strickland's kind of simplifications" (43). I agree with this and would add that it is at this moment, when the reader has absorbed the wildness and profundity of the experiences presumably set down in the log, that he is most conscious of the narrowed possibilities of Strickland's self-serving ways. The beating he will receive in a few pages from the goons who take the logs from him (and whose psychopathic gaiety is perfectly rendered) seems like fair payment. We join Stone in ushering his limited cousin from the novel so that we are left with Anne, the healthiest of the principals, as the appropriate survivor, struggling to meet her responsibilities to Maggie and the world.

Falling Through

What Browne increasingly speculated on followed from his sense of the disintegration of all big pictures. Instead of suggesting that any Melville quote in Browne's log was from *Moby-Dick*, Strickland would have done better to invoke Melville's next, far more tortured novel, *Pierre* (1852). Melville's plots usually contain a moment when the protagonist "falls through" a tolerable, familiar world into one that is suddenly, frighteningly, alien. The most meticulously documented fall comes in *Pierre*, when the eponymous protagonist falls through the first "story" of his identity into ambiguities of existence so pervasive than he can eventually escape them only through suicide. Indeed, *Pierre* is subtitled *The Ambiguities*.

Stone has long argued that we live by telling ourselves stories of who we are. Browne completed his fall through a story that let him live in the world when he looked out of the window of a spectral house on an uncharted island and saw

in place of the declining sun . . . innumerable misshapen discs stretched in limitless perspective to an expanded horizon. . . . Each warped ball was the reflection of another in an index glass, each one hung suspended, half submerged in a frozen sea. They extended forever, to infinity, in a universe of infinite singularities. In the ocean they suggested, there could be no measure and no reason. There could be neither direction nor horizon. It was an ocean without a morning, without sanity or light.

On this ocean, Browne thought, goodbye to almanacs and hope in Stella Maris and the small rain down. This is a game beyond me. A diver, he felt as though he were breathing from an emptying tank. . . . He felt the suspension of hope and wished for it back. He regretted lying. (*OR*, 362)

We must backtrack if we are to understand how Browne has come to such an erosion of fundamental trust that, in his eyes, the sun itself has been reduced to constituent parts. The eruptions that begin after his return from Annapolis do not seem to me significant aspects of a turn

away from the ideals that have shaped Browne's life: the upheavals follow from his sense of how little he acts out his heroic conception of himself and his resistance to the obedience that has brought him to his
midlife shoals. Nor is there significance—in the last months before setting sail—in the humiliating waves of fear Browne finds rising in him,
"as if some rat lived around [his] heart," as if he were overpowered by his
"late brother, the infant reprobate, beaten senseless by the rod, by the
drill sergeants and the good nuns of life" (*OR*, 168). A bit inappropriate-
ly, Stone here transfers from his own experience to Browne's the cringing
victim of childhood abuse that he placed within Hicks of *Dog Soldiers* and
Mackay of "Absence of Mercy." A courageous man, Browne will, once at
sea, quickly dismiss excessive physical fear as the residue of the fearful
lives crowding him on land. There's some truth to this, but I think that
the fear on shore is not so much of death at sea as of the revelation—to
himself and to the world—of his fundamental inadequacies, of his lack
of the virtues of the heroic adventurers he so admires. Inasmuch as
Browne carries within him an abused child, it is a "late brother" who
emerges under sufficient stress and is still vulnerable to his father's derision or withholding of approval.

At sea, sufficient courage quickly ceases to be an issue. Just 48 hours
into the sail, Browne fears that the infection from a cut might develop
into tetanus, and his desire to turn back, to hear his wife's voice, is overwhelming: "He felt whipped and frightened." As Napoleon observed,
the hardest kind of courage to come by is the 4:00 A.M. variety, but
Browne, awakening afflicted in the dark, musters it:

> To be sure, his neck was stiff, his jaw ached; he was still very feverish. But
> this time the accompanying panic failed to strike him. It was as though
> he had not the energy for panic.
>
> If I die of tetanus, Browne thought later, or gangrene or botulism
> or whatever else, then I will simply die of it. I will lie here as long as it
> takes to die and call no one. I will not run puking home to her or the
> Coast Guard or anyone else.
>
> . . . .
>
> It was so much in the mind, Browne thought. The logic of ordi-
> nary life was the logic of weakness and fear. The imperatives of weakness
> and fear were persuasive. . . . The time to treat the cut had been before
> the race began and he had chosen to ignore it. He would live with his
> own decision, excused from further responsibility. There were ways of
> coping with everything, even despair.

And it was useful to think of the dividing world overhead, the gates of Altair sliding closed, Orion leading on. He was in a zone of transit between his lost world and the one beginning to take over. (*OR,* 215–16)

Buzz Ward speaks for the author when he tells Anne that one cannot have moral courage until one has physical courage. Browne still has the latter, but the moral expansion he had hoped for—his growth at sea into the stability, the self-confidence, and the connectedness with the world around them of the memoirists—does not happen. For one thing, before Browne has been two months at sea, he is struck by the essential falseness of these accounts, and he thinks that he could simulate the style of heroic stoicism. Then he contemplates what it would be like to skirt the faked style of the conventional travel narrative; he thinks of "what it might be like to record the reality of things, matched with the thoughts and impressions it brought forth. To find the edge on which the interior met the exterior space" (*OR,* 249). Thus we have the origins of the two sets of logs Browne will begin keeping, and it is fair to say that he is killed by the collision between the two kinds of truths they pursue: the superficial accuracy, the degree of untruth in the simulation of the false; the writing that justifies its existence in every line. Browne will say in the last hour of his life, "The truth's my bride, my first and greatest love" (*OR,* 383). He's wrong about this, for he does not take truth as his bride until, at sea, he tears off the wrappings of the heroic package he bought during his boyhood.

Intrigued by the possibilities of both heightened literary creation and simulation, Browne finds his attempts at the first mode unsuccessful and fatally attempts the second after he has discovered that the structural shoddiness of his boat precludes actual competition. So he competes imaginatively. Having found his way to the waters around an island that, perhaps to symbolize the experiential extremities that will befall him there, is not on the chart, Browne, "[a]t his chart table [makes] a game of calculating where he might have been if the winds had held, if the boat had hung together, if the world had been different from what it was." And so he marks off 280 miles and adds the sort of upbeat comment typical of the man who would have written the book of the voyage he had contemplated writing before he sailed, the "book of a stern, steady man, a man for long solitary passages" (*OR,* 332–33).

This assertion of his literary preferences is part of Browne's much larger declaration of independence, as he rebels in different ways against the obedience that dominated his past. When he is less than a month at sea, Browne does not bother to read a fax stating his competitors' positions, "as though he wanted not to be in a race. Which was not to say, he thought, that he wanted not to win one. . . . Not checking it was a little stupid but he was in his own house, in his own kingdom, and he supposed he would find out about the others soon enough. Is this self-confidence or cowardice, he had to ask himself, independence or spite? The church lady's broadcast had put him in a vein of self-examination. He felt as though he might be in rebellion" (OR, 231–32).

Stone ingeniously inserts into the narrative the imagined broadcasts of an actual missionary station to excite both Browne's atheist assertions of independence and his agnostic longings for support on the utterly indifferent ocean.[16] Bill Pinckney, a recent solo circumnavigator, attributed his successful voyage to prayer, along with experience and judgment: "There are no atheists at sea," according to Pinckney.[17] It is as an amused atheist who, having scratched his genitals and opened a can of fruit, sits to listen to "the grimly English religious lady" discourse on man's obligation to God. If Browne can politely disagree with her claims—"To be in rebellion . . . is to be alone. It is to be insane. For all reality belongs to God," she asserts—he is intimidated enough by the ferocity of her sermon to silently offer "by way of prayer . . . Let Him with Whom we have to do have nothing to do with me" (OR, 230–31).

A few weeks later Browne is surprisingly moved by a dramatization of the process by which Jacob gained first Esau's birthright and then the latter's blessing from the dying Isaac. Central is the force of Browne's identification with the anguish of the African actor playing the deprived Esau: "Who knew, Browne thought, over there in Africa, what his life was like, what things he'd seen?" But this alone cannot explain the tears that course down Browne's cheeks as he listens. Though he is infuriated by the missionary lady's ensuing homily, which defends God's favoring the manipulative, dissembling Jacob over Esau, and then moves into a paean celebrating His power, Browne is forced "to admit that a weak God would not be worthy of love." Later he considers the severity of God's will and then dreams that he is in the water, beneath a gray sky, trying to swim away from the turmoil of an angry voice behind him, which Browne identifies as that of his father. One line of the dramatization hits Browne with particular force, for it is one "he had often heard his father use. . . . 'The smell of my son is as the smell of a field the Lord has blessed' " (*OR*, 285). Just before he goes to sleep, between his considerations of God's will and the dream, it suddenly strikes Browne "that there might be some form of false thought, notions that had their origin outside the brain and even outside ordinary reality" (*OR*, 287). Ordinary reality prevails here: Browne's dream of his father might be triggered by his complex response to the idea of God; his anger toward God might follow from his unresolved conflicts with his dead father. What is certain is that Browne's father and God are for Browne essentially punitive presences or absences whose approval he sometimes longs for, and who sometimes merge in his mind—though, in his crucial last moments, they do not.

Browne reflects after hearing the second Christian station theatrical—a dramatization of Christ walking upon Galilee—that with all of the biblical stories, "[c]oncealment was a constant theme. Someone was always being played for a fool." In this story, what is concealed is Christ's protection of the fishermen; the fool is Peter, for not assuming the protection. In a fury, Browne proceeds to argue to himself that the true concealment is the uncertainty of God's existence, but because our need to have comfort is so strong, we make the leap of faith and so are kept from the freedom we might have. Concealment in Stone's earlier fiction is most obviously evidenced by the agony of characters like Rainey and Egan over God's hiddenness, and certainly this is part of Browne's distress. When he realizes the dramatization will be of the walking on water, he is filled with mocking hilarity. Yet, as with the story from Genesis, he weeps, and he repeats out loud Peter's "Lord save me" (*OR*, 321). And after his bitter rejection of the hope that the stories of miraculous manifestations give their auditors, he ponders the possible relationship, both in name and divine causality, between Peter and the petrel he has seen that morning.

Obviously, *Outerbridge Reach* deals with Browne's attempt to conceal himself from man; less obvious is his attempt to conceal himself from God. In the final broadcast of the missionary station that Browne listens to, the text is the temptation to sin that is offered to Job (22:12–14) by one of the counselors: God is so far away and the dark clouds that obscure the earth are so thick that God cannot see what we're doing. Stone has analogized the logic here with a circumnavigation race conducted when the contemporary eyes of heaven, the satellites, are down, and, most of all, with what happened in the presatellite 1960s when Crowhurst tried to pull off his hoax: "That incident always stayed with me; it struck me as an amazing existential incident" (Solotaroff 1991).[18]

By the time Browne hears the text from Job, he is stricken at having
called in a false position, and precludes the missionary lady's inevitably
ensuing homily about the impossibility of hiding from God with his own
maddened conclusions: "So Browne knew that things had found him
out, down to the deepest level of his dreams. He thought of the shadow-
less beach, skuas descending out of the sun. The snares were like land
crabs whose bustling caused hallucination. The fear was the loss of reality, never quite retrievable once your share in it was put aside" (OR, 369).

"To be in rebellion . . . is to be alone. It is to be insane. For all reality
belongs to God," said the missionary lady in her first broadcast. Were
Browne, by now deranged, decisively able to believe in this God, or even
the less frightening Berkeleyan one who might not own all reality but
whose thought keeps all things in existence, then—having fallen
through, seven pages and several weeks earlier on the island of the skuas,
land crabs, and hallucinations—he would not have to assume the impossible task of playing God by connecting enough disparate realities into
the coherence he needs to live in the world. The God of Job is reduced in
the God-playing Browne's mind to one of the malevolent "things" that
oppose. After a few more weeks of "trying to organize reality into a series
of angles," in the last hour of his life, Browne thinks of making his way to
a port, to a white city, where he might partake of the consolations of
belief by going to the cathedral square. There, "he might kneel and walk
on his knees across the cobblestones of the plaza and strike his brow
across the lowest step of the temple until the blood flowed. Until sleep
came, an end of calculation." But the mocking, atheistic father who has
gained ascendency in Browne's stricken mind decisively separates himself
from the God who has sometimes pursued, sometimes stayed hidden
from Browne throughout the voyage: "What's this, Browne's father said,
religion? Unctuous religiosity in extremis? That's for women my son. For
little Juanito, swart Maria and your lady mum" (OR, 382–83). Thus
Browne denies himself the religious support that could have saved him.

When Browne discovers his boat is breaking up, there is no longer
any question of being "in his own house, in his own kingdom." Given his
new sense of his radical vulnerability at sea, it's as if he's a furry cartoon
creature in a disintegrating flying machine: "Flightless furry me" (OR,
302). He follows what might be the heaven-sent petrel in the direction
of an island he earlier thought he saw reflected in a sunset but finds,
when he lands, not God but, as Leonard has observed, Darwin (493): the
stench from the thousands of birds around him, stacks of whalebones;
above all, a flock of skua gulls in screaming descent tearing the flesh

from a young, blind penguin. The hallucinations he has grown used to at
sea follow him onto land as, entering an abandoned house, he hears
"mocking sprightly music," thinks that he sees a woman's head among
the quilts on a chair—indeed, hears the woman lasciviously invite him to
her as the wind brings to his ears " 'Midshipman Browne.' "

His psychic disintegration accelerates. Just before he hallucinates the
woman, he looks out the window and sees that the sun is occupying
exactly the same position on the horizon that it had hours earlier. He
regards this as a punishment for having "taken liberties with time and
located himself falsely." As he speaks to the hallucinatory woman, a
strain of compensatory megalomania is added to his disorientation. First
he tries to make the sun move by moving his hand from horizon to horizon in the clockwise deasil motion[19]; then he seeks to protest his
unavailability to the illusionary woman—who excites him with what he
experiences as her shameless sexual appeal—by pointing out to her what
connects him to wife and daughter: "bone hooks fastened to his flesh,
inserted under the muscle so that he could swing free. Hide lines bound
him to a pole, the central pole, the axis of the world. He swung around,
in the ancient deasil motion, at varying angles to the blue horizon, supported by the trusty hooks beneath his ligaments. . . . He himself sang
in the grip of the hooks, glad to be there, exhilarated by the dips and
turns. The rational, algorithmic Sun Dance" (*OR*, 350–51). The new
strain is megalomaniacal, for with the hand motion Browne is trying to
make the sun move, and with the hallucination of himself as sun-fetcher, he imagines that he is making it move. Indeed, when he leaves the
house and looks "at the horizon again, to his great relief the sun was
down" (*OR*, 352).

Riding upon this megalomania, Brown returns to his boat and fate-
fully calls in to Duffy a position that is about 1,300 miles to the east of
his actual one. The enormity of what he has done is hinted at a few minutes later when Browne remembers himself as an information officer in
Vietnam, "transfigured by his own forthrightness . . . the reporters [sens-
ing] his honesty. . . . I am neither that person . . . nor the person remembering that person. There had been something like a death." The
Browne who has survived the young man who bought the Vietnam
package then decides that "[t]he power of command over reality consisted in being party to its nature and possessing the knowledge exclusively"—withholding this reality from the rest of the world. "All at once
Browne understood that such power would always be denied him" (*OR*,
359–60). On his way back to the house, Browne is moved to envious

tears by the sight of salmon, making their way back to their origins. And when he returns to the house, he discovers that the figure in the chair he had mistaken for a woman was, with its "rotting quilts and horsehair," a crab's nest. He sees the fragmented sun from the window, thinks, "I'll go home . . . before I take a crab's nest for a wife," but then perceives that "[i]t [is] too late for that. He [is] a new man with a new fortune" (*OR*, 361–62).

Maddened as he is, why can Browne not go home? For one thing, if his lust for the heroic life has dissolved, the idealism that enabled it to persist has not: he wildly exaggerates the importance of plotting different false positions and calling in one of them. Here is Stone in a 1992 interview on Browne's sense of what he's done when he looks at the fractured sun:

> He thought that by trying to deceive the world about his precise location in such a precise way, by trying to hide himself on the grid of the world, he's performed an act against all measure, and against all proportion. There's something almost blasphemous for him about pretending to locate the sun at an angle it isn't at. It's as though he's creating a universe with this deception which is utterly without order, which consists of singularities—in other words, where things can happen without any relationship to each other, where anything can happen and there are no laws, not even physical laws. Everything that happens is a singularity. Nothing is predictable. Nothing can be defended against. It's the world with a vengeance, an absolutely arbitrary godless, meaningless, unfathomable world in which he has now located himself. (Benson and Solotaroff)

In the last week of his life, when the preparations for his celebratory return to Devon were under way, Donald Crowhurst tried to think his way out of the bind in which he found himself. In the desperation that would steadily bring his mind closer to total breakdown, he postulated the existence of a hierarchy of four systems. In ascending order, he called them matter, biological (animals), human (apes with minds), intelligence (gods). His great "discovery" was that a supremely gifted human, like himself, could with an act of will ascend from his place in the human system to take his place with the gods; he could escape his body—and the particular situation he was in—and become pure mind. Of course, he had to die to achieve this, and Tomalin and Hall's account of his gradual perception of this—indeed, their entire fascinating account of the 25,000 words Crowhurst wrote in his last week—is particularly poignant.

As he retreats from the fateful island and sails northwest, back into the Atlantic, imprisoned within his sense of the radical disparateness of all truths and of his own apostasy against the gods of just measure, Owen Browne cannot attempt such an integrated paradigm. At night he might be able to connect some stars into new constellations, but the struggle of learning to live in a world "in which no one action or thought connected certainly with any other and no one word had a fixed meaning," though it had "its satisfactions . . . put a great burden on concentration" (*OR*, 371). This, the penultimate section in which Browne appears, is set an indeterminate number of weeks after he leaves the island. We next see Browne on the last day of his life, within 600 miles of the equator (about 3,500 miles northwest of the island) and perhaps two months after his fall into the world of singularities. Whatever the duration of time, he is exhausted by his struggle to impose order on the wildly disparate world he now sees. Browne tells himself that "[h]e had never stopped wanting to prevail and go home"—which is not true, for Browne's crazed perfectionism rejects any form of the life he had. Buzz Ward had told him his sense of the secret of life: to value one's family and, above all, to value one's life, "shitty as it may be. . . . The war's over and you're alive. Do it in honor of the men who aren't" (*OR*, 155). This Browne cannot do. For a moment he thinks that "it would be wonderful to have back the man he had once been. The honest innocent drone who had never seen the blue forties or heard the crab songs." But the maddened perfectionist takes over: "Then he reflected that the man he had once been had never been satisfactory. In any case it was too late. The lie had been told and sustained" (*OR*, 383). And when, in his last moments before jumping, it seems as if he still might return home, his perfectionism suicidally blends with his sense of the fragmented world: "A single step was so charged with ambiguities. A single word, the smallest gesture, was a compromise. . . . Every whimper, every fidget, every argument defamed the truth. He would never be satisfied. He would always be ashamed" (*OR*, 385). And so Browne jumps.

Closing Thoughts

Leonard has claimed that "the last couple of hundred pages of *Outerbridge Reach* are as dazzling as anything in American literature" (490). While I think this is excessive—one thinks of any 200-page stretch in *The Sound and the Fury* or *The Great Gatsby*—the last half of the novel, which begins with Browne finally at sea, is extremely impressive writing, and the novel as a whole seems to me to be very close to a great one. So much of my available space has been devoted to offering an explanation of what Browne is about that a good deal very much worth discussing has been scanted: complexities of Anne Browne's and Strickland's characterizations, the workings of the interactions between them, vivid minor characters like Pamela, Riggs-Bowen, Hersey (Strickland's assistant), Fanelli, and Crawford, the literary allusions, the variety and palpability of setting, and, particularly, the quality of the prose. As William Pritchard has written,

> The novel's movement is leisurely, but the narrative has shapeliness and great cumulative power. The source of that power—and pleasure—is, of course, Mr. Stone's language as it creates a style. On every page something verbally interesting happens: the insolent voice of a Hylan executive "suggested gulls over India Wharf"; Strickland's 1963 Porsche has rusty fittings, "but the engine reported like a Prussian soldier on the first turn of the key"; Captain Riggs-Bowen . . . "had a brick-red blood-pressure mask around his eyes which resembled those of a raptor"; Anne's father, who disapproves of Browne, calls the sea a desert ("Nothing there but social cripples and the odd Filipino") while his 60-year-old secretary, Antoinette Lamattina, looks "as though she thrived on chaste bereavement, frequent communion and the occasional excursion to Roseland Ballroom."[20]

In a comment about the way in which his teenage participation in Operation Deep Freeze III helped to prepare him for the writing of the novel, Stone wrote, "After more than thirty years, I found I could still recall the hallucinatory icebergs, the uncanny colours, the silences and the light. Also the shingles of Cape Hallett, the swarms of penguins and the stark mountains, entirely black and white beside the steel blue sea" ("Genesis," 14). For me, the two sections where he most fully exploits this experience, those set on the island, achieve a visionary intensity and suggestiveness that are extraordinary. These remarkable sections serve as the peaks—but often not by much—of the second half of the novel: Strickland's love for Anne and her fascination with the subtly twisted moviemaker propel these other two principals into psychic terrains that are almost as frightening to them as the island and the annihilating seas that Browne traverses are to him. In the beauty and expansiveness of its prose and the diversity of its locales and concerns, *Outerbridge Reach* justifies the aspiration implied by its title.

Chapter Seven

The Stories and The Nonfiction

Since *Outerbridge Reach* was Stone's fifth novel it meant that at the time of its 1992 appearance, he had published one less story than he had novels. In 1981, midway in the 12-year period between the publication of his second and third stories, Stone responded to Kay Bonetti's question about the extent of his activity in the short-story form:

Well, I started out writing quite a few. I find that I'm difficult to satisfy in terms of my own stories. I think I have destroyed many more than I have ever submitted. My stories are rather different from my novels. They're a bit more surreal, perhaps there's more humor in the short stories. The concerns, though, are the same. Perhaps I find I don't have the opportunity to really address those concerns in what I consider to be a serious way, in the story, in quite the same way that I can get to them in the novel because in the novel I can go off in different directions. I can find resonances by setting up things like parallel structures where two different sets of people are doing totally different versions of the same thing, whereas in the short story everything must be particularly impacted. So I'm always waiting for some story to occur to me that I consider to be inevitable. Because I don't actively pursue the form but rather wait to be struck by some story that will come together in my mind, I don't do many. (Bonetti, 91)

The earlier stories, the 1969 "Porque No Tiene, Porque Le Falta" and the 1975 "Aquarius Obscured," move in the same medium, are oiled by the same lubricants, as are large parts of Stone's first three novels—alcohol, drugs, paranoia. But the focus in the stories is so limited to the drug-addled sensibilities of the protagonists that, of the novels' major concerns—anomie and injustice in America, the consequences of the pursuit of American interests abroad, the damage that people do each other, the quest for spiritual transcendence or a transformed sensibility—only the last is confronted, and that from a perspective that is so chemically canted that the transformation is a source of comedy. The stories published after Stone's response to Bonetti's question, "Absence of Mercy" and "Helping," both of which came out in 1987, were written between the time he finished *Children of Light* and began *Outerbridge Reach*. Though these two dramatize or discuss relatively extreme emotions and actions, there is no drug-induced surreality about them; one never has the sense, as one does with the earlier pair, of Stone taking time out from his normal fictional broodings and instead batting out brilliantly extended jokes or jeux d'esprit. In fact, the stories signal a temporary return to Stone's brooding over brutish behavior in America before he created the least diseased social world of his five novels, the one in *Outerbridge Reach*. In the latter pair of stories, as with the earlier pair, all data are filtered through just one sensibility, that of the protagonist, but in "Helping" and, much more, in "Absence of Mercy," Stone wove into the plottings complementary intentions and actions by secondary characters. The distances between what the various characters intend and what they do, between what they want and what they suffer, combine with Stone's sharp eye for telling detail and a characteristically mordant narrative tone to bring to the stories—though, of course, in small—the force, seriousness, and grim vision of the first three novels.

"Porque No Tiene, Porque Le Falta"

"Porque No Tiene, Porque Le Falta" is obviously the result of Stone's association with Ken Kesey, particularly the trip to Mexico in September 1966 for the article that *Esquire* had commissioned from Stone but, upon completion and submission, would not accept. Stone also appropriated and transformed the names of two characters from the La Honda scene of the preceding three years: the sobriquet Pancho Pillow, used to describe an irritating hanger-on there, surfaces in the story as Sinister Pancho Pillow; the name of an aging Methedrine freak, Willie Wings, seems to be a comic tip of the hat to William Wong, the federal narcotics agent who supervised the 23 April 1965 raid that resulted in Kesey's first arrest on charges of possession of marijuana. On 17 January 1966 Kesey was found guilty and sentenced to six months on a work farm and three years' probation. Two days after the sentencing, he was again arrested for marijuana possession. Before the eventful month had ended, Kesey staged a fake suicide and fled to Mexico.

Stone gave Fletch, the story's protagonist, a fair amount of the paranoia that understandably plagued Kesey in Mexico, but with far less reason: there is no suggestion that Fletch is in flight from the law. He is merely an American poet who is living on what seems to be the Pacific coast of Mexico with his wife and two children; he is also the principal in the whole of Stone's fiction for whom the author has the least sympathy. Since Fletch "had developed an odd passion for constancy; he liked things to stay as they were," he seems likely to spend the remainder of the story's dramatized day in his hammock, accompanied by a jug of Coca-Cola and alcohol.[1] Occasionally, he varies his intake by dipping into the cedar box of marijuana and makings underneath the hammock. But Willie Wings and Fencer, an American whose consumption habits are similar to Fletch's, bully him into joining them on a trip they had earlier agreed to make to the top of a nearby volcano. Willie's conversation tends to support Fletch's contemptuous appraisal—Willie's is a mind "running off its reel," its possessor bound "to end up in a speed museum" ("PNT," 203)—but Fencer seems sane and affable enough to render paranoid Fletch's conviction that the two intend to offer him up on the volcano as a ritual sacrifice.

The story is a very funny one, particularly the pages describing the drive. Funniest of all is the middle-aged Willie's Methedrine rhapsody of "the most beautiful night of my life spiritually" ("PNT," 210). That night occurred "years and years ago at the start of my career" ("PNT," 207), when he was the only white bellhop in Chattanooga, and it consisted of his watching through a peephole while a man entertained himself sexually with apparently indescribable imagination and energy. This demonstrated to the lad, at the start of his perverse career, "how groovy it is to be human! What a beautiful thing to be alive and conscious." "You fucking repulsive baldheaded rat . . . who wants to hear about your lousy life?" ("PNT," 210–11) is one of Fletch's responses, not a tactful one to make to a speaker who is crazed by Methedrine and has a pistol strapped to one of his legs.

Out of the car and, in the gathering darkness, on the track up the volcano, Fletch moves into his Errol Flynn mode as he hurls his thermos of Coke and whiskey into Willie's face and leaps down the side of the hill. Willie shoots and misses, Fletch races out of range and at a safe distance finds "the remnant of a joint in his trouser pocket and, having no matches, [eats] it." Then, the pot calling the kettle black, he justifies his escape from his former traveling companions, whom he judges "overripe, deracinated by years of smoking grass in the tropics, consumed by maniac ravings." Below, the lights in Corbera, a nearby town, take to flickering and reappearing, and then heat lightning begins flashing.

> Fletch stretched out his arms and with Jovian fingers began to play the
> illuminations one against the other—with one hand he dispensed light-

ning for the firmament, with the other darkness for the sons of men. The
lightning and the town's electricity followed the bidding of his fingers
with precision.
 Fletch cried out joyfully from his Promethean rock.
 "I'll be screwed if I'm not stout Cortez," he said.

Similar self-congratulations accompany the walk to Corbera, even
after he has to make his way through jungle: he judges himself "all perception . . . a fortress beset by flying men"; he feels "his presence electri-
fy the night," for he is "the sentient consciousness here"; even his
walking is an occasion for him to experience his "animal grace" ("PNT,"
218–19). In a Corbera bar he executes what he thinks is another dazzling escape from the Mexican known to Fletch and his crowd as Sinister
Pancho Pillow, a reputed body snatcher (an agent who kidnaps American
fugitives and turns them over to American lawmen). But reality has a
way of toppling self-adulatory structures, particularly in any work by
Robert Stone. Fletch arrives home to find that he has been replaced in
his hammock by Willie and in his bed by Fencer, who, naked, is joined
by and to Marge, Fletch's wife. Fletch watches them "do it for a while"
but does not seem to experience the exaltation that Willie did decades
earlier in Chattanooga. Still, there's room for self-congratulation: he
judges his five-minute crawl to the front door to be "a masterpiece of
silence," and he boasts to Willie of his trip up and then down the mountain. The whole trip had been intended by Fencer to break down the
barriers between Fletch and the other two men, and finally a very low
level of acceptance is achieved as, in the last line of the story, Willie
moronically says, "Fletch, babe . . . I had you wrong, brother. You really
are a poet" ("PNT," 225–26).
 The title is from "La Cucaracha," the third line of the song's four-line
chorus, which Stone took as the story's epigraph. In Samuel Garren's note
on the story, he translated these lines as "Cockroach, cockroach, you no
longer can walk because you don't have—because you lack—marijuana
to smoke." (Whatever Fletch lacks, does not have—the words of the
title—it is not marijuana.) Garren observes, "To these lines Stone adds the
ironic comment, 'A Song of the Revolution' "; he continues, "Stone's story
thus is a humorous commentary on the attempt in the 1960's to create a
revolution of the sensibility through drugs. Whereas Tom Wolfe in *The
Electric Kool-Aid Acid Test* presents Kesey . . . as a sincere prophet of the
new consciousness, Stone through the character of Fletch presents a man
whose 'revolution,' like the one in the song, is based from first to last on

drugs."[2] In the note's preceding three paragraphs Garren had pointed out a number of similarities between Kesey's Mexican experience as Wolfe describes it and Fletch's: in particular, Kesey's standing out in an electrical storm, "high on acid," and feeling that he can "make the lightning break out where he points" (Wolfe, 325).[3]

"Porque" can certainly be read as a negative comment on 1960s drug-fed grandiosity in general and on Kesey's mission in particular, but there are problems. First are the factual errors in Garren's attempts to equate Fletch and Kesey[4]; most obviously, Fletch is a mean-spirited loner who experiences as visual entertainment the wasting away of his wife's body from amoebic dysentery and who gets the cuckolding he deserves. Kesey was a charismatic leader who, a few months after the lighting experience, told a critic with some accuracy that he had been working to further the revolution of consciousness "with every fiber in my body" (Wolfe, 31). To a certain extent, Stone divided Kesey between Fletch, who gets an altered lighting experience, and Fencer, whose equanimity, generosity, easy acceptance of zany ravings, down-home way of speaking, and flamboyant dress are reminiscent of Kesey. Fletch seems to me to be too much of a paranoid crank who uses nothing stronger than marijuana for his "electrification" to stand for the delusion of the acid revolution, but it might be in the story. "La Cucaracha" was indeed a revolutionary song, but Stone's reminding the reader of this primarily works to emphasize the very partial and temporary revolution of Fletch's senses.

"Aquarius Obscured"

The second story Stone published is an outgrowth on a road he chose not to follow in *Dog Soldiers:* "I meant for there to be an aquarium scene, but not that story" (Solotaroff 1991). On the night of his return to Oakland, Hicks calls Marge and arranges to deliver the heroin at a time no more precise than early the next morning. In the morning, at no designated hour, Marge awakens from a night of frightening dreams, strung out on her Dilaudid addiction. When Hicks arrives a few minutes later, she tells him that she doesn't have his $2,500: "I missed the bank. I went to the aquarium. . . . I was going to go to the bank today. . . . Somehow I thought you'd come at night." We might expect Hicks to say something like, "What is this insanity? We agreed ten hours ago that I'd come in the morning, and you didn't have time to go to the aquarium anyway." Instead he says, with the mean terseness that characterizes so much of the novel's prose, "I hope you got off on the fish. . . . You're not getting shit until I get paid" (*DS*, 93). Whether Stone was nodding here, or simply offering up their weird collaboration over the time of the meeting and the phantom trip to the aquarium as a prelude to the strange liaison that will follow, he did give Alison, the protagonist of "Aquarius Obscured," the need and the opportunity to get off on the fish, or at least on a porpoise.

For Alison has fallen upon hard times. If Big Gene, the man she lives with, has stopped beating her since he became addicted to heroin, he has eased into outer dysfunctionality: for example, opening the story by answering what might be a telephone call to her with his version of "Dutch": "Geerat, Geroot. Neexat, Nixoot."[5] He will soon be after her weekly pay for his next fix, and Alison badly needs the $80 for herself and Io, her three-year-old daughter: as a part of the past night's degradation, she was fired from wherever she was a danseuse in some form of undress. In addition to Io and Big Gene, Alison has, for extra stress in her life, a "vicious and unhygienic doberman" ("AO," 162) who will tear the apartment apart if he's left alone in it. Since Gene will not stay with the dog, Alison has to bring him to the aquarium and tie him up outside. To endure the trip "more gracefully," Alison comes up with the kind of zany 'appropriate response' favored more by the principals of *Fear and Loathing in Las Vegas* (1971) than by other Stone druggers: she swallows a *handful* of "white cross jobbers . . . synthetics manufactured by a mad chemist in Hayward" ("AO," 163).

In Stone's earlier fiction, underwater imagery tends to equate the feeding frenzy that goes on beneath the sea's surface with the different forms of voracity that exist between humans above the surface and on land. But, occasionally, visions of the ocean's depths or other aquatic imagery soothe a jangled sensibility. For example, when Marge first takes Dilaudid, "she passed into a part of the sea where there was infinite space, where she could breathe and swim without effort through limitless vaults. She fancied that she could hear voices, and that the voices might belong to creatures like herself" (*DS*, 72). It is appropriate that, as Marge's fictional descendant,[6] Alison responds to Io's suggestion that they go "[s]ee the fishies" by recalling

> the fragment of an undersea dream. Something in the dream had been particularly agreeable and its recall afforded her a happy little throb.
>
> "Well that's what we'll do," she told Io. "We'll go to the aquarium. A capital idea." ("AO," 161)

Io's suggestion was in response to Alison's "What'll we do?"—a question fearfully directed more toward their economic futures than toward the next few hours. Even before they leave for the aquarium, then, it figures as a significant experiential alternative.

Standing before the tank in which a porpoise is describing elegant turns, Alison begins to fuse it with a benign paternal presence and divine order by telling Io that it comes from the Atlantic Ocean, where her father, in Providence, lives. The name of the city brings to her an intense reexperiencing of "the dream feeling . . . the memory of some loving presence in it and a discovery." But then, in a negative rush that interestingly anticipates one of Pablo Tabor's, she thinks, "God . . . it's all just flashes and fits. We're just out here in this shit." When she realizes that this sense of radical nakedness is also a part of the dream, we suspect that Alison is undergoing a continuous déjà vu, so that almost any thought triggers her sense of a prior experiencing of the content of the thought. Whether or not this is the case, her encounter with a talking porpoise certainly follows from a mindset that creates desired causes for particular flashes and fits.

An astronomer who has never practiced her profession, Alison thinks of herself as "a trained scientist [who] loved logic above all." Now she moves to what seems to her a massive logical breakthrough: every effect has a cause; her 'dream' could not have ended with her being "mercifully carried into a presence before which things had been resolved" had not the resolving presence existed somewhere in the universe. Another writer might have pedantically corrected Alison, perhaps comparing her to one of the medieval theologians who—for all we know, experiencing a childish need for a protective father—argued that the idea of an omnipotent and omniscient God had to have been implanted in his mind by Same. Robert Stone proceeds differently. Having laid the ground for an "I think, therefore it is" ontology, he has Alison first ask the porpoise if it put the sense of a resolving presence in her mind, and then hear the porpoise say, "Yes, it was." The part of her that needs the comfort of a transcendently spiritual parent easily fights down the part that is declaring her state "prepsychosis" ("AO," 164–65), and seven brilliant pages recording the conversation between a stoned woman and a porpoise, in a public place, with her child playing or reclining nearby, follow.

In a wonderful parody of the first meeting between an initiate and a transcendently superior being, the porpoise quickly separates its modes of perception from those of rank, fumbling humankind. Being in a tank in an aquarium in a city does not bother the porpoise because it has never left an ocean that is other than the ones we comprehend. The primary visual reality in an aquarium is the porpoise's meeting and observing the humans, registering how *dry* they are. Porpoises are not held captive by the needs and appetites that soil human lives: "We don't require the same things. Our souls are as different from yours as our bodies are." When Alison opines that porpoises' souls are superior, the beast responds with surreal objectivity: "I think they are. But I'm a porpoise" ("AO," 166). Just as funny is how Alison deals with her annoyance at "its blank, good-humored face appear[ing] utterly oblivious of her presence" by reminding herself that "the hollow dissembling of human facial expression was beneath its nature."

For about half its length the conversation wittily works within a standard sci-fi format: the porpoise is there to execute the purpose of the superior race, in this case, to bring select initiates like Alison to a realm beyond the self-indulgence and banality of humankind. Alison is not one of the stoned or schizophrenic who hear personal directives on the radio; the momentary messages she had been hearing were for the purpose of bringing potential initiates to the aquarium, where the porpoise could begin raising their consciousnesses. But as it begins explaining just what it wants from Alison, the porpoise's austere kindness and serenity begin modulating into something else. It will be "her privilege to assist the indomitable will of a mighty and superior species. The natural order shall be restored. That which is strong and sound shall dominate. That which is weak and decadent shall perish and disappear" ("AO," 169–70). Different sci-fi or B movie scenarios begin intruding now—Alison's versions of the "dime store badness" (*FS*, 64), the upsetting flashes that will cause Pablo to shoot his dogs. She is still a counterculture storm trooper, squaring her shoulders, bringing her heels together, crying "right on!" But as the porpoise invokes "a final solution" and talks of reducing cities to rubble, its "distant, euphonious voice [assumes] a shrill, hysterical note"—the note I tend to associate with the high times at Nuremburg Stadium—as it rants of how they will "strike without mercy at the sniveling mass of our natural inferiors. Triumph is our destiny." Alison then beholds, not Der Führer on high, but "the image of a blond-bearded man wearing a white turtleneck sweater and a peaked officer's cap," with the gray cylindrical shape of the porpoise having changed into a periscope. Didn't the crewcut underlings on the U boats of the World War II movies all wear black turtlenecks, the behatted captain a tunic over his black turtleneck? No matter; Allison now denounces the porpoise as a fascist, even denounces as "a cheapo routine" its Nazi Song of the Sirens: *"Surrender to the Notion / Of the Motion of the Ocean."*

New alternatives swarm in the mind of the skilled logician, in the new pop-cult role of dauntless defender of endangered humankind:

> The voice, she suspected suddenly, might not be that of a porpoise. It might be the man in the turtleneck. But where?
>
> Hovering at the mouth of a celestial Black Hole, secure within the adjoining dimension? A few miles off Sausalito at periscope depth? Or—more monstrous—ingeniously reduced in size and concealed within the dolphin?
>
> "Help," Alison called softly.
>
> At the risk of permanent damage, she desperately engaged her linear perception. Someone might have to know.
>
> "I'm caught up in this plot," she reported. "Either porpoises are trying to reach me with this fascist message or there's some kind of super-Nazi submarine offshore."

But other explanations now come to Alison: a "momentary warp . . . [a] trifling skull pop, perhaps an air bubble"—never a handful of white cross jobbers. Her return to less unusually drugged reality is not eased by the young man who has been watching her and now sidles over, filled with a pothead's palaver about how "groovy" fish are, how "spaced out" Alison appeared while she was "really tripping on those fish" ("AO", 171–72), as he calls the porpoise, how "far out" is the luncheon engagement she invents to refuse his invitation "to go smoke some dope" ("AO," 173). Whether Alison is undergoing a sort of hangover when she insults him and steals two of his camera lenses, or protesting in some way either against drugs or against his totally accepting counterculture style, or asserting her return to depraved humanity, becomes the mystery with which we leave the story.

Like "Porque No Tiene," "Aquarius Obscured" is a satiric puncturing of the potential of drugs for genuinely spiritual experiences, but to so much more intense and sustained a degree that it is possible, but not necessary, to see the story as a rejection of Stone's claims that he experienced a spiritually resolving presence during his acid trips of the early 1960s. The title alerts us to the thoroughness of the story's rebuttal to the claims that astrology buffs and counterculture types had been making in the decade before the story's composition: the planetary configuration had just occurred or would soon occur that would initiate (or had initiated) the Age of Aquarius. With the planets guided by peace and the stars steered by love, the authors of "Aquarius" (from the 1960s musical *Hair*) might celebrate the way in which our fully liberated minds will now enable us to live with the fullest honesty, empathy, and harmony, but this aspect of Aquarius will always be obscured in a writer who will soon bring the Gnostic vision that had been a part of him for decades to its fullest realization in *A Flag for Sunrise*. If Alison temporarily cast herself as a potential savior of humanity, she also created the fascist vision she resisted. The desire to destroy or to subjugate others is not about to give way to drugs or to benign astral configurations.

"Absence of Mercy"

The grueling "Absence of Mercy" is Stone's only attempt at roman à clef. In the mid-1980s he found that he was almost obsessively regaling friends with an account of a scrape he had had in 1964 or 1965, and so he decided that he would try to rid himself of this need to tell the story by transforming it into fiction. Here is Stone's 1992 account of the fracas:

> It happened in the Seventy-second Street station of the IRT subway. What happened was this kind of well-dressed man was haranguing a very small, elderly black woman, and against my better judgment and everything I had been conditioned to do, I interfered and he really came at me. . . . I started to get the better of him and he started to yell help. The train pulled in and my contacts left, including the lady I imagined myself assisting, and everyone else on the platform who had seen what had happened got on the local that I had been waiting for and disappeared. So I was left with the guy and when I started getting the better of him, he started to yell help. I had a peajacket on, I had a beard, and my hair was long—it was the midsixties—and what people coming down the steps were seeing was a young long-haired guy who was slamming around an older, fiftyish man who was yelling help. So people started yelling "Help!" and "Police!" up the stairs, and it suddenly occurred to me that I had better get out of there and I fled. That was it. (Solotaroff 1992)

In his dramatization, Stone brought a number of sharply rendered complexities to this sequence. The woman does not appeal quite so immediately to the sympathy of a white with large sympathies, for there is no suggestion that she is small or black, though she is elderly. As the assailant harasses her, Mackay, the Stone figure in the story, sees her face

as not only "convulsed with fear" but "sheeplike, vacant and repellent."
When she boards the local, she looks through the window at Mackay,
fighting on the platform, "with a disapproving frown." The assailant's
clothing displays the attractive distinction Stone spoke of, but his handsome face, carriage, and behavior bespeak the assurance of someone who
is completely at home in a world in large part of his own construction.
When Mackay asks the elderly woman if anything is wrong, the stranger
first says, then half screams, " 'You!' . . . His cry of recognition seemed to
transcend the merely personal. He seemed indeed to be recognizing in
the person of Mackay everything that had ever been wrong with his life,
which Mackay suspected had been quite a lot." This strain of detached
sympathy continues when, with a European inflection, the maniac twice
says, "You are from Doc," and Mackay notes "the unnatural brightness
of his eyes and the starvation gauntness of his bony face. It was frightening to imagine what kind of life had to be endured behind such eyes.
They were without order or justice or reason." We might pause to pon-
der the nature of this man's fatherhood of, or descent from, Weitling, the
blue-eyed psychotic killer with the European accent in *Flag*, but there's
little time left for reflection for Mackay: with a final crazy recognition—
"You are an English queer" ("AM," 66–67)—the man attacks.

The description of the fight is detailed and lengthy, more than 600
words, and captures the sense of being in a terrible struggle that has
already gone on for too long and seems likely to go on forever or until
one of the combatants is killed. For this is not just a fight with a crazy,
frighteningly strong stranger; it is occurring on a narrow platform beside
a space that is intermittently filled with arriving or onrushing trains.
Mackay quite literally fights for his life, for the maniac tries to push him
in front of the local Mackay had been waiting for, then in front of an
express hurtling through the station. Punched, kicked, teeth broken
from a head butt, Mackay breaks both his hands on his adversary's face
before the older man sits down on the platform and begins calling for
help. An ebbing of Mackay's strength, "subverted by guilt, by weakness,
by fear and indecision and lack of confidence," a terrified flow of
strength when the maniac grabs him around the throat, the assailant's
evil smell, the way he seizes "Mackay's arms at the biceps, trying to
gather strength for the shove that would impel him off the platform"—
these are a few of a good many powerfully convincing details. Just as
arresting is Mackay's panicked, bloody-handed flight through a crowd
that seems "monstrous, like the mob in a Bruegel crucifixion," a crowd

that curses and punches at him as a "driven creature, with fists and elbows, he [cuts] his way up to the light" ("AM," 67–68).

Stone made Mackay, at this point in his life, not a married father of two toiling at an an apparently unfinishable novel while he made up exposés for a sensationalist tabloid, but a married father of one who is returning from a second job as a house painter when he meets the maniac in the subway station. Most of Mackay's working time is absorbed by an apprenticeship as a photographer's assistant, a job that "would lead to his working as a news photographer and then to his becoming an artist" ("AM," 66). But back in the early spring of 1966, as the maniac cried for help and Mackay "leaned against a signboard, breathing with difficulty . . . [h]is vision seemed peculiar; it was as if he saw the dim empty station around him in spasms of perception, framed in separated fragments of time. The disconnectedness of things, he saw, was fundamental. Years later, photographing a civil war in Nigeria he would find the scenes of combat strangely familiar. The mode of perception discovered in the course of his absurd subway battle would serve him well. He would go where the wars and mobs were, photographing bad history in fragmented time. He had the eye" ("AM," 68).

What comes through here is the sense of the subway battle as an initiatory experience, one in which Mackay's full employment of primary process, to use a phrase Stone likes—or, to use others, his access to the flight-or-fight mechanism, the rush of terror and adrenalin that comes with engagement of the adrenal-sympathetic pole of the autonomic nervous system—brings him a new, disconnected way of seeing. His discontinuous art form, the still photograph, can capture the essence of the continuous and collective violence he sees because of the disconnected mode of seeing individuals in combat.

This sense of the fight as ushering in something new runs counter to the rest of the workings of this strongly integrated story. When Mackay tells the maniac to clear out, "his voice had to him the quality of a dream. It was as though upon addressing the man, he had entered something like a dream state." That this is a bad, recurrent scenario that he has had to live through many times in his waking and sleeping life is made clear just after the fighting begins. "Aware of the unheeding crowd, Mackay felt all the deeper bound by a dreaming state. In one of his recurring dreams he would always find himself alone in a crowd, a foreign unregarded presence, the representative of Otherness. At the height of the nightmare some guilty secret or possession of his would be exposed to the crowd and draw their pitiless alien laughter ("AM," 67–68).

The subway scene constitutes the last part of this five-part story. The first two parts are shaped by Stone giving Mackay his schizophrenic mother and the years at St. Ann's, renamed in the story for that fighting divinity, St. Michael. This is where Mackay's "experience of violence began"; St. Michael's is surely the source of the nocturnal scenarios in which damage is to be done to the helpless, largely blameless dreamer. After all, it would later often "seem to Mackay that his grade-school years were a single continuous process of being found out in transgression and punished. At other times he would recall them as a physical and moral chaos of all against all."

Here I want to add a few comments only to my discussion in chapter 1 of St. Ann's-St. Michael's. Fairly early in the story Stone lays out the taxonomy of abuse at St. Michael's. The sixth paragraph concerns the unregulated violence done to the "scholars . . . as they were referred to, quaintly." Since we have earlier been told that "a significant minority . . . were statutory delinquents," since "[m]any were suffering from emotional disturbances of varying severity," and since "[a]ll were unhappy and unloved or unwisely loved or loved ineffectively," this amount of violence is, by itself, considerable. The seventh paragraph concerns the violence wreaked by the staff, whether spontaneously and informally in class or more formally by the prefect. The eighth paragaraph describes the "weekly smokers," the boxing matches in which a scholar "found himself confronting both the authority of the institution and the mob spirit of his fellows." Though Mackay lost most of the hearing in one ear as the result of an injury sustained in a smoker, what clearly most fascinates the author are the nocturnal beatings that the prefect, Brother Francis, administers in his chambers. Stone devotes all but the last paragraph of the story's second section to these horrific scenes. For the grown Mackay, the worst of it was not the hours of "stark sick-making terror" that followed Brother Francis's theatrical declamation, "You will stand by my room . . . tonight" ("AM," 61–62, author's ellipses), or the "ceremonial nature of the punishments," their "perverse religiosity," or, the lashings of the palms completed, the children, "flying weeping toward their pillows, their burning hands tucked under their armpits, scuttling barefoot over the wooden floor like skinny little wingless birds." It was "the absence of mercy. Once the punishment began, no amount of crying or pleading would stay the prefect's hand. Each blow followed upon the last, inexorably, like the will of God. It was the will of God. Brother Francis, implacable as a shark or a hurricane, carried out what was ordained on high. If a scholar withheld a trespassing hand, Brother Francis would wait until it was duly extended. He seemed to have nothing but time, like things themselves" ("AM," 63).

With the last three words we are back to that obsessive theme of Stone's, the absence of innate, positive, moral structures in the world—a large part of the Gnostic vision of *A Flag for Sunrise*. The absence of humane order—of mercy—or justice or properly informed reason in the maniac echoes the absences in the Pauline Brothers at St. Michael's, or, in their ignorance, in the crowd on the stairs of the subway station. Individual humane gestures like Mackay's defense of the abused woman might arise, but as with the recognition he receives from the crowd, they might not be appropriately comprehended or reciprocated. At the center of existence is whirl, contingency.

This theme is both reinforced and ironically varied in the two sections that intervene between St. Michael's and the subway station. The third section touches upon several aspects of a period of about eight years that begins when Mackay's mother leaves the hospital and he leaves St. Michael's to join her "in a single bathless room at a welfare hotel on the West Side" ("AM," 63) and terminates with an account of Mackay's experience in Navy boot camp. In the latter segment the emphasis is on one of Mackay's instructors drilling, infuriating, and terrorizing Mackay out of the instinctual cringing before authority figures he had picked up at St. Michael's; thus one severe regimen might partially mend the damage wrought by another. These details are from Stone's life, as is Mackay's teenage membership in a West Side gang that gets into a nocturnal Central Park scrape with another gang in which knives are drawn. But now Stone weaves imagined happenings into the story. A member of the other gang is wounded, and when Mackay and Chris Kiernan—a gang member Mackay has known since he was six, when both were scholars at St. Michael's—mercifully take the bleeding youth to an expensive private hospital, an attendant locks the inner door in their faces. Kiernan figures in another incident in this section when he knocks out Mackay in a poolroom brawl. The proprietors have no patience with losers and throw Mackay down "the many steps that led to the street. Mackay, tasting defeat, learned a certain embittered caution. Kiernan, on the other hand, came to regard his own belligerence too indulgently, as events years later would make clear" ("AM," 63–64).

The whole of the fourth section is a development of this sentence as Stone pushes further with his doubling of the two characters. Both struggle hard to put behind them the world of St. Michael's, welfare hotels, and poolroom brawls. By 1964, when Kiernan is about 27, he, like Mackay, is married and a father, but Kiernan's ascendancy is more obvious: he is a college graduate, a former army officer, and an account executive with one of the most important advertising agencies in the world. But on a southbound subway, "an unemployed immigrant from Ecuador" begins harassing a middle-aged woman who looks to the large, respectably dressed Kiernan for help. At a station about three miles north of where Mackay will, perhaps seven months later, be attacked by the maniac, Kiernan wrestles the Ecuadorean out onto the platform and shoves him a distance from the train. But the doors of the train don't close; the Ecuadorean reboards and stabs Kiernan through the heart.

Both before and after his death, Kiernan receives appropriate recognition for his behavior: other passengers cheer when he pushes the Equadorean clear of the train; newspaper accounts of the incident refer to him as a Samaritan, list his achievements, and quote friends' assertions of his "sterling character." Moreover, "[i]n Albany, a legislator introduces a bill to benefit the survivors of people who incur injury or death assisting their fellow citizens in an emergency. It is referred to as the 'Christopher Kiernan Bill.' " But as Mackay realizes, Kiernan wanted to distance himself from all contacts with the meanness and violence of lower-class life: "How he must have hated to die in the subway," the survivor thinks. And how much does the recognition of others weigh against the loss of the enjoyed and valuable life of a man in his twenties?

Mackay and Kiernan were so much "of the same stuff," that "Mackay felt his existence threatened by Kiernan's death. He felt diminished." Still, he cannot bring himself to attend the funeral or to write to Kiernan's wife or to stop "by the wake to sign the book. In the end he did nothing. He did not want the world of his childhood to touch him. He wanted it gone utterly, buried with Kiernan." Mackay comes out of the incident with a stronger resolve to eschew violence in his own behavior, to protect his children from it; "he adopted a mode of politics he believed would place him in opposition to war. . . . He felt as though he had earned the right to work for peace and human brotherhood. He embraced these things with joy" ("AM," 65–66). Of course, in the next section, Mackay learns that an assertion of communality may tug one into violence and that there is no guarantee that the originating generosity will be recognized. Small wonder that as he runs from the revengeful mob out into the street, "[f]or neither the first nor the last time . . . he wondered just how far he would run and where it was he thought to go" ("AM," 68). Mackay is the most blameless of the 19 principals in the fiction Stone has so far published, the least deserving of his sufferings. Could Stone have so abjured autobi-

ography in his fiction because he feared that it would lead him into the
self-pity he would seem, at some early age, to have deemed unafford-
able?

"Helping"

The first words of "Absence of Mercy" are, "Mackay once described
himself as 'the last orphan' " ("AM," 61). In terms of his longing for a
guarantor of gentleness and justice, Mackay might have asked—as
might have Father Egan, Lu Anne Bourgeois, and Owen Browne, and as
in a somewhat different context, Ishmael did ask—"Where is the
foundling's father hidden?" (Melville, 406). Grace Elliot of "Helping"
has an answer: "the sky is full of care and concern." But the speaker of
these words is not Grace, articulating a part of the credo that underlies
her work as a lawyer employed by the county in worthy causes, but the
story's protagonist, her husband Chas, who adds a few moments later, "I
swear I would rather be a drunk . . . than force myself to believe such
trivial horseshit."[7] And in the past few hours, this is indeed what Elliot, a
social worker who works for a state hospital, has chosen again to be.

"Helping" is divided into five unnumbered sections. The first three
detail the process by which Elliot, an alcoholic who, after 18 months of
sobriety and 15 months of AA meetings, falls off the wagon; the last two
parts follow Elliot through the 16 or so hours after the fall. The whole of
the story brilliantly charts the way a man who has for some time been
losing his balance, simultaneously topples and uses his fall to move
toward regaining his equilibrium. The terms of the struggle for balance
have large social reverberations: Elliot is simultaneously undermined by
his sense of the breakdown of civility and the futility of what has become
his life's work—of organized "helping"—to deal with this breakdown.
So far, the story could have the reductiveness of a good-guy-dragged-
down-by-the-bad-guys scenario. Stone convincingly complicates things
by giving Elliot a mean edge and by having him identify more with the
dregs of the social order, the crushers of civility, than with most of the
people and social structures on his side.

The story's first three paragraphs move quickly over the first three
months of winter; one month, one or more corrosive presences per paragraph. Boston, on the gray November day Elliot visits the city, "seemed
cold and lonely. He sensed a broken promise in the city's elegance and
verve. Old hopes tormented him like phantom limbs, but he did not
drink." Nor does he on Christmas Day, "a festival of regret" for childless

Elliot. Blizzards come with January, then severe cold. As the ferocity of the outer world increases, his stays against chaos undergo painful compression: "Elliot could hear the boards of his house contract and feel a shrinking in his bones." During parts of the night he lies sleepless, "listening to the baying of dog packs running [starveling deer] down in the deep moon-shadowed snow." But the most enervating event was the sense of collapsing culture in Boston back in November: "In his mind's eye he could see dead leaves rattling along brick gutters and savor that day's desperation. The brief outing had undermined him."

In difficult February—winter having gone on for so long, spring being so far away—Blankenship, "a sponger and petty thief," brings his "red hair . . . brutal face, and . . . sneaking manner" into Elliot's office and pushes over the rickety structure of his sobriety. There's a subtle doubling going on between the two men. To a limited extent Elliot is working the immense welfare system to his advantage: though he has only a master's degree, he draws a slightly higher salary than a colleague with a Ph.D. because the two are employed by different branches of the state government. Having completed an apprenticeship among the undeserving poor, Blankenship swims about in the welfare system like a well-fed carp. His schooling in social work was administered by his family, which "made their way through life as strolling litigants . . . [who] had threatened suit against half the property owners of the southern part of the state. What they could not extort at law they stole" ("H," 2240–41). When, after his unnerving meeting with Blankenship, Elliot asks a probation officer about Blankenship's "present relationship with his family," the officer lists the different correctional institutions inhabited by Blankenships and wittily adds, "Their dog's in the pound" ("H," 2243). As for the branch of this ignoble tree, "young Blankenship's speciality was slipping on ice cubes. Hauled off the pavement, he would hassle the doctors in Emergency for pain pills and hurry to a law clinic" ("H," 2241). This February day, Blankenship has left his abode, a Goodwill depository bin, for some psychiatric counseling to help him deal with upsetting recurrent dreams about his Vietnam combat. (Blankenship frequently describes himself as a veteran of the Vietnam War and often wears army camouflage fatigues.) But Elliot, seven different times in less than two pages, points out the problem behind the problem: Blankenship was never in Vietnam.

Here Stone recasts a motif he used in *Dog Soldiers*. Danskin sarcastically mentions the middle-class kids who, feeling entitled to every acquisition, demand the right to be revolutionaries with guns. Lower-class appropriation makes a less serious surfacing when Smitty tells Converse that he had been in Vietnam, but as with the women Smitty tells this to, he's only trying to impress strangers. Blankenship's appro-priation is more substantial: as Elliot concedes, after his harrowing hour with the impostor is over, Blankenship now fully believes that he was there. Elliot reflects that his client "had trouble with alcohol and drugs. He had trouble with everything." We might then expect Elliot to play the indulgent social worker and reason that if Blankenship, in his dregs-of-the-social-world style, appropriates every sort of difficulty and every sort of social service to help him deal with the difficulty, why should he not have trouble with Vietnam and why should not Elliot help him to deal with the dreams?

For one thing, because Elliot detests the way Blankenship, a master of passive-aggressive manipulation, uses his various weaknesses to bully. For another, Elliot, who did serve in Vietnam and seems to have been considerably damaged by the service, feels that "[i]t was unfair of Blankenship to appropriate the condition of a Vietnam veteran." The protagonist continues to reason with a degree of fatalism we like to think is not characteristic of the social welfare industry: Blankenship had been born into "the poverty, anxiety, and confusion that would always be his life's lot" in the same arbitrary and unfair way Elliot and his com-rades had been elected for service in Vietnam. The unstated conclusion is that Blankenship should accept the misery of his situation and not appropriate the misery of others.

It is understandable that, in these thoughts that conclude the story's first part, Elliot should try to dismiss Blankenship in such an uncharita-ble fashion: the supposed Vietnam dream has really rocked the unsocia-ble social worker. The first dream detail, the sense of floating in rubber, catches much more of Elliot's attention than he wants to give: "Elliot had caught dengue in Vietnam and during his weeks of delirium had felt vaguely as though he was floating in rubber." The second set of details is offered by a genuinely frightened man as Blankenship remembers look-ing up at a sky filled with a blackness that might be smoke. To a terrify-ing degree, Elliot is pulled into the other's world: "In a waking dream of his own, Elliot felt the muscles on his neck distend. He was looking up at a sky that was black, filled with smoke-swollen clouds, lit with fires, damped with blood and rain" ("H," 2242–43). The relationship of the waking dream to Elliot's own experience is ambiguous. When Elliot again confronts Blankenship's dream that night, he resuffers what he clearly had undergone in Vietnam: "He saw the bunkers and wire of some long-lost perimeter. The rank smell of night came back to him, the dread evening and quick dust, the mysteries of outer darkness: fear, combat, and death" ("H," 2255). But the imagery of the waking dream is of black clouds obscuring daylight. Had Blankenship appropriated a dream that Elliot had had, or one that awaited the protagonist? The latter alternative seems more likely, and it is because Elliot sees himself being pulled into a world both magical and diseased—one for which a Blankenship, a collector of grievances, is better suited than himself—that dread creeps over him, "like a paralysis":

> Blankenship had misappropriated someone else's dream and made it his own. It made no difference whether you had been there, after all. The dreams had crossed the ocean. They were in the air.
>
> . . . .
>
> It was possible to imagine larval dreams traveling in suspended animation undetectable in a host brain. They could be divided and regenerate like flat-worms, hide in seams and bedding, in war stories, laughter, snapshots. They could rot your socks and turn your memory into a black-and-green blister. Green for the hills, black for the sky above. At daybreak they hung themselves up in rows like bats. At dusk they went out to look for dreamers. ("H," 2244)

With this surreal vision, Stone offers a causal explanation for the infection of the American psyche by the Vietnam experience—as he did not with the many analogies between Vietnam and the United States in *Dog Soldiers*.

After leaving work early and visiting an older cousin who works in the local library, Elliot senses that "[h]e had run away from a dream and encountered possibility." Because the library had been his launching pad for a good many earlier drunks—he would spend the afternoon reading there until he left to hit the bars—he realizes, as he stands in the snow outside the library, "that he had contrived to promise himself a drink." How appealing, after the uncanny onslaught at the hospital and the do-gooder sanctity of his Quaker cousin, is the boozy camaraderie of the Midway Tavern, with its fill of factory workers in after the afternoon shift, with Bruce Springsteen on the jukebox, with the bartender—"a club fighter from Pittsfield called Jackie G."—offering all those little supportive strokes: the familiar "Say, babe" greeting; the "Good move . . . Scotch"? after Elliot tries to explain his presence; the "Happy hour, babe" ("H," 2247–48) that accompanies his return of one of the two dollar bills Elliot proffers for his drink.

Although Grace is bitterly disappointed by Elliot's slip, her day has been of the sort to drive her to join her husband in depleting the bottle of scotch he's brought home. Acting as the prosecuting attorney attempting to deprive the Vopotiks, a biker and his obese wife, of the custody of their three-year-old, she lost the case when her three witnesses did not appear. They were to testify that the couple had burned the child on a radiator and broken some of its fingers.

Two lines that have been often quoted since Yeats first published them in 1920 apply here, as they have to so many laments over the dissolution of civilization: "The best lack all conviction, while the worst / Are full of passionate intensity."[8] Sorting out "the best" in a Stone fiction is usually a thankless task; here we should be concerned with the energy of the worst, the brutes who increasingly seem to be the wave of the future. Within the workings of this story, predators with an aggressive-aggressive style are even better suited to profit by existing social structures than professional victims with Blankenship's passive-aggressive style. Grace describes the courtroom milieu with bitter wit: "The court convened in an atmosphere of high hilarity. It may be Hate Month around here but it was buddy-buddy over at Ilford Courthouse. The room was full of bikers and bikers' lawyers. A colorful crowd. There was a lot of bonding. . . . They didn't think too well of me. They don't think too well of broads as lawyers. Neither does the judge. The judge has the common touch. He's one of the boys" ("H," 2252).

Vopotik's sense of entitlement extends to the Elliot home, which he three times invades by telephone. During the first call he is demanding to speak to "the skinny bitch" when Elliot hangs up. During the second call his threats to harm Grace for trying to break up his happy biker's family widen to include Elliot after the latter wittily baits him. Stone's fine ear is never better than when he employs it to catch the accents of lower-class brutes; Vopotik, in particular, speaks with the authority of someone whose energies are inhibited by no superego whatsoever. But Elliot responds to Vopotik's threats and assured commands ("You put your woman on, man. Run and get her") with somewhat surprising solidity: he either refuses to put Grace on or baits the caller, or hangs up. With his third call Vopotik finally 'communicates' with Grace as, with the inspired brutality Stone loves to catch, he plays his chain saw for her. The mordant humor in the description of Elliot's preparation for the biker and his buddies is also vintage Stone. As he cleans his shotgun, Elliot announces to his wife a commitment to a new mode of social welfare: "Most of the time . . . I'm helpless in the face of human misery.

Tonight I'm ready to reach out. . . . I'll grease his ass" ("H," 2253–54). But in the bitterly cold early morning, as Elliot, poisoned with anger and alcohol, patrols his Massachusetts perimeter with his shotgun, he meets a much different sort of sojourner, his neighbor Loyall Anderson.

Here a bit of backtracking is helpful. Just before he sees Anderson, Elliot thinks, "Fear, anger and sleep were the three primary conditions of life. Once he had thought fear the worst, but he had learned that the worst was anger. Nothing could fix it; neither alcohol nor medicine. It was a worm. It left him no peace. Sleep was best" ("H," 2256). But this is not the way the central movement of the story—Elliot's lurch away from, then back toward, stability—works. Alcohol serves to release anger in Elliot. Once home, he nastily and unfairly mocks Grace's concern for him and for others. Before this, just after she smells the liquor on his breath, he tells her that he intends in the morning to string head-high razor wire across the trail on which the Andersons frequently ski. They constitute what Strickland might call an up-to-date wholesomeness package. A full professor of government at what seems an early age, Anderson is over six feet and blond, as is his wife. They have two blond children, "who qualified for the gifted class in the local school but attended regular classes in token of the Andersons' opposition to elitism." If, when the whole Anderson family is attractively out skiing together, they encounter a snowmobile, "Darlene Anderson would affect to choke and cough. . . . Elliot was picturing razor wire, the Army kind. He was picturing the decapitated Andersons, their blood and jaunty ski caps bright on the white trail." The Andersons share their attractiveness, their wholesomeness, with the world; Elliot shares his violent fantasies with his wife: "Know what I mean? One string at Mommy and Daddy level for Loyall and Darlene. And a bitty wee string at kiddie level for Skippy and Samantha, those cunning little whizzes." For, "[a]lthough Elliot hated snowmobiles, he hated the Andersons far more" ("H," 2248–49).

Indeed, Elliot hates the Andersons' collective self-satisfaction, their smug certainty of the rightness of their politically correct behavior in a complexly flawed world, more than he does the Vopotiks' psychopathy or Blankenship's uncanny parasitism. Much more than he wanted to, he identified with Blankenship's dream, and his fantasy of killing the Anderson children aligns him with the Vopotiks, who Grace is sure will kill their child. And showing a bit more of the kind of controlled otherness we might expect from an intelligent social worker, Elliot thinks of how much Grace must remind "the cherry-faced judge and the bikers and their lawyer [of] the schoolteachers who had tormented their childhoods, earnest and tight-assed, humorless and self righteous" ("H," 2252).

But for Anderson on this icy morning, Elliot can only silently offer the fantasy of blowing out his neighbor's white teeth with some of the deershot in his shotgun and, perhaps, a veiled threat. A bit after he tells the professor that he is out for "[w]hatever there is" ("H," 2256), he announces that he's been drinking most of the night and then contentedly recognizes a certain thickness in Anderson's tongue, a certain slowness in his jaw. Now Elliot wants to be agreeable: the fear he's inspired in Anderson seems to wipe away some of his accumulated anger, and more evaporates when Elliot shoots at a bird and misses. Having armed himself against the violent rabble, quietly but successfully threatened a member of the ranks of the virtuous, and tried to take life, Elliot now wishes "no harm to any creature." Though he sarcastically turns on the tenderness he now feels for himself, with his anger spent he is ready to approach what had been the loathsome process of "helping" from a much different perspective. Stone renders this shift subtly. Elliot's corrosive negativism is still in charge when, after missing the bird, he sees his naked wife at the window: "What had she thought to see? Burnt rags and blood on the snow? How relieved was she now? How disappointed?" But he shifts into a more profitable way of thinking:

> The length of the gun was between them, he thought. Somehow she had got out in front of it, to the wrong side of the wire. If he looked long enough he would find everything out there. He would find himself down the sight.
> How beautiful she is, he thought. The effect was striking. The window was so clear because he had washed it himself, with vinegar. At the best of times, he was a difficult, fussy man.
> Elliot began to hope for forgiveness. ("H," 2258)

The cleanness of the window symbolizes the clarity with which Elliot now sees his wife: as a lovely woman; at the shooting end of a rifle (that is, with justifiable power over him); someone with beauty and help to give, both of which he badly needs. And though he sees himself negatively, there's an absence of the anger, dread, and melodrama that have characterized his behavior for the past day. The story, then, ends with Elliot reaching out not a shotgun but a hand as he waits for Grace's grace, for a response that (as he returns to AA's "One day at a time") will give him a day to build on.

Of course, it is possible to look at his "recovery" as sourly as Elliot has been looking at the world around him. He would seem to have enough resentment to qualify to be what AA people call a dry drunk, even if he stays away from liquor. And it is easy enough to see the pressure building for the next slip. Finally, there is Grace Elliot's description of her sense of loyalty: "In my family we stay until the fella dies. That's the tradition. We stay and pour it for them and they die" ("H," 2250). How optimistic should we expect the end of a Robert Stone fiction to be?

The Nonfiction

The 24 nonfiction works Stone published between 1968 and 1992 can be divided into five groups: reviews, other pieces on the arts, travel writings, social and political commentaries, and a biographical sketch. But, in fact, a number of efforts bridge two categories. For example, "Changing Tides," which is about New York Harbor, appropriately appeared in a special travel section of the *New York Times* but is also social history; "Havana Then and Now" could as easily be placed under the rubric of social and political commentary as travel. Since Stone has written only one pure travel piece—a two-paragraph effort cataloging the beauties of Albania's Ionian shore for a many-authored feature called "Dream Vacations"—the number of nonfiction categories can be cut to four.

Reviews   In October 1991, two weeks after the publication of the seventh of Stone's eight reviews—this one of Pete Dexter's *Brotherly Love* (1991)—I asked him how he felt about this string on his bow. Stone seemed to be having second thoughts about the amount and degree of praise he had just lavished upon Dexter's novel, for he said, "I don't think I always do a good job. Sometimes I think I'm good when I write about a very established writer whose reputation I don't think I can affect. I like what I've written about Graham Greene. . . . I have a great hatred for Greene's work. I did a review of Bruce Chatwin's last novel I feel good about. . . . Otherwise, I think I tend to overpraise, get enthusiastic, and end up somewhat displeased with the results" (Solotaroff 1991).

Stone's review of Greene's *The Human Factor* (1978), "Gin and Nostalgia," which explains why his recent sojourn in Greene's work caused his preexisting distaste to ripen "unpleasantly into contempt," is certainly written with a pen of fire. For starters, he denounces Greene's "phony

ideological commitment, phony religiosity, phony self-discovery . . .
[and] phony personal decency." The last, which Stone claims suffuses
Greene's stupid and world-weary protagonists, particularly angers him:
"[B]y employing the stance of personal decency as a shallow device of
motivation, he has attempted to rob us of our last refuge from cant. In
an age past patriotism, he has delivered up personal decency as a refuge
for scoundrels." In these sentences Stone got about as close to critical
hysteria as he ever has. Greene betrays representational novelists as well
as all of us who aspire to decency: "He is not much of a stylist, and the
half-baked characterizations and pseudo-insights that have fallen in his
work with the insistence of that tropical rain on those corrugated iron
roofs have laid the convention of character open to all the criticisms of
the anti-novelists." The onslaught continues: "His beef and ale moralists
. . . are for the most part monuments of petty snobbery, timely cliché,
and unconscious self-satisfied hypocrisy." They effect a "boozy alienation
and a massive sense of superiority to the poor bastards who take any of
these things seriously." "These things" are the distorted versions of
Catholicism, Marxism, and Freudian thought that surface in the novels.
For "in this world of world-weariness and the self-consciously second-
rate, ideas exist to be vulgarized, blended, aged in wooden language, and
employed as a substitute for characterization."[9] Having tried to sink the
whole of Greene's novelistic achievement, Stone proceeds to disembowel
The Human Factor.

Stone's attack is certainly vivid, but it seems to me somewhat unfair:
of the three Greene novels I have recently read, it captures *The Quiet
American* (1955) but not at all *The Honorary Consul* (1973) and *Our Man
in Havana* (1958). Usually, Greene does not write as badly as Stone
claims he does. But we must realize that Stone's attempted kneecapping
of Greene is something of a special case. Published in *Harper's* in April
1978, "Gin and Nostalgia" was written when Stone had completed
about half of *A Flag for Sunrise*—his novel of anguish, alcoholism,
Catholics, and revolution, in a Central American police state, with the
world-weary, anguished, alcoholic, Catholic-born Holliwell as the prevailing sensibility. Surely he was anticipating the reviewers who would
describe him as being influenced by Greene or of being a member of
some literary brotherhood that included the English writer. Which is not
to say that Stone is not offended by dishonest advocacies, shallow and
unconvincing characterizations, unrealized settings, and loose and inac-
curate prose wherever he sees them. He seems to have a strong sense of
belonging to a community of novelists who will only publish the best

that they can write at any particular time. For the most part, Stone reviews the novels of members in good standing of the community, and then praises their efforts proportionately.

In two different senses, however, his other six reviews of novels are not all praise. (Stone also reviewed the 1991 production of *Miss Saigon* and largely used the occasion of seeing the musical to reminisce about Vietnam.) First, with one exception, Stone is very good at economically laying out the propelling tensions of a novel, of offering the prospective reader a fair sense of its terrain. Second, some negative strictures are present in his reviews of Bruce Chatwin's *Utz* (1988), Pete Dexter's *Brotherly Love*, Ward Just's *The American Ambassador* (1987), and Peter Matthiessen's *Far Tortuga* (1975). And in the only novel he has reviewed since his comment about his excessive generosity, Stone handles Julian Barnes's *The Porcupine* (1992) quite harshly.

As an example of Stone's economy, the opening paragraph of his review of *Utz* describes the novel's opening scene: "alive with shrewd observation, pathos, absurdist humor," with a "dead-on" sense of place and "lapidary . . . component prose"—all of which typifies the precision and suggestiveness with which the novel is written. Stone moves on, justifying as he goes his claim that the collisions of Utz, the partly Jewish, aesthete protagonist, with first Nazi then Russian totalitarianism provide the novel's readers with "a rich and rewarding meditation." But Utz's raison d'etre is so consistently aesthetic that Stone must challenge the novel's "spiritual landscape . . . so high and dry . . . that any display of principle (other than artistic) is a mark of vulgarity, and good intentions are equivalent to philistinism." Thus, after quoting Chatwin's celebration of " 'the true heroes of this impossible situation . . . people who wouldn't raise a murmur against the Party or State—yet who seemed to carry the sum of Western Civilisation in their heads,' " Stone tartly comments, "This is very civilized indeed but a trifle too much, not to say a trifled unearned in a book by a writer for whom 'the role of the artist in a totalitarian state' has always been someone else's problem. But then, Bruce Chatwin's irony relentlessly pursues any expression of near-political concern."[10]

Stone's political concern has, of course, been much complicated by negative forces, whether his pervasive sense of human limitation or his knowledge of the dross that has crept into the revolutionary gold of a particular upheaval. (The vagueness concerning the success of the Tecanese revolution in *A Flag for Sunrise* is probably a consequence of the tension between his hopes and doubts.) As a matter of course, Stone praises in his reviews the excellences of plotting, characterization, dialogue, scenic description, and so on, that he seeks in his own fiction. Only in the review of Thomas Keneally's *To Ismara* (1989) does a certain envy for what is unattainable to him creep into Stone's writing. The novel is set in Eritrea, the eastern province of Ethiopia that has been in a war of rebellion since 1961, "one of the world's longest running and least understood wars." Keneally so convincingly argues the rightness of the rebel cause and behavior, so believably documents the brutality of the Ethiopian government, that what Stone finds most remarkable in a novel he very much admires is how Keneally "has presented in his description of the Eritrean struggle a vision of that good fight many of us had long ago given up on locating. . . . [S]truggling Eritrea . . . democracy's best hope in the region, [is] an African beacon to the world."[11]

Only in his review of Peter Matthiessen's *Far Tortuga*, an account of a turtling expedition in the Caribbean, did Stone fail to offer any sense of the ways in which a novel is propelled by its characters' goals and interpersonal tensions. Admittedly, *Far Tortuga* is an extremely atmospheric effort, and, largely through extended quotation, Stone communicates well the way in which Matthiessen connects skeins of vivid images to render the setting. Toward the end of the piece, the reviewer suggests that the characters are subordinated to the novel's "single insight, the unity of things beneath an ever-changing multiplicity of forms." But he observes that the characters "are very much the carefully individuated, positivistic creatures of traditional good fiction, outfitted with speeches, histories, destinies," so that "the reader becomes thoroughly involved in their fate, and the book works well even on what I take to be its secondary levels." But Stone offers no sense of the workings of these secondary levels. And it's as if he realized the problem but just wanted to get the damn review done; with a logical and tonal clumsiness rare in his writing, he immediately moves, within the same paragraph, to his conclusion: " 'Far Tortuga' is an important book, its pleasures are many and good for the soul. Peter Matthiessen is a unique and masterful visionary artist."[12]

No stumbling or praise mars the surface of Stone's most recent review, of Julian Barnes's *The Porcupine*. Stone has always been proud of his autodidacticism, but I think it took the success of *Outerbridge Reach*, both in achievement and reception, for him to make a claim like, "[Marx] was the first to attempt the fusion of art and life that would make the 20th century so entertaining." I know both that I don't know what this might mean and that, if I did know, I lack the mighty historical sweep Stone is flaunting here to know if he is right. In the review, Stone's most negative save for the one on *The Human Factor*, he certainly lives up to his 1991 decision not to be excessively generous. He chides Barnes for thematic obviousness, sketchy characterizations, inadequate language, and goes so far as to suggest that the novel might work better as a play. Here Stone invokes Arthur Koestler's fine novel of totalitarian trial and punishment, *Darkness at Noon* (1940), which was made into a very successful play. Earlier, Stone had asserted that Koestler "offered a premise to explain the Moscow purge trials of the 1930's: that the old Bolshevik defendants in those trials abased themselves and duly accused one another out of an existentialist loyalty to their own youthful values." Stone finds this claim "improbable, a touch melodramatic and obvious."[13] I think he misses what was propelling Rubashov, the protagonist of Koestler's novel: a commitment to act out the consequences of his materialist assumptions so that he could finally be freed to confront the mystical body of experience that Koestler had had thrust upon him, as a prisoner sentenced to death, two years before he wrote the novel.

Other Pieces on the Arts When asked in a 1984 interview if he had "a fully articulated theory of fiction . . . in the sense, say, that Conrad framed his in the preface to *The Nigger of the 'Narcissus,'*" Stone responded that he was "beginning to frame one—and along rather Conradian lines." He went on to assert that prose fiction "must first of all perform the traditional functions of storytelling. We *need* stories. We can't identify ourselves without them. We're always telling ourselves stories about who we are: that's what history is, what the idea of a nation or an individual is. The purpose of fiction is to help us answer the question we must constantly be asking ourselves: who do we think we are and what do we think we're doing" (Woods, 49).

So far this seems to be a good distance from Conrad's credo, which begins with the assertion that "art itself may be defined as a single-minded attempt to render the highest kind of justice to the visible universe, by bringing to light the truth, manifold and one, underlying its every aspect." The artist who is sufficiently talented, persistent, and fortunate achieves his goal by descending, "within himself . . . [to] that lonely region of stress and stir" and, by exercising the most rigorous selection and organization, communicates to the senses of the audience some of what has entered there through the portals of the author's senses. Through these latter faculties, then, the artist "appeals to that part of our being which is not dependent on wisdom; to that in us which is a gift and not an acquisition—and therefore, more permanently enduring." In that unacquired, essential part of us, the artist "speaks to our capacity for delight and wonder, to that sense of mystery surrounding our lives; to our sense of pity, and beauty, and pain; to the latent feeling of fellowship with all creation; and to the subtle but invincible conviction of solidarity that knits together the loneliness of innumerable hearts . . . which binds together all humanity—the dead to the living, and the living to the unborn" (145–46). Conrad does not suggest whether the aspect of the self to which the successful artist descends is as untouched by social patternings as the primal center of the audience that is the final repository of his communications.

It is instructive to contrast some of the stances of Conrad and Stone, two ironic moralists who are much concerned with the workings of style. There is no shortage of conjecture about the insubstantiality of identity in Conrad's work: one thinks of his different secret sharers or of Martin Decoud in *Nostromo* (1904), who literally cannot endure life once his easy social identities are stripped from him. But for the Conrad who wrote the *Nigger of the "Narcissus"* preface, art must first of all minister to more exalted needs than our bewilderment over who we are. However much Conrad recognized "the warlike conditions of existence" (145) or "the heartless secrets which are called the Laws of Nature" (148), however much he lamented the isolation in which we usually live, he was still a sort of transcendentalist who believed both that a single, multiplicitous, apparently benign truth underlies all aspects of the universe and that there is, at the deepest level of humankind, a common, humane core that is fundamentally untouched by the external ravenings that bear down on us.

Conrad's credo is eloquent kin to all those late nineteenth-century poems, fictions, and paintings that, in different ways, render men warming themselves around a common fire during the God-less, post-Darwinian, late Victorian night. Whether as certain private patternings within his own mind, or the articulations of Saussure about the nature of language, or the world wars, or the camps, the psychic and social events of the intervening years have made warming assurances like Conrad's inaccessible or unbelievable to Stone. The need "to render the highest kind of justice to the visible universe," which has "a truth, manifold and one, underlying its every aspect," has a hierophonic sound to it; these are the accents of a sort of priest prostrating himself before a sort of deity. As

Stone said in 1983, fiction "serves to mythologize in a positive way a series of facts which of themselves have no particular meaning. . . . Reality as a phenomenology, as a primary process does not have any meaning. So you create a kind of artificial phenomenology. You create artificial events" (Schroeder, 155). As for the human animal trying to make his way within this inherently unvalenced swarm, he has no essential core that responds automatically, sympathetically, to what is noble in human behavior and beautiful in the external world. The most significant psychic fact is swarm:

> If we took the composite mentality within this room, if we took the fantasies, the perversities, the madnesses, the weirdness, the strangeness, the odd directions, our own crippled making-it-through-life psyches— because we are only people, we are only this imperfect play which is only so much—if we took our mentalities, or even mine, and projected it on a wall, we'd drive each other mad. . . . We have only the responsibility, not to compete in terms of moral status but simply to get on with each other, and to extend to each other the civility that we do, and above all, if we are artists, to try and transcend this level of our lives, which is *of* us and which *is* us. ("MU," 233)

The reference to the others in the room and the assertion of the need to avoid moral competition speak to the special conditions for which "Me and the Universe," the short essay these lines come from, was written. Speaking during a November 1984 symposium on writers' political responsibility, Stone was obviously committed to emphatically protesting his pessimism as a way of puncturing some of the moral smugness in a Gathering of the Right-minded. For example, in one of the discussions he defended his contentiousness (in this case, telling Barbara Foley that she was "the prisoner of a verbal machine") by saying, "That's what I'm here for."[14] Stone began "Me and the Universe" with the account with which I began this book: of his first contact with war; of his consequent recognition of—and sense of complicity in—human "depravity and craziness and weirdness and murderousness" and of his sense that we can transcend this level of depravity only through art. But the collective effect of the transcendence is at best quite limited: "[I]f we can turn [the barbarism] into art, it means that on some level the world's consciousness gets that tiny bit higher, and maybe, somehow, in some unforeseeable distance, we can get beyond this and it will stop" ("MU," 233). On the one hand, Stone insists that we never lose sight of the current state of human depravity; this, he grandiosely said during a question-and-answer session, "is part of the medievalism which I'm going around, centuries after the fact, attempting to reestablish, because my plan is to start western civilization all over again" ("Session III," 243). On the other hand, responding to another symposiast's (Terrence Des Pres's) belittling of the nineteenth-century poets and cultural philosophers who identified with and sought fulfillment in the universe, Stone argued that his version of the romantic, unencumbered self was the source of moral acts he did perform. As Stone put it in the essay's last sentence: "I've been drawn into politics only because what concerns me is me and the universe, and if me and the universe is not the bottom line, then is my preaching vain, then is your faith vain."

For Stone, literary transcendence is necessarily incomplete: "Words are not life, they're only words" ("MU," 233–34). Surely Conrad was enough of a modernist to believe that perfect combinations of words or sounds or pigment or stone were equal to the task of reaching the innermost self through the capturing of selected aspects of the magically connected external world. Early in "Me and the Universe," Stone elaborates on the limitations of language: "I know that words are words, and life is life, and that between them stands an absolutely unbreachable gulf. Language is language. It's a series of symbols. Life is something altogether different from language. They must not be confused, they are not the same. Language makes its flying leap at life, but it is not life. It is a function of life, a small part of life. Life is something altogether different. We can write our little poems. We can organize our series of words about the experiences that we undergo. But they cannot ever be brought into balance with living because living is living" ("MU," 229).

For the more positive stances he has taken toward the function of art, we should turn to Stone's closest approach to the articulation of a post-Conradian credo, the 1988 essay "The Reason for Stories: Toward a Moral Fiction." Here his rhetorical position forces Stone to what is for him the celebratory, for the essay is a rebuttal to William Gass's "Goodness Knows Nothing of Beauty" (1987), published in *Harper's* a bit more than a year before Stone's response. Gass's essay, in Stone's words, "toyed with the proposition that art and moral aspiration were mutually distant." Stone finds in Gass a tendency "that goes back at least to Nietzsche," one that polarizes the moral and the aesthetic by depicting the former as a stodgy, dull affair and the latter as "nothing but beautiful. Art is like a black panther. . . . Art is radical, the appealing cousin of crime. Morality, in this view, is not only its opposite but its enemy." Stone strangely calls this tendency "antinomian"—what it has to do with the doctrine that salvation can be gained by faith alone eludes me—and sets about undermining it by belittling the self-congratulation of its adherents, posturing over what they think is their daring illicitness.

This ad hominem attack is not overwhelming but strikes me as less problematic than the next one, which offers up Alain Robbe-Grillet's antinovels as examples of what the novel "freed completely from moral considerations might be like . . . novels without any moral context, but they are similarly without characters and plots, beginnings and endings." In a characteristic Robbe-Grillet antinovel like *Jealousy* (1957), the author certainly used the laborious, repetitious, and contradictory listing of objects—and of the agents as objects, with the effaced narrator never offering a single conjecture about motives or moral disposition—to disrupt the reader's normal sense of plot, character, and moral context. Still, I can imagine readers who bring their moral angles to the text, who sympathize with the effaced narrator's unspoken anxiety as he tries to read projected or completed adultery into the gestures and statements of his wife and neighbor, readers who judge the potential or actual adulterers as immoral. Correspondingly, it could be argued that a strongly plotted novel, in which the characters (the moral dispositions of the agents) are made quite clear, might not offer moral signposts more evident than those in *Jealousy*. Such an argument could be made for Vladimir Nabokov's *Laughter in the Dark* (1938), in which the spectacle of a wife and her lover tormenting her blind husband is offered up for the reader's entertainment. I am not suggesting that Stone's reasoning is muddled here, just that his argument wanders into extremely complex issues—for example, precisely what is a moral context—that demand a good deal more clarification than he offers.

The oversimplifications continue when Stone tries to define the comic novel as essentially moral because "laughter is itself a primary moral response. Laughter represents a rebellion against chaos, a rejection of evil, and an affirmation of balance and soundness" ("RS," 71–72). In the greatest study we have of laughter, Henri Bergson argues that, though laughter may be used for moral ends, it is not primarily moral but spiteful, an assertion of superior flexibility whose "function is to intimidate by humiliating" (188). I would add that laughter's content may be not moral but sadistic (we remember Baudelaire's "When we smile, it's a chance to show our teeth"[15]), and that laughter may celebrate chaos as well as assert order.

Of course, Stone could have admitted that laughter can celebrate immorality and then taken the easy way out by arguing that the greatest achievements of comic writing, tragic writing—all imaginative writing—celebrate the moral. Correspondingly, he could have cited examples to support the claim that individual writers' greatest achievements tend to be works concerned with large moral issues. For example, how many readers of racist comic novels like *Scoop* (1938) and *Black Mischief* (1932) anticipated that Evelyn Waugh could produce anything with the depth and range of *Brideshead Revisited* (1945) and the *Men at Arms* (1952–61) trilogy? I mention Waugh because Stone uses him as an example in an argument I cannot follow. Waugh, "one of the worst human beings ever to become a major novelist," used "the certainties of Catholicism . . . to infuse his best work with the moral center that makes it great." I would agree that an author who tries to eschew moral considerations is overlooking a primary ingredient of successful fiction, but how does the *source* of Waugh's morality "provide us with a ringing confirmation of the dependence of serious fiction on morality"? ("RS," 72).

"The Reason for Stories" has some fine, reasonable things in it, particularly about the good fiction can do as it tells us who we are and what parts of the world are, as it offers us models of behavior we sometimes attain, as morally centered fiction (in a very Conradian assertion of solidarity) ministers to the reader in his solitude, "hoping to see his lonely state reflected across time, space, and circumstance" ("RS," 74). But the sort of ambition that has helped him to create such fine novels will not permit Stone to rest with the modest claims of even so obsessive a ruminator on the relationship between morality and fiction as Bernard Malamud. When asked in a 1975 interview if he was suggesting that art is moral, if it changes the world, the most Malamud would assert was, "It tends toward morality. . . . It changes me."[16] But Stone actually attempts a defense of the validity, both in life and in art, of Keats's association of beauty with truth and truth with beauty.

His claim for the reciprocity of truth and beauty in life is relatively modest and quite reminiscent of the relationship between art and morality Malamud claimed: it "tends to be true." The support Stone offers for the assertion is strange. He invokes the perceptions of Job and the medieval mystic Julian of Norwich, both of whom felt that the goodness and beauty of God pervade the universe. Fine, if we experience the wonderful body of feeling that goes with their inner lives, but what if we do not? As for a proof that does not depend on experiencing God's presence, "the grimmest principles of existence have their symmetry." That's it.

The argumentative core of the essay—the claim that in art it is "always true" that truth is beauty, beauty truth—is no more convincingly defended but certainly asserts Stone's aesthetic preferences. For example, "Surely every aesthetic response entails a recognition. What standard do we hold up to art, other than things themselves?" ("RS," 73–74). But many standards besides verisimilitude have been held up: for example, Tolstoy's demand that art join people together; the art object must be well made; it must make the reader contemplate the sublime; it must be truly original—no end of standards. But apart from his sojourn into expressionism and surrealism in the last third of *A Hall of Mirrors*, this has certainly been Stone's desideratum. As he said in his 1985 "Art of Fiction" interview, "There's only one subject for fiction or poetry or even a joke: *how it is*. In all the arts, the payoff is always the same: recognition. If it works, you say that's real, that's truth, that's life, that's the way things are. There it is" (Woods, 32).

Between this interview and "The Reason for Stories," Stone wrote "Portrait," an introductory essay of about 2,300 words for the portrait section of *Legacy of Light* (1987), a collection of Polaroid photographs taken by many different photographers between 1960 and 1986. His emphasis in earlier interviews had been on the usefulness of fiction in helping us to better understand who we are. Here Stone focuses not so much upon the swarming multiplicity of the self as upon human isolation and the helpfulness of art in familiarizing the other to us, in helping us to feel more at home in the world. If the facet of the self that he is considering is different, the criterion for appropriate aesthetic ministering to it is the same. "All art has truth as its object"; is the artwork so convincingly representational that we respond to it in the same way—"That's how it is!"—we do to a good joke, a jazz improvisation, a painting, a novel?[17]

Sometimes the recognition is of the limitation of our perceptual control of the other, as with Stone's discussions of his visual encounters with Bronzino's "Portrait of a Young Man" and a Dürer self-portrait. With his subject's condescending smirk, Bronzino seems to be mocking both his arrogance and that of the viewer who feels certain he understands the young man. In the latter painting, Dürer has tried to capture his own confidence. "At the same time there is a suggestion of wonder, and even timidity, as though he could not continue this bold confrontation with himself or face his own steady gaze for very long. It appears he has decided to be pleased with himself, but his expression is questioning. He has reversed the game and rendered Self as Other. Before him lie all the arcana of humanity" ("P," 63).

This is quite intelligent and interesting, but the aesthetic game's a bit fixed. Portraits are by definition representational; Stone's claim for the representational nature of all art simply does not apply, for example, to nonobjective painting or to a vast amount of great music. To say, "That's the way it is" in praise of the totality of colors and shapes in a Kandinsky painting or of the combination of sounds in a nonprogrammatic piece of music is to say very little. Stone is really on more comfortable ground when he speculates not about the morality of all representation but, for example, about how "all the socialization in the world can not remove completely the partly threatening nature of the Other. The possession or contemplation of another person's image really does provide us with a degree of power over that person" ("P," 59).

Social and Political Commentaries   Probably Stone's most successful piece of social or political commentary is his essay on the 1988 Republican National Convention, "Keeping the Future at Bay: Republicans and Their America," published the same year. Late in the essay he mentions that many at the convention attributed Bush's choice of Dan Quayle as his vice-presidential candidate to the fact that Bush's media consultant was also employed by Quayle: "a dream deal in the Hollywood mode, a media fix so pure it could almost be called nonpolitical" ("KFB," 65). This is about as far as Stone goes in the way of apocalyptic revelation. There's no attempt to come up with the sort of startling news that Mailer sifted, for example, from the 1960 Democratic and 1968 Republican conventions: JFK was America's cinematic prince who could liberate the buried dream life of the nation; Richard Nixon might be a "new and marvelously complex improvement of a devil, or angel-in-chrysalis or both."[18]

But given Stone's more modest mode of political reportage, the project was a sort of dream deal. Here he was back in New Orleans, a place so evocative for so many but particularly charged for him as the site of most of the first year of his marriage, of his first child's birth, of the real beginnings of his political education, of the novel that would transform his life, of his brief careers as factory worker, performing poet, census collector, and much more. And if the French Quarter had been tackily upgraded, if the black slums whose inhabitants offered the northern census-taker lemonade and life stories had been replaced by the Superdome—where convention spectators could gain some contact with the tiny, talking figures in the distance only by watching them on the television sets spread throughout the vast, impersonal building—why, then, the whole of the essay could be structured around the disparity between the poignancy of what was and the existential distancing of the political doings at the convention. If the essay has a flaw, it is Stone's failure to invoke and capture some of the heat of the disruptive forces throughout America from which the Republicans were trying to distance themselves. Then again, Stone's stance tacitly assumes a fraternity with the hip *Harper's* readers who know all about these forces and how essentially out of it the Republicans are.

The evocations of times past are sharply written, particularly the account of Stone's attempt to glean census information from several black families assembled around a dying relative. A consideration of what kind of a man George Bush really is can hardly compete with this sort of vividness, but, as a whole, Stone's reportage of the convention is sharp and some of the snapshots of faces in the crowd are arresting. A few examples: A priest at a party given by the National Rifle Association has a face "that would have looked a lot more appetizing on a plate with parsley and horseradish than it did on the front of his head"; he eyes Stone's "press pass as if it were a turd or a squirting boutonniere." Members of "what used to be called the Eastern Republican Establishment, now reduced to a grim band of *conversos*, practice their ancient faith in secret. For at least the last four years, they had been sporting kelly green slacks and white loafers, trying to pass as right-to-life Holy Rollers, while stealthily sipping scotch and dreaming that Nelson Rockefeller is alive in the heart of a mountain somewhere" ("KFB," 63–64).

A good deal of the essay's success follows from the "then and now" structuring: one senses that the past has such a powerful presence to the writer that he has to struggle to keep it from continually effacing the present moment. To a certain extent, Stone attempted to employ the same strategy in his piece on Havana; the essay is even titled "Havana Then and Now." Then, the author tells us, was 1955, when the *U.S.S. Chilton*, en route to the Mediterranean, docked at Havana and the 17-year-old Stone enjoyed his first shore leave. According to the information Stone gave me about a week after he returned from Havana, the ship was the *U.S.S. Muliphen*, the year was 1956, and he was 19 (Solotaroff 1991).[19] Apart from making us aware of Stone's probably unconscious desire to tell the best story he could by making his avatar as young and callow as possible, the slippage in facts does not much affect the account of the shore leave. Whether 1955 or the following year, Stone was still taking his "first step into that problematic otherness that would so tax our country's moral speculation: the un-American world." (No problems here if we agree that the Montreal to which he traveled with his mother was really "American.") It would seem also to have been Stone's first trip into the problematic otherness of sexual relations, but his account of his first visit to a brothel is, depending upon the state of the reader's curiosity, tactful, vague, or disingenuous: "I have many recollections of that day, but I can recall neither the woman's face nor her name nor the details of our encounter. I do recall there was a certain amount of laughing it up and pretending affection and also that there was paying." Then it was off to the Superman Show at the Teatro Shanghai: "a melancholy demonstration that sexism, racism, and speciesism thrived in prerevolutionary Havana." (The principals of the Superman Show were a nearly naked blonde, "a large muscular black man who astonished the crowd and sent the blonde into a trembling swoon by revealing the dimensions of his endowment. . . . [There were] other performers as well, principally a dog and a burro.")[20]

Chastened by his debauch, Stone went the next day with a shipmate to do "some of the cool foreign-type things experienced world travelers did, like drinking black coffee very slowly from very small cups." Then follows a paragraph that describes very well the vibrant and various life the coffee drinkers found on the grand boulevard that runs between the ocean and the city's central park. Stone claims that he was "struck less by the frivolity of Havana than by its unashamed seriousness," which for the teenaged Stone was best symbolized by the "formal elegance and polite luxury" of the Hotel Inglaterra and by the adjoining building, "the overdone but monumental Teatro Nacional, a structure besotted with its own aspirations toward high culture, fearlessly risking absurdity, all trumpets, angels and muses. It was a setting whose pleasure required a dark side—drama, heroism, sacrifice. All this Spanish tragedy, leavened with Creole sensuality, made Havana irresistible" ("HTN," 39).

Though there are prostitutes in the lobby of the Inglaterra 35 or so years later, Creole sensuality seems to have taken off for other parts. In fact, the hotel now serves Stone as a "melancholy souvenir" of Marxism. While the communist bloc toppled from Central Asia to East Germany, "Cuba, of all places, was imperfectly replicating Warsaw or Bucharest in the age of Brezhnev" ("HTN," 36). And the middle-aged Stone is less infatuated with the Latin obsession with "drama, heroism, sacrifice." To the Fidelista rallying cry of "*Socialismo o muerte*," he invokes a Cuban tradition more committed to survival and reasonably queries, "Why not socialism or somewhat less socialism? Why not socialism or regulated private enterprise?" ("HTN," 45). At different places in the essay, however, Stone documents how nearly a century of American exploitation of and condescension toward Cuba has strengthened the resistance of Castro and a good many followers to any gesture that seems like a capitulation to the *Yanquis.*

And what is the blend of support for and resistance to Castro's Draconian measures? In Cuba—no, in Havana—for just a week, Stone can offer only some rough conjectures. A fair number of intellectuals and artists are strongly opposed to the regime's suppression of civil liberties. Many of those who have had enough courage to appeal for reform have been punished in different ways; many of them have been jailed. But there are also a fair number of "artists and professionals whose attachment ranged from enthusiasm to sympathy to resigned acceptance. . . . Many of the enthusiasts were people of principle who resembled not at all the cynical apparatchiks I used to encounter on visits to Eastern Europe. Still the mood of the city seemed forlorn and surly." Stone goes on to describe how "a surprising number of young people, encountered casually on the street, denounced the government in bitter and obscene terms" ("HTN," 43).

The ideal center of the essay—intelligent conjectures about how the inner and outer lives of this expressive people have changed between Battista's corrupt and flamboyant Havana of 1956 and the straitened city of Castro's austere 1991 Cuba—is missing. And how could perhaps ten days' acquaintance—two or three then, seven now—have provided the material for such conjectures? For example, when Jacobo Timerman traveled throughout the country in 1987, one of the many curious phenomena he found among vivacious Cubans was a nearly traumatic inability to think or talk about political issues. But Timerman, whose native language is Spanish, was in Cuba for a whole summer, not a total of ten days separated by three and a half decades. Moreover, all but a very few aspects of Havana life were closed to Stone during his first stay.

Yet Stone is used to writing with considerable authority about what he feels is most important, and perhaps his sense of the absence of this authority contributed to the essay's strangest aspect: the virulence and frequency of his attacks on the Cuban lifestyles of his two famous literary predecessors in Havana, Ernest Hemingway and Graham Greene. There are some witty and appropriate moments in Stone's account of his visiting Hemingway's home outside Havana, like the way in which the mounted animal heads are "absurd and obscene, looking less like trophies of the field than something a mafioso would send to his least favorite Hollywood producer. That had been the first vertiginous moment, seeing the room imperfectly embalmed in the past yet seeing it with the eyes of the present; realizing that the front ends of twelve antelope pasted to a single wall no longer look the way they did in the Fifties, when such a sight suggested virile jollity and Old Grandad." How nicely the sort of double time he describes extends the previous paragraph's meditation on the way the fantastically finned cars from earlier decades, Russian cars, "and the largest number of motorcycle sidecar combos assembled since the Blitzkrieg" combine with the painted slogans and crumbling buildings to make of Havana "a dream state being grimly and desperately prolonged." But referring to Hemingway and Greene as "two macho coxcombs who had so much trouble staying at the right end of their own firearms," or to Greene as someone "who hated all vulgarity but his own," has something of the abrasiveness of the sportswriters who try to set themselves up as realists by belittling on a daily basis everything that passes before them ("HTN," 42–43). This was not the best way for Stone to protest how far he had come from the 19-year-old who, filled with reverence for Hemingway, tried to sip coffee Papa-style on the Paseo del Prado.

Stone's reference to the American pragmatism so many Cubans resist turns up in a much enlarged context in his contribution to the op-ed pages of the *New York Times* in March 1992. For Stone, the recent willingness of mafiosi to inform on each other and to give up their businesses rather than go to prison was an example of "one more fissure in the general erosion of every imaginable standard beyond self interest." A Vietnamese immigrant once told Stone, "Our Vietnamese culture is of steel. . . . But yours is acid that dissolves the steel"; the mafiosi's behavior signals the dissolution of their peculiar version of a long-standing Mediterranean code of honor and "can be seen as yet another triumph of Yankee pragmatism over ancient culture."[21]

Stone traces our eschewal of "the heroic mode" to our long-standing resistance to aristocratic stances. It is "this refusal to honor doctrines and accept the authority of tradition that makes the elites of Europe and Latin America profess to despise us." Our doctrine of immediate self-interest may have prevented us from making some of the terrible errors that convulsed countries like Germany and Italy in this century, "[b]ut self-interest can take us only so far." What follows comes naturally enough from a writer who, for decades, has been concerned with the quest for the numinous, one who had recently finished writing of the consequences of Owen Browne's idealism and longing for a genuinely worthy opponent: "At a certain point, human nature rejects it as an end, requiring something higher and finer"—something of the transcendent stances we traditionally scorn. "We can tell our children to just say no from now until doomsday; eventually they will require something to say yes to. If we cannot furnish them with a cause beyond the realization of their individual desires all our past success may be rendered meaningless" ("EP").

"Just say no" is, of course, a mocking repetition of Nancy Reagan's advice to actual or potential drug users. Toward the end of his 1985 essay "A Higher Horror of the Whiteness," Stone put his finger on the mechanism that makes it so hard for many, particularly the young, to just say no to an immediate pleasure: "[W]e live in a society based overwhelmingly on appetite and self-regard. We train our young to be consumers and to think most highly of their own pleasure" ("HHW," 54). Stone asks, can enough adults in America provide admirable, alternative models of behavior? The preceding 3,000 words of "A Higher Horror of the Whiteness" implicitly argue that they cannot.

The essay is subtitled "Cocaine's Coloring of the American Psyche." Were Stone into the recent mode of supposedly riveting punning ("en*gender*," "*his*tory"), he might have added something like "An Ap*pall*ing Process." Mercifully, he seizes upon "The Whiteness of the Whale" chapter of *Moby-Dick* as his trope for the horror of the whiteness of cocaine, particularly the words Melville used to describe Lima, Peru: "the strangest saddest city thou canst see. . . . [T]here is a higher horror in the whiteness of her woe" ("HHW," 50–51). The frissons of a summer 1984 walk through Manhattan—the number of men signaling the crack they had to sell by snapping imaginary whips, the strangers trying to sell him Elavil (used to relieve "the depression attendant on the deprivation of re-refined cocaine—'crack' "), the sense that most of the pedestrians in the Wall Street area were wired to their cocaine use, the particularly demonic nature of the traffic—all combined to make Stone feel that in a Manhattan that seemed given over to cocaine he had found not the California of the mind where the beatnik pot smokers of *A Hall of Mirrors* longed to live, but "a Lima of the mind" ("HHW," 49, 51).

Cocaine and crack are, of course, national or near-national problems. And in discussing the pervasiveness of the problem, Stone frequently speaks nationally. For example, "[T]he ubiquity of cocaine and its derivative crack [has] helped the American city to carry on its iconographic function as Vision of Hell" ("HHW," 49–50). But to most Americans

New York already is the ultimate in urban hellishness. When some moviemakers came up with a particularly amusing dystopia—an island city isolated as a penal colony—they knew what they were doing when they titled their effort *Escape from New York* and shaped the plot accordingly. That the film's Manhattan is ruled by a psychopathic black named the Duke of New York, and that the midwestern vision of descending into the subway system is rendered by having unspeakable subhumans crawl out of the manholes at night, strike me as particularly shrewd appeals to the audience's fantasies. With the national sense of New York as the cutting edge of urban disintegration, with the 1985 statistics on cocaine use that Stone quotes—more than one in ten Americans, and more than one in six high school students, have tried the drug at least once—with the surfeit of television and movie drug deals and drug busts, with drive-by shootings and the national inability to deal with the problem, Stone has a fair amount of argumentative leverage for his suggestion that he was very much picking up the way America is going on that summer day when he walked among an apparently cocained populace. This is a good deal easier to agree with than the implicit argument in *Dog Soldiers:* that the smuggling of the heroin and all that followed fairly represented the malign influence of the Vietnam adventure upon the social fabric of the United States. (Then again, every page of that novel is so well written that this implausibility does not seem to me to weigh very much.)

Stone tries to explain the appropriateness of the vision that came to him in the Wall Street area by invoking Bartleby, and than moving from there to quote Melville on the horror of whiteness. But his interesting conjectures on cocaine as the "success drug" fit in nicely with the Wall Street locus: " 'I thought of cocaine as a success drug,' one addict is reported saying in a recent newspaper story. Can you blame him? It certainly looks like a success drug, all white and shiny like an artificial Christmas morning. It glows and it shines just as success must. And success is back! The faint sound you hear at the edges of perception is the snap, crackle, and pop of winners winning and losers losing." And though a friend agrees with Stone

> that what cocaine mainly gave you was the jitters . . .
>
> ". . . sometimes," she said, "you feel this illusion of lucidity. Of excellence."
>
> I think it's more that you feel like you're *about* to feel an illusion of lucidity and excellence. But lucidity and excellence are pretty hot stuff, even in a potential state, even as illusion. Those are very contemporary

goals and quite different from the electric twilight that people were pursuing in the sixties.

The essay captures a good deal more than Stone's fascination with drug use and his ability to write fine dark comedy, like his account of the addicted stockbroker who began telling his clients that "the world was coming to an end and that he was supervising their portfolios with that in mind. The world would end by water, said the financier, but the right people would turn into birds and escape. He and some of his clients were already growing feathers and wattles." The users of the drugs of choice of earlier decades—marijuana, LSD, heroin—tended to be dropouts. Given the immense economic consequences of the buyouts, junk bonds, and insider trading of the 1980s, much of it done by relatively young men whose appetites included cocaine, Stone's 1985 association of the drug with success, Wall Street, and the New Hedonism was prescient indeed. Of course, the majority of cocaine users are at least one of the following: poor, young, a dropout. Stone accommodates their use of the drug with his claim that, in one way or another, the contemporary American mind tends to associate cocaine with success: "The poor and the children have always received American obsessions as shadow and parody. They too can be relied on to 'go for it' " ("HHW," 53–54).

A Biographical Sketch   One piece stands alone here, "The Man Who Turned on the Here." The "man" is Ken Kesey, holed up in Manzanillo on the Pacific coast of Mexico, anxiously hiding out from American and Mexican law enforcement agents and body snatchers. In August 1966, when Stone drove into Manzanillo, he was on a roll. He had in the last two months finally completed *A Hall of Mirrors*, and, in Tom Wolfe's account, he arrived in style at the abandoned Purina factory where Kesey was living: "Even Bob Stone sails in. . . . He pulls in in a Hertz car. He flew into Mexico City. He has an assignment from *Esquire* to do a story on Kesey in Exile." Wolfe offers several funny stories of Stone's antics there: driving, wholly strung out on Dexedrine, *beneath* a giant road-building machine, which he is convinced is a monster waiting to devour him; a drive with Kesey north, toward California, in which "Stone . . . nice and high on speed . . . thinks he's behind tinted glass in a cab, although he is doing the driving. So like a taxi!" (321–22).[22]

But in the sketch Stone stays so far in the background that he is merely "a friend," who suggests that Kesey can best deal with a Mexican who has been taking pictures of the fugitive's house and asking about him by pulling the native into the "here," into a Kesey-present-moment movie: an on-the-spot remaking of *Casablanca*. After this reference to himself as a friend, Stone disappears from the narrative completely, and so it is quite strange that the *Esquire* editor who commissioned the piece refused to publish it because of what he felt was its excessively personal angle of vision.

Stone begins the piece with a brief introduction that describes Kesey's October 1966 reentry into the United States under the guise of Singin' Jimmy England, "somebody's hard-times cowboy," who had supposedly been robbed of all identification in Mexico. Then the author moves back two months but forward from the past to the present tense, to the moment when Kesey "is sitting in the garden of the Casa Purina" and one of the Pranksters with him in Mexico bounds in to announce the dapper Mexican and his camera across the road.[23] Stone stays in the present tense to describe the very funny interactions among such Merry Pranksters as Ken Babbs, Neal Cassady, Kesey, and the Mexican, who cuts short his first observation by driving off without a word but who, having mysteriously learned to speak English over the siesta hour, returns to talk, eat, drink, and boast.

The Mexican's cover story is wonderful: "He is from Naval Intelligencia. He is looking for a Russian spy, whose description is incredibly like Kesey's. The Russian spy is spying on the coast of Mexico. Occasionally, Russian ships appear off the bay and they flash lights to him. Russian spies are Commies, the man explains, and mean America no good. The Pranksters are Americans No? Ah, the man likes Americans very much indeed. He hates Russians and Commies. Might the Pranksters assist in investigating this nastiness?" While this is happening, Cassady is throwing a six-pound hammer at a brick target while exuding his usual nutty rant: " 'Um yass, quite indeed,' Cassady says, retrieving his hammer. 'Quite a set-up, yaas, yaas, yaas. Bang, bang, bang,' he sings, 'bang bang, went the moto-sickle' " ("MWTH," 58). Kesey, who has been in the house taking all this in through the blinds, now goes for the walk in which Stone lays out the *Casablanca* caper, and they join Babbs and the Mexican in a Polynesian restaurant down the road. By this time the small Mexican is in macho orbit, boasting of the killers he's turned into compadres, the way they call him "El Loco . . . at the office . . . because he takes on the cases no one else wants," the snarling contempt with which he shivered the resistance of the movie stooge who tried to keep him from meeting Elizabeth Taylor. Then there is the display of a badge emblazoned with the rampant eagle and struggling snake. He is a Federale, and his badge number is One. He is agent Number One.

> "Number Uno," Kesey says. He looks at the badge.
> Babbs whistles softly through his teeth.
> "Do you have a licence to kill?" Babbs asks.
> Agent Number One cocks his head in the Mexican gesture of fatality. ("MWTH," 67)

It's hard to say whose movie predominates: the Pranksters', with Babbs commencing "to tell outrageous stories involving Russians and people who appeared to be Russians whom he has encountered in and around Manzanillo. . . . Sometimes it has seemed that there were more Russians than Mexicans about," and Kesey then telling "of *his* encounters with Russians" ("MWTH," 68), and Kesey and Babbs's inviting Agent Number One to their next Acid Test along with the 150 federal agents he claims wait only for his report to act; Agent Number One's, with his letting it drop that he specializes in narcotics cases and his taking Kesey's picture so that, as he claims, he can add it to a collection that includes Elizabeth Taylor's.

Twice Stone moves away from "The Pranksters Prank the Federale" to offer wittily written accounts of the two drug busts that drove Kesey to Mexico. Stone is in good form in capturing the squareness of the American narcs, particularly when he is on the case of William Wong, the agent with the Federal Bureau of Narcotics who prodded the country sheriff into making the raid on Kesey's house that led to his first arrest. For example, Wong was convinced that "Kesey was, in addition to being a novelist, a dealer in both marijuana and heroin on an international scale." To bring this nefarious drug lord to justice, Wong took to eavesdropping in North Beach coffeehouses: "perhaps his hat is pulled low across his countenance, perhaps he counterfeits the stupor of narcosis." For their part, the local police believe that Kesey "was so confirmed a dope pusher that he felt able to devote his spare time to enrich the literature of narcotics, perhaps with an eye toward drumming up a brisker business" ("MWTH," 62–63). Praised be narcs like Agent Number One, whose inventiveness has zaniness and color to it. Indeed, the piece ends in tribute to the diminutive swashbuckler:

> "What a great cat!" Babbs says. "How about that guy?"
> "Definitely a man with something going for him," Kesey says.
> "Definitely." ("MWTH," 69)

Notes and References

Preface

1.   Robert Stone, "Me and the Universe," *Triquarterly* 65 (Winter 1986): 233, hereafter cited in text as "MU."

2.   "Absence of Mercy," *Harper's* 275 (November 1987): 61, hereafter cited in text as "AM."

3.   William Crawford Woods, "The Art of Fiction XC: Robert Stone," *Paris Review* 27, no. 2 (Winter 1985): 28, hereafter cited in text.

4.   Steve Benson and Robert Solotaroff, "Talking Sense," an interview with Robert Stone, KUOM, Minneapolis, 1 May 1992, hereafter cited in text.

5.   When Eric James Schroeder asked him if he felt that the United States would ever recover from the damage caused by its involvement in Vietnam, Stone drew the analogy of "a piece of shrapnel that the organism has built up a protective wall around, but it is embedded in our history; it is embedded in our definition of who we are. We will never get it out of there." But then he added, "I don't think that it is a mortal wound for this society. . . . I would never write off the pliability of American society. America is really a very tough, endurable thing, and I would be very surprised if it was actually laid low by this kind of thing" (Eric James Schroeder, "Two Interviews: Talks with Tim O'Brien and Robert Stone," *Modern Fiction Studies* 30, no. 1 [Spring 1984]: 154, hereafter cited in text).

6.   Charles Ruas, *Conversations with American Writers* (New York: Alfred A. Knopf, 1985), 280, hereafter cited in text.

7.   Roger Sale, "Robert Stone," in *On Not Being Good Enough* (New York: Oxford University Press, 1979), 72.

8.   Joseph Conrad, "Preface to *The Nigger of the 'Narcissus,'*" in *The Nigger of the "Narcissus,"* ed. Robert Kimbrough (New York: W. W. Norton & Company, 1979), 145, hereafter cited in text.

9.   A. Alvarez, "Among the Freaks," *New York Review of Books* 33 (10 April 1986): 23, hereafter cited in text.

Chapter 1

1.   Robert Stone, with Russell Banks, Jan Morris, and William Styron, "Itchy Feet and Pencils: A Symposium," *New York Times Book Review*, 18 August 1991, 24, hereafter cited in text as "IF."

2.   Steve Chapple, "Robert Stone Faces the Devil," *Mother Jones* 9 (May 1984): 35, hereafter cited in text.

3.   Robert Stone, interview with author, 27 October 1991, Westport, Connecticut, hereafter cited in text as Solotaroff 1991.

4.   Paul Gray, "Flowers of Evil," *Time* 104 (11 November 1974): 111, hereafter cited in text.

5.   Maureen Karagueuzian, "Interview with Robert Stone," *Triquarterly* 53 (Winter 1983): 254, hereafter cited in text.

6.   I date Stone's comment in 1981 because a shortened version of the Ruas interview, containing Stone's comment in slightly different words, appeared in the *New York Times Book Review* (34–36) on 18 September of that year.

7.   Sybil Steinberg, "Robert Stone," *Publisher's Weekly* 229 (21 March 1986): 72, hereafter cited in text.

8.   Stone also said that he still receives requests for contributions from the school, renamed Archbishop Manning when St. Ann's moved to Queens. Though he never received a diploma, and it always gets some of his titles wrong, the school lists him among its celebrated graduates.

9.   Telephone interview with author, 26 January 1992, hereafter cited in text as Solotaroff 1992.

10.   Janice Burr Stone, interview with author, 27 October 1991, hereafter cited in text as JBS interview.

11.   Robert Stone, "Keeping the Future at Bay: Republicans and Their America," *Harper's* 277 (November 1988): 58, hereafter cited in text as "KFB."

12.   "New Orleans Seizes Seven in a Lunch Sit-In," *New York Times*, 10 September 1960, 14.

13.   Edward F. Haas, *DeLesseps S. Morrison and the Image of Reform* (Baton Rouge: Louisiana State University Press, 1974), 261, hereafter cited in text.

14.   *New Orleans States-Item*, 6 August 1960, 1. A. J. Liebling calculated that though the state saved only $61 a year for each child struck from the rolls, with the cutoff of federal aid, "the grass-eaters running the state under Davis thus got as a free bonus another $244 worth of revenge on a child for being colored" (*The Earl of Louisiana* [New York: Simon and Schuster, 1961], 245, hereafter cited in text). As for the federal challenges in 1960: on 9 May the Justice Department demanded the voting records of East Carroll Parish, which had a large black population but no black voters; on 7 June the same agency filed suit in district court in Shreveport to order the names of 56 black voters returned to the voting rolls in Bienville Parish.

15.   Ivan Gold, "Apocalypse in New Orleans," *New York Times Book Review*, 24 September 1967, 3.

16.   Judging from several comments by people who knew Stone well in the 1960s, he certainly seemed to have a streak of paranoia. In 1984 Ken Kesey told Steve Chapple that Stone was "a professional paranoid. . . . He sees sinister forces behind every Oreo cookie. This is one of his endearing characteristics when you get to know him" (Chapple, 35). What seems to have been Stone's special blend of fearfulness and recklessness is nicely captured in what Tom

Wolfe heard about the Stone who visited Kesey in Mexico in 1966: "[Stone is] still hypersensitive, seeing the FBI and Federales behind every cocoa palm—or else scorpions—and in that very moment, plunging head first, as always, into whatever chaos debacle any Prankster cares to dream up, crying lissen this is dangerous as he swandives off every handy cliff" (Tom Wolfe, *The Electric Kool-Aid Acid Test* [New York: Farrar, Straus and Giroux, 1968], 321, hereafter cited in text). The Stone I spoke with for more than three hours in October 1991 seemed serenely confident, save for the moment of heightened affect that emerged when he discussed his mother's symptoms. As I was leaving, I half-jokingly told him how unfair were the descriptions of him as a paranoid; he smiled and said, "It comes and goes."

17.   Kay Bonetti, "An Interview with Robert Stone," *Missouri Review* 6, no. 1 (Fall 1982): 111–12, hereafter cited in text.

18.   Hugh O'Haire, "The Search for Transcendence in the Novels of Robert Stone" (unpublished master's thesis, City University of New York, Queens campus, n.d.), 76, hereafter cited in text.

19.   Although Chapple is not the most reliable of interviewers, Stone's obvious thirst for a pervasive sense of rightness in the world conforms with what he has written. For example, in a 1988 essay, as part of an attempt to prove that there is always a moral component to beauty, he argues that this should be true in Western culture because we want so badly for it to be true. Then, to exemplify what is for him the peak of human yearning, Stone quotes the following utterance by the medieval mystic Julian of Norwich: "[A]ll shall be well and and all shall be well and all manner of things shall be well" ("The Reason for Stories: Toward a Moral Fiction," *Harper's* 276 [June 1988]: 73, hereafter cited in text as "RS").

20.   Wallace Stegner, "Hard Experience Talking," *Saturday Review* 50 (August 1967): 25, hereafter cited in text.

21.   Raymond Carver, "Fires," in *In Praise of What Persists*, ed. Stephen Berg (New York: Harper and Row, 1983), 38, hereafter cited in text.

22.   In my 26 January 1992 telephone interview, Stone said, "I took fatherhood in stride; it didn't throw me. I got so much support from Janice. Both of us were a little bit young; Raymond was even younger than I was, but it was common for people our age to have kids. With someone other than Janice, it could have been very difficult, but she was very good, a wonderful person. She made it fairly easy." When I said, "I surmise that Janice was a near ideal mate for you," Stone responded, "I would have to agree with you. It's so much easier with somebody sticking up for you and helping you out."

23.   In the May 1992 radio interview "Talking Sense," Stone talked of his sense of getting what he called the "soundings" of a character.

> I think you have to discover something about your characters as you go along. You start with a situation and a handle on the principal characters. I think there are three things necessary for me to undertake a

novel, and one is the situation the people are in; the other is the characters themselves—what they're like—and then, usually, I have a scene in mind toward the end. Once I get a fix on the characters, it's then time for me to bring them to some kind of life, to some kind of psychic and verbal existence. What I call "soundings," the discovery of the dimensions of the character, is something like an impersonation. It's less like you're being possessed by a spirit than it's like acting. It's as though you do the voice, you impersonate the character, you take on the character's psychology and mentality. You speak with the character's voice, and, as you do this, you discover leitmotifs, and your prose will take on a certain quality and sensibility, which will be reflected in the quality of the prose. The savor of the prose will reflect what the person is like, and this is an ongoing discovery. And so that's what I mean when I talk about soundings.

24.   In 1967 Stegner mistakenly attributed the intercranial tension to psychosomatic origins and described Stone as "quiet, nervous, given to black depressions and psychosomatic ailments" (25). Jane Burton, described by Bruce Weber as "a friend from the sixties," remembered Stone as "very dark, very black" (Bruce Weber, "An Eye for Danger," *New York Times Magazine*, 19 January 1992, 20).

25.   The negative review appeared in *Publisher's Weekly* 192 (31 July 1967): 53. The only evaluative comment blended in with the summary offered in the 7 November 1966 issue was that the novel "is very well written" (62). The final review had it this way: "A very, very good first novel. . . . It's a tragicomedy (but that's not saying it all) about present day America, set in New Orleans. And it's ribald, sad, poetic, raucous, coarse and fine—all things, in short, that a novel should be" (*Publisher's Weekly* 194 [2 September 1968]: 61).

Chapter 2

1.   When I interviewed her, Janice Stone told me that her husband copied their apartment on St. Philip Street for the one that Rheinhardt and Geraldine inhabit.

2.   Morris Dickstein, *Gates of Eden* (New York: Basic Books, 1977), viii.

3.   Robert Stone, *A Hall of Mirrors* (Boston: Houghton Mifflin, 1967), 252–53, hereafter cited in text as *HM*.

4.   Herman Melville, *Moby-Dick*, ed. Harrison Hayford and Hershel Parker (New York: W. W. Norton & Co., 1967), 235–36, hereafter cited in text. The most insistent example of the way fish and water figure in *Hall*'s grim, evolutionary prophecy comes toward the end of the novel. The morning after the racist riot that killed 19, Bogdanovich is reading a book called *Living Fishes of the World* and shows Rheinhardt a picture of a deep sea lantern fish, bearded, armed with a luminous appendage and rows of dagger teeth.

"Look at the teeth, Rheinhardt. The little son of a bitch is nothing but a mouth full of teeth. It says these fish gotta be all teeth because at the bottom of the sea it's like very competitive. The book comes on very straight and explains this jive. I mean, what a wiggy world! *Que Vida!*"

"It's very competitive," Rheinhardt said.

"On land, on the sea and in the air," Bogdanovich exclaimed. "Like last night. I never made a scene like that before."

"There'll be a lot of scenes like that now. That's evolution is what that is." (*HM*, 391)

For a thorough discussion of this aspect of the novel, see L. Hugh Moore's "The Undersea World of Robert Stone," *Critique: Studies in Modern Fiction* 11, no. 3 (1969): 43–56.

5.   Robert Lowell, "Inauguration Day, 1953," in *"Life Studies" and "For the Union Dead"* (New York: Noonday Press, 1970), line 8, hereafter cited in text.

6.   To take one example, here is Stone, in 1986, speaking quite accurately about the California experience: "Life in California was in a way the affluent American experience at its peak . . . but at the same time there were other strong forces at work: civil rights activism, the rebellion against the 50's, a new sense of freedom, even a spirit of anarchy; the refusal to buckle down to arbitrary norms. All of these things collided in one enormous explosion" (Steinberg, 72–73).

7.   The one example that comes to mind is in *A Flag for Sunrise*, when the narrator tells us that "Justin was innocently snobbish in the extreme" (New York: Alfred A. Knopf, 1981), 237, hereafter cited in text as *FS*.

8.   An exception, again, is *A Flag for Sunrise*, which centers 5 of its 43 sections in the sensibility of a fourth character, Father Egan.

9.   Again, the exception is *Flag*, in which, in one scene, the author gives the reader access to the thoughts of two revolutionaries who do not know the principals, and whom we do not see again.

10.   Saul Bellow, *Herzog* (New York: Viking, 1964), 5.

11.   Henri Bergson, *Laughter* [1900], in *Comedy*, ed. Wylie Sypher (Garden City, N.Y.: Doubleday Anchor Books, 1956), 137.

12.   Although *Hall*'s acknowledgments give Lowell's 1946 collection *Lord Weary's Castle* as the source of "Children of Light," Stone used the version that appeared in the poet's 1944 collection *Land of Unlikeness*. The major change in the two versions of the poem was Lowell's substitution of "by an empty altar" for "in a hall of mirrors," a change that much more surely suggests that materialism is celebrated in a religiously faithless land. The later version fits in much better with the content of *Hall*, in which the most flamboyant con man, Farley the Sailor, once played Christ in a passion play and dresses up in clerical garb

(as Father Jensen) to run some of his cons. By the end of the novel all is out in the open: still in religious garb, he is bludgeoning and murdering so that he can roll his victims.

13. T. S. Eliot, *The Waste Land*, in *T. S. Eliot: The Complete Poems and Plays, 1909–1950* (New York: Harcourt, Brace, and World, 1952).

14. "Looking out of the bus window at the outskirts of New Orleans, Rheinhardt finds it 'the sodden end of folly.' The roads are 'wasted,' running past rows of 'blank houses' with 'futile little lawns, bottles of milk on peeling steps, haunted chairs propped against the shingles.' Boats look like 'grounded fish, moored to docks that stood rotting in mud.' The bus passes a freight yard 'ringed with monstrous tank towers where solitary Negroes shambled solemnly along the smoky sidings.' Lake Pontchartrain is fringed with 'skeletal trees bent like gibbets under grave-beards of unwholesome Spanish Moss.' Black cormorants fly in a 'black sky' " (O'Haire, 10). O'Haire argues that the novel is, in part, "a literary allegory based on both Dante's and Milton's treatment of the revolt and fall of Lucifer" (4). While Stone plays a bit with allusions—as I point out above, Rheinhardt quotes from *Inferno* and later refers to himself as "the evil fool of the Air" (*HM*, 254)—I do not see patterns of parallel actions sufficient to constitute allegories.

15. David Thorburn, "A Fearful and Mindless Violence," *The Nation* 206 (1 April 1968): 452.

Chapter 3

1. Robert Stone, "We Couldn't Swing with It: The 'Intrepid Four,' " *Atlantic Monthly* 221 (June 1968): 61.

2. The length of Stone's Vietnam stay is a conundrum. He told Schroeder that he "spent something under two months there in May of 1971" (151). Something has to be wrong here, and so, when I interviewed Stone in October 1991, I asked him if it was correct that he was in Vietnam for five or six weeks in May and June of 1971. He responded, "Essentially." A few weeks later, I looked more closely at the piece in the *Guardian* of 17 July (see note 4). It begins, "Last month I went to Vietnam and stayed there for a couple of weeks."

3. Robert Stone, "There It Is," *Guardian*, 17 July 1971, 9.

4. Robert Stone, *Dog Soldiers* (New York: Penguin Books, 1987), 25, hereafter cited in text as *DS*. This edition has the same pagination as the original 1974 Houghton Mifflin edition.

5. Frank W. Shelton, "Robert Stone's *Dog Soldiers:* Vietnam Comes to America," *Critique: Studies in Modern Fiction* 24, no. 2 (Winter 1983): 74.

6. Joan Joffe Hall, "*Dog Soldiers* by Robert Stone," *New Republic* 172 (4 January 1975): 31.

7. D. H. Lawrence, *Studies in Classic American Literature*, in *The Shock of Recognition*, ed. Edmund Wilson (New York: Farrar, Straus and Cudahy, 1955), 965.

8. William H. Pritchard, "Novel Sex and Violence," *Hudson Review* 28, no. 1 (Spring 1975): 160.

9. Some of the preceding correspondences (and a good many more) were first pointed out to me in a splendid paper that Michael Young wrote in 1978 for a course at the University of Minnesota.

10. Sharon Lee Ladin, "Spirit Warriors: The Samurai Figure in Current American Fiction" (unpublished doctoral dissertation, University of California, Santa Cruz, 1979), 186.

11. For me, the artwork that most economically sums up the collapse of the ethical into the aesthetic in the 1960s is a movie made in London by an Italian. In Michelangelo Antonioni's *Blowup* (1966), a photographer discovers by progressive enlargements of a picture he took that a murder has been committed. Though he has apparently become a shallow and thoroughgoing hedonist, the blowup is not simply a combination of shades and shapes, or proof of his command of the photographic medium, but evidence that something is *wrong*, in a way that some things, like murder, were *wrong* when he was a child. But he never makes it to the police with the blowup. It disappears, he has an orgy, amid purple paper, with two teenyboppers, he gets stoned at a party, and the next morning he joins members of a surrealistic mime troupe who are playing tennis without a ball.

12. Converse's attempts to think through moral issues collapse as much as his behavior does. At the end of the first dramatized day of the novel, he thinks about how moral objections to the destruction of a termite colony are overridden by the obvious fact that "people were more important than termites." From this he tries to rebut moral objections to his helping to smuggle heroin: "So moral objections were sometimes overridden by larger and more profound concerns" (*DS*, 41). This is chop logic, for the assertion of the primacy of humans is as much of a moral claim as the objection to the destruction of termites. His chance to offer a higher good comes when Hicks asks him if "worldsavers," like Converse and his wife, are not bothered by "all these teeny-boppers OD-ing on the roof." All Converse can come up with is, "We've dealt with the moral objections" (*DS*, 54). Marge's justification of the drug caper is at least as illogical: "The way things are set up the people concerned have nothing good coming to them and we'll just be occupying a place that someone else will fill fast enough if they get the chance. I can't think of a way of us getting money where the money would be harder earned and I think that makes us entitled" (*DS*, 39).

13. Saul Bellow, *Mr. Sammler's Planet* (New York: Penguin Books, 1985), 147.

14.   Daisetz T. Suziki, *Zen and Japanese Culture* (New York: Pantheon Books, 1959), 74–75.

15.   Stone has said that "I didn't really mean him to kill Gerald. Gerald, the writer who OD's, is not supposed to die. I didn't make that clear enough. I left it open. I should have been more specific. In my mind, anyway, Gerald doesn't die" (Schroeder, 157).

16.   They could have dropped through the cave and joined a Mexican neighbor on their side of the road out, but it's impossible to tell whether or not Angel has blocked the way to Hicks's Land Rover with his truck.

17.   Norman Mailer, *The Presidential Papers* (New York: Bantam Books, 1965), 191.

18.   I take O'Haire's word that what Hicks recites—"Gate, gate, parasamgate bodhi swaha"—is indeed the Prajna Paramita Sutra; I have not been able to find a neat compilation of Buddhist sutras that contains it. William Malandra, of the Classics Department at the University of Minnesota, told me that the sutra works here as a declamatory mantra, not a statement in vocative form. Professor Malandra translated the successive words as, "way, course, course to the beyond, enlightenment, amen."

Chapter 4

1.   When I mentioned to Stone that the coasts in Honduras are on the north and south sides of the country, not on the east and west (as they are in Nicaragua and Tecan), he responded, "The average person thinks of the coasts as being east and west." The year after he completed the novel, Stone told Charles Ruas that Tecan is "not a portrait from life of prerevolutionary Nicaragua, nor is it Honduras, nor is it Guatemala, but in certain ways it resembles all those places" (287).

2.   After I wrote the preceding, I mentioned the problem to Stone. He spoke of how hard it was to think his way back into the much different political framework that existed in Central America in the late 1970s and then said: "I think that what I was suggesting was that the process was tainted. I meant Ortega to be admirable, but he's got historical baggage—the conditions, the contradictions of the country—to carry" (Solotaroff 1992).

3.   Hans Jonas, *Gnostic Religion* (Boston: Beacon Press, 1958), 42, hereafter cited in text.

4.   As Ronald Schiller has written:

The Gods of MesoAmerica were innumerable, implacable and voracious. Unless they were fed, they would not permit the rains to fall, the crops to grow or life to continue—and the food they lived on was human blood and human hearts. To assure survival, human sacrifice was practiced from the earliest times. Indeed, it may have been considered the principal reason for man's existence. Favored victims were hunchbacks and other deformed people, who were believed to possess magic powers, and children, whose tears were particularly precious to the rain Gods. . . . The bodies of slain children were buried at the corners of the pyramids of Teotihuacan. Lying beneath an altar at Cholua, archeologists found the skeletons of boys six to eight years old, with artificially deformed heads, who may have been reared for sacrifice . . . Considering the thousands of pyramids that existed, and the necessity of feeding the gods *every day*, the slaughter is believed to have been enormous.

As for the ball game mentioned by Egan, it was played with teams of two to seven on a side, and "scores were made by sending the ball through a vertical stone ring set high in the wall." Players were often maimed or killed by the ball, or died of exhaustion. The winning players sometimes executed the losing ones—who then supposedly gained automatic divinity—and could also "strip spectators of everything they had, including their clothing, provided they could catch them" (Ronald Schiller, *Distant Secrets* [New York: Birch Lane Press, 1989], 146–48).

5. Stone told me during the October 1991 interview that he had been reading about the Gnostics, off and on, "ever since high school, when I came across a religious pamphlet refuting every imaginable heretic. It all struck me as rather sublime then and has continued to do so." When I asked him if he found Gnostic doctrine a real experiential alternative to canonical Christianity, he responded, "It has a great aesthetic attraction, and it also has a degree of truth. There is a way in which life, like a dome of many-colored glass, stains the white radiance of eternity. . . . I think there is truth in it; I always found it sublime and on a certain level true."

6. Richard Poirier, "Intruders," *New York Review of Books* 28 (3 December 1981): 37, hereafter cited in text. The next sentence—"Drugs or alcohol are in that sense also intrusive, a self-inflicted assault upon the mind"— is fine, but then in his attempt to support his claim, Poirier has hallucinogenic drugs coming to America from Vietnam (peyote was around centuries before Vietnam, and the dispersal of LSD began in California), and he exaggerates the effects of Rainey's welfare visits in *Hall*.

7. Religiousness A includes all those whose lives are shaped by any body of religious belief; the existences of those in Religiousness B center on their acceptance of the paradoxes of canonical Christianity. Each level of existence contains lower ones. Thus, for example, Justin's ethical existence encloses her aesthetic experience. She will give herself to Holliwell only when it seems that she no longer has an ethical cause to fight for.

8. Two years later, Stone told Eric James Schroeder that "just what's down there is awful. It's Unknown. It's things themselves" (163).

9. Stone's feelings about the innocence or malevolence of annihilating

nature—both within man and without—would seem to vary considerably from month to month.

10. When the interviewer Kay Bonetti remarked that the name suggested to her a hollow well, Stone first disagreed, then conceded, "Well, there's a kind of hollowness too. I mean you can't always control what's coming into your mind" (98–99).

11. "Every time this Colossus of the North turns on the edge of its bed, poor little Tecan is practically overthrown. This American presence—its turns cause all this upheaval—it's almost unaware of itself, unaware of its effects. It doesn't specifically mean to cause harm. It's serving its own interests as it sees them, but is inflicting great hardship and great harm on Tecan. It's a due bill coming up for payment" (Ruas, 291).

12. On the same page Poirier suggests that the reference to Justin being nailed "also refers to the lost love of Father Godoy and to the bloody giving of herself to Holliwell," and that the faith expressed in this scene "is still a cheat and is known to be by the victim." I disagree with all of this. Though I do not take an author's declaration of intentions as the last word on an interpretation, I feel that the following comment of Stone's, made in a comparison of Justin's wholeness with the broken psyche of Lu Anne Bourgeois (from *Children of Light*), captures much of what is embedded in the text of this scene: "Psychologically, spiritually, Justin is a person whose integrity remains unbroken. There's a kind of upward progression. Justin's despair is redeemed, even though what happens to her is fatal" (Jean W. Ross, "Interview with Robert Stone," *Contemporary Authors*, vol. 23, ed. Deborah A. Straube [Detroit: Gale Research Co., New Revision Series, 1981], 403, hereafter cited in text as *Contemporary Authors*).

13. Carol Kennicott is the relatively cultured, city-bred heroine of Sinclair Lewis's *Main Street* (1920) who languishes among the crude inhabitants of Gopher Prairie, Minnesota.

14. After putting the coin on the counter with that one word, Stone elaborated: "A tradition of rectitude that genuinely does exist in American society and that sometimes has been translated into government. Enlightenment ideas written into the Constitution. Emerson and Thoreau. The whole tradition so wonderfully mythologized in John Ford's Westerns—the Boston schoolmarm seeking service on the frontier" (Woods, 56).

15. William H. Pritchard, "Novel Discomforts and Delights," *Hudson Review* 35, no. 1 (Spring 1982): 175. Pritchard's context is as follows: "In some of his Hemingwayesque life-is-meaningless-but-we'll-live-it-and-only-occasionally-weep moods, Stone is prey to a corresponding sentimentality (I know, Holliwell is a *character*, but . . .) [Pritchard's ellipsis]." If Pritchard's point is that Stone's language is sometimes pulled into excessive sentimentality by Holliwell's sensibility, I agree with him. When I asked Stone in the 1991 interview about whether he felt that Holliwell's ruminative loquaciousness cost the

author his usual trenchancy, he said, "There's a level on which you have to give a character his head. You want to keep control but I think you ought to take out the parts when you're just reminding yourself who the character is. I tried to keep a tight rein on Holliwell."

16. I am indebted to Derik Newman for pointing this out in a paper he handed in to me in December 1992.

17. Walter Clemons, "The Making of a Quagmire," *Newsweek* 98 (18 November 1981): 88.

Chapter 5

1. Robert Stone, *Children of Light* (New York: Ballantine Books, 1987), 19, hereafter cited in text as *CL*. The title is from the First Letter of Paul to the Thessalonians, and the context comments ironically on the often drunken or drugged or deranged world of the novel, one in which God is absent or nonexistent:

> Ye are all the children of light, and the children of the day: we are not of the night, nor of darkness.
> Therefore let us not sleep, as do others; but let us watch and be sober.
> For they that sleep sleep in the night; and they that be drunken are drunken in the night.
> But let us, who are of the day, be sober, putting on the breastplate of faith and love; and for an helmet, the hope of salvation. (I Thessalonians 5:5–8, King James translation)

2. Robert Stone, "A Higher Horror of the Whiteness: Cocaine's Coloring of the American Psyche," *Harper's* 273 (December 1986): 54, hereafter cited in text as "HHW."

3. Jean Strouse, "The Heebiejeebieville Express," *New York Times Book Review*, 16 March 1986, 1, hereafter cited in text.

4. "Well, she might have [played with skeleton's bones]; something happened in Louisiana that rings a bell to me. Somebody being told not to get a Sno-ball because he would be exposed to something. Maybe there was a flood and the bones were exposed; maybe that really happened, maybe it just happened once" (Solotaroff 1991). Lu Anne sometimes feels that it is her fault that she is a schizophrenic. Late in the novel, in the party scene, she explains that she was warned that playing in the graveyard "would make us sick and we didn't listen. All summer we would creep over in the middle of the day. Inside it was cool and awful smelling. We played with the bones until old black Pelletier come [*sic*] yelling at us." Then Stone used his dim memory of some infectious disease being associated with Sno-balls, the local name for flavored, shaved ice:

"My sister would run across the street, eat a Sno-ball—never even wash her hands" (*CL*, 298).
5. Donald Spoto, *Lawrence Olivier: A Biography* (New York: Harper Collins, 1992), 18.
6. Larzer Ziff, *The American 1890s* (New York: Viking Press, 1968), 305.
7. Cynthia Griffin-Wolff, "Thanatos and Eros: Kate Chopin's *The Awakening*," *American Quarterly* 25 (October 1973): 469. Griffin-Wolff invokes R. D. Laing's ideas about the workings of schizophrenia to discuss the tensions between Edna's inner self and her socialized, conformist self. I have no quarrel with her conclusions about these tensions, save for the repeated description of a nonpsychotic psyche as a schizophrenic one. What Professor Griffin-Wolff does with Edna's narcissism—with the persistence in her of the infant self, which demands limitless gratification—is quite convincing.
8. George M. Spangler, "Kate Chopin's *The Awakening:* A Partial Dissent," *Novel* 3 (Spring 1970): 254–55.
9. Not understanding at the time Stone's almost Buddhist emphasis upon the illusory nature of disparate entities, I asked, "The great continuum of the *Liebestod?*" and Stone tried to explain his intention from a different perspective: "It is a *Liebestod*, but it's a *Liebestod* seen by people who know what Tristan and Iseult don't know, that this is all a much bloodier business."
10. Solotaroff 1991. Struck by the way in which Lu Anne revels in the manure here but later, even after a shower, claims that it, blood, and milk are still on her, I asked Stone if her initiation of the pigshit fight with Walker, then her concern with scrubbing off the blood and pigshit, were her attempts, first to get back to Yeats's "foul rag-and-bone shop of the heart" where all poetry begins (from "The Circus Animals' Desertion"), then, by cleaning herself, wanting out of this human mire. Stone agreed (perhaps too generously) and added, "Another Yeats line that crossed my mind there is, 'Love has pitched his mansion in / The place of excrement' [from 'Crazy Jane Talks with the Bishop']."
11. To cite just a few examples, Frank Rice has Stone "attempting to inflate a film location and its scurvy denizens into a spiritual seismograph of a national malaise" ("The Screenwriter's Revenge," *New Republic* 194 [28 April 1986]: 33), and according to Jeff Danziger, Stone gives the reader a set of characters "who get no compassion from each other or their author" ("Disappointing Tale of Hollywood from Critically Acclaimed Robert Stone," *Christian Science Monitor*, 23 May 1986).
12. Thus Robert Jones claims that we cannot be moved by the scenes with the Long Friends because "Stone has written these episodes with the pitch of a Grand Guignol melodrama. . . . Everything is 'literary' in the most artificial sense. There is no naturalness to Stone's prose, nothing that makes one feel that this disintegration is happening to a human being" ("The Other

Side of Soullessness," *Commonweal* 113 [23 May 1986]: 306). A. Alvarez refers to the Monte Carmel scene as "more like *grand guignol* than *King Lear*" (25).

13. Peter Prescott, "A Wasteland of the Heart," *Newsweek* 107 (17 March 1986):73.

Chapter 6

1. Robert Stone, *Outerbridge Reach* (New York: Ticknor and Fields, 1992), 73–74, hereafter cited in text as *OR*.

2. John Leonard, "Leviathan," *The Nation* 254 (13 April 1992): 490, hereafter cited in text.

3. F. Scott Fitzgerald, *The Great Gatsby* (New York: Charles Scribner's Sons, 1953), 23, hereafter cited in text.

4. Ernest Newman, *Stories of the Great Operas and Their Composers* (Garden City, N.Y.: Garden City Publishing Co., 1930), 133.

5. Nicholas Tomalin and Ron Hall, *The Strange Voyage of Donald Crowhurst* (London: Hodder and Stoughton, 1970), 283. Toward the end of the book Tomalin and Hall consider other alternatives—that Crowhurst is still alive somewhere, that he died accidentally—and conclude that "the theory we have advanced is, we are convinced, the only one that fits all the facts" (282).

6. Amid the ensuing furor over the relationship between his work and Tomalin and Hall's, Stone began his piece defending himself, "The Genesis of *Outerbridge Reach*" (*Times Literary Supplement* [5 June 1992], hereafter cited in text as "Genesis"), by saying he came across the hoax in 1968. The story broke a year later.

7. For the similarities between the two texts, see Dominic Loehnis, "Stone Best Seller Called a Copycat Work of Fiction," *New York Observer*, 25 May 1992, and Gordon Burn, "Where Mine Is At," *London Review of Books* (28 May 1992): 20–21.

8. Katherine Stephen, "A Dangerous Voyage," *London Sunday Times*, 24 May 1992. Two weeks later Stone wrote that he "referred only to an 'incident that actually took place' " because he was "anxious that no one would mistakenly believe that I was writing about Crowhurst the man or about his family" ("Genesis," 14).

9. Robert Stone, "Outerbridge Reach," letter to the editor, *Times Literary Supplement* (26 June 1992): 15.

10. Robert Towers, "Navigating through Reefs," *Atlantic Monthly* 248 (November 1981): 86.

11. Since we're told that Browne returns to Annapolis 20 years after he graduated in 1968, I assume the novel begins in 1988. As with his first two novels, though, Stone is a bit careless about dates. Browne speaks of a crisis in the stock market as having occurred in "eighty-seven" (*OR*, 42); one thinks

that, in 1988, he would have said "last year." Some other small inconsistencies: Browne's house is both "outsized, a mansion," and "not a large house" (*OR*, 12, 133); Browne lies to Fowler about solo sails to Bermuda and the Azores, along with "a couple of transatlantic deliveries" (*OR*, 106), but he remembers the lie, one he would not miscast, as being told to Riggs-Bowen, concerning a solo sail around an island off British Columbia.

    12.   Mark Edmundson, "America at Sea," *New Republic* 206 (20 April 1992): 43.

    13.   Robert M. Adams, "Fall of Valor," *New York Review of Books* 39, no. 6 (26 March 1992): 29.

    14.   Saul Bellow, *Dangling Man* (New York: Plume Books, 1974), 88–89.

    15.   Browne discovers that "the tie rods were not stainless steel rod but appeared to have been rigged out of galvanized wire" (*OR*, 302). More importantly, he realizes that the fiberglass is crazing, or cracking, throughout the boat, but he does not speculate about the reason. Stone offered it in the KUOM interview: "[T]he particular boat is a knockout. The worst thing is that if you don't keep a crew on 24 hours, when the laminate cools on fiberglass it just doesn't provide a suitable lamination. The fiberglass won't hold up to extreme conditions. . . . What they'll do in the Orient sometimes, they'll keep one crew on, and the guys will work 16 hours, but then they'll have to go home. In the meantime the laminate will cool. The way to do it right is to keep adding the laminate around the clock; it stays hot so that it isn't allowed to cool between the layers of fiberglass" (Benson and Solotaroff). A salesman, Browne does not know this much about boat making.

    16.   When I asked Stone if he had ever heard of a station like the one he uses in the novel, he responded:

There is such a station. It transmits from various places. It used to originate on the island of Bonaire in the Dutch West Indies, and it covers just about the entire earth, and they broadcast to a large extent to seamen, and they broadcast in Tagalog and Cantonese and English, and they do these dramatizations, and the actors are not professional actors; they are a very mixed lot. And the English speakers are variously Africans, British, Canadians, Americans. You get this mixture of accents of spoken English from all over the English-speaking world, and it's quite fascinating to listen to. And there are speakers like this woman I have speaking. It's geared, really, for people in the Third World; I mean, they're speaking to people in Africa, and this sometimes makes the biblical situation tremendously relevant. I mean, they're talking about goats and sheep and camels. They're addressing situations that are close to the ones people are in: tribe against tribe and so on. Stuff in the Old Testament is right there in the lives of the people they're broadcasting to. So it's sometimes very moving. (Benson and Solotaroff)

17. Grant Pick, "Race against Time," *Chicago Tribune*, 4 October 1992. Pinckney's sail was a leisurely effort, running from August 1990 through June 1992, with 6 months on shore and 16 at sea.

18. Playing the familiar novelistic God, Stone had some revolutionaries blow up the satellite receiver so that Browne's position could no longer be determined and he could attempt concealment from a race that had become degrading for him.

19. According to *Webster's Third New International Dictionary of the English Language* (Springfield, Mass.: G. & C. Merriam and Co., 1976), a deasil is "a charm performed by going three times about an object in the direction of the sun and sometimes carrying fire in the right hand."

20. William H. Pritchard, "Sailing over the Edge," *New York Times Book Review*, 23 February 1992, 21.

Chapter 7

1. Robert Stone, "Porque No Tiene, Porque Le Falta," *New American Review* 6 (April 1969): 199, hereafter cited in text as "PNT."

2. Samuel B. Garren, "Stone's 'Porque No Tiene, Porque Le Falta,' " *Explicator* 42, no. 3 (Spring 1984): 62, hereafter cited in text.

3. Wolfe quotes Kesey describing the experience: he explains that a recent casting of the I Ching had told him that "we had reached the end of something, we weren't going anywhere any longer, it was time for a new direction," and he went out into the storm, pointed to the sky, "and lightning flashed and all of a sudden I had a second skin, of lightning, electricity, like a suit of electricity, and I knew it was in us to be superheroes" (25–26). From all this came Kesey's decision to sneak back into the United States and try to move the culture beyond LSD.

4. For example, Garren writes, "Like Kesey on the lam, Fletch lives in a cheap hideaway on the west coast of Mexico with a lovely blonde wife and two young children" (61). There's no suggestion that Fletch is on the lam and his house is a hideaway—he tells Willie and Fencer that he has nothing to fear from the supposed body snatcher Sinister Pancho Pillow. Kesey had three children and his wife's hair was, according to Wolfe, "sorrel brown" (27). There is no evidence that Sinister Pancho Pillow is shadowing Fletch, as Garren claims. In fact, the story works much better if Fletch's paranoia is wholly unrealistic, as Kesey's was not.

5. Robert Stone, "Aquarius Obscured," *American Review* 22 (February 1975), 134–51, reprinted in *Many Windows*, ed. Ted Solotaroff (New York: Harper Colophon Books, 1982), 160, hereafter cited in text as "AO."

6. They both live in the Bay Area, where they use drugs, have one

child (a girl of about three), and work in locales that offer sleazy sexual gratification. Both are conscious of speaking with a whine.

7. Robert Stone, "Helping," *New Yorker* 63 (8 June 1987), 28+,
reprinted in *The Norton Anthology of American Literature*, 3d ed., ed. Nina Baym,
et al. (New York: W. W. Norton and Co., 1989) 2:2253, hereafter cited in text
as "H."

8. "The Second Coming," *The Collected Poems of W. B. Yeats* (New York:
Macmillan, 1956), 185.

9. Robert Stone, "Gin and Nostalgia," *Harper's* 256 (April 1978): 78.

10. Robert Stone, "The Connoisseur as Survivor," *New York Times Book
Review*, 15 January 1989, 3.

11. Robert Stone, "Imaginary People in a Real War," *New York Times
Book Review*, 1 October 1989, 42.

12. Robert Stone, "A Visionary Novel of the Sea," *New York Times Book
Review*, 25 May 1975, 2.

13. Robert Stone, "The Cold Peace," *New York Times Book Review*, 13
December 1992, 3.

14. "The Writer in Our World: "Session III: Questions and Answers,"
Triquarterly 85 (Winter 1986): 238, hereafter cited in text as "Session III."

15. Charles Baudelaire, "On the Essence of Laughter," in *Comedy:
Meaning and Form*, ed. Robert W. Corrigan (San Francisco: Chandler Publishing
Co., 1965), 451.

16. Daniel Stern, "The Art of Fiction: Bernard Malamud," *Paris Review*
61 (Spring 1975): 51–52.

17. Robert Stone, "Portrait," introduction to *Legacy of Light*, ed.
Constance Sullivan (New York: Alfred A. Knopf, 1987), 60, hereafter cited in
text as "P."

18. Norman Mailer, *Miami and the Siege of Chicago* (New York: New
American Library/Signet, 1968), 50.

19. Stone, who was born on 21 August 1937, left radio school at
Norfolk and boarded "the *U.S.S. Muliphen* during September of 1956"
(Solotaroff 1991).

20. Robert Stone, "Havana Then and Now," *Harper's* 284 (March
1992): 37–38, hereafter cited in text as "HTN."

21. Robert Stone, "Everything Possible, Nothing Sacred," *New York
Times*, 15 March 1992, hereafter cited in text as "EP."

22. Wolfe tells *his* version of the encounter with Agent Number One on
pages 336–42 of *The Electric Kool-Aid Acid Test*. It diverges from Stone's account in
at least ten different ways. Stone defended his version in my October 1991 interview with him; with obvious annoyance he said, "I was the one who was there."

23. Robert Stone, "The Man Who Turned on the Here," in *One Lord,
One Faith, One Cornbread*, ed. Fred Nelson and Ed McClanahan (New York:
Anchor Books, 1973), 55–56, hereafter cited in text as "MWTH."

Selected Bibliography

PRIMARY SOURCES

Novels

Children of Light. New York: Alfred A. Knopf, 1986.
Dog Soldiers. Boston: Houghton Mifflin, 1974.
A Flag for Sunrise. New York: Alfred A. Knopf, 1981.
A Hall of Mirrors. Boston: Houghton Mifflin, 1967.
Outerbridge Reach. New York: Ticknor and Fields, 1992.

Short Stories

"Absence of Mercy." *Harper's* 275 (November 1987): 61–68.
"Aquarius Obscured." *American Review* 22 (February 1975): 134–51.
"Helping." *New Yorker* 63 (8 June 1987): 28+.
"Porque No Tiene, Porque Le Falta." *New American Review* 6 (April 1969): 198–226.

Sections of Novels Printed Elsewhere

"The Ascent of Mount Carmel" (*CL*). *Paris Review* 27 (Winter 1985): 58–81.
"Farley the Sailor" (*HM*). *Saturday Evening Post* 240 (14 January 1987): 42–44.
"A Hunter in the Morning" (*FS*). *New American Review* 26 (November 1977): 118–34.
"In a Mexican Garden" (*CL*). *Esquire* 104 (August 1985): 112–16.
"Not Scared of You" (*OR*). *Gentleman's Quarterly* 59 (March 1989): 259+.
"Our Lady of the Revolution" (*OR*). *Esquire* 117 (February 1992): 104–6+.
"Thunderbolt in Red, White, and Blue" (*HM*). *Saturday Evening Post* 240 (28 January 1967): 62–70.
"To Find the Edge" (*OR*). *Harper's* 283 (October 1991): 66–82.
"War Stories" (*FS*). *Harper's* 254 (May 1977): 63–66.
"WUSA" (*HM*). In *On the Job*. Edited by Thomas O'Rourke. New York: Vintage Books, 1977.

Books Edited

The Best American Short Stories: 1992 (with Katrina Kenison). Boston: Houghton Mifflin, 1992.

Nonfiction

"Albania's Byronic Shore" (a contribution to "Dream Destinations"). *New York Times*, 4 March 1990.

"Blows to the Spirit" (with Ken Kesey). *Esquire* 105 (June 1986): 266–68+.

"Changing Tides" (a contribution to "The World of New York"). *New York Times*, 4 April 1987.

"The Cold Peace" (a review of *The Porcupine* by Julian Barnes). *New York Times Book Review*, 13 December 1992, 3.

"The Connoisseur as Survivor" (a review of *Utz* by Bruce Chatwin). *New York Times Book Review*, 15 January 1989, 3.

"East West Relation." *Harper's* 279 (November 1989): 279–93.

"Everything Possible, Nothing Sacred." *New York Times*, 15 March 1992.

"The Genesis of *Outerbridge Reach*." *Times Literary Supplement*, 5 June 1992, 15.

"Gin and Nostalgia" (a review of *The Human Factor* by Graham Greene). *Harper's* 256 (April 1978): 78–83.

"Havana Then and Now." *Harper's* 284 (March 1992): 36–46.

"He Knows They Are Coming for Him" (a review of *Brotherly Love* by Pete Dexter). *New York Times Book Review*, 13 October 1991, 3.

"A Higher Horror of the Whiteness: Cocaine's Coloring of the American Psyche." *Harper's* 273 (December 1986): 49–54.

"Imaginary People in a Real War" (a review of *To Ismara* by Thomas Keneally). *New York Times Book Review*, 1 October 1989, 1, 42.

"Itchy Feet and Pencils: A Symposium" (with Russell Banks, Jan Morris, and William Styron). *New York Times Book Review*, 18 August 1991, 1, 23–25.

"Keeping the Future at Bay: Republicans and Their America." *Harper's* 277 (November 1988): 57–66.

"The Man Who Turned on the Here." In *One Lord, One Faith, One Cornbread*. Edited by Fred Nelson and Ed McClanahan. New York: Anchor Books, 1973.

"Me and the Universe." *Triquarterly* 65 (Winter 1986): 229–34.

" 'Miss Saigon' Flirts with Art and Reality" (a review of the musical drama *Miss Saigon*). *New York Times*, 7 April 1991.

"Portrait." In *Legacy of Light*. Edited by Constance Sullivan. New York: Alfred A. Knopf, 1987.

"The Reason for Stories: Toward a Moral Fiction." *Harper's* 276 (June 1988): 71–76.

"Terrorist in the Family" (a review of *The American Ambassador* by Ward Just). *New York Times Book Review*, 15 March 1987, 1, 22.

"There It Is." *Guardian*, 17 July 1971, 9.

"A Visionary Novel of the Sea" (a review of *Far Tortuga* by Peter Matthiessen). *New York Times Book Review*, 25 May 1975, 1–2.

"We Couldn't Swing with It: The 'Intrepid Four.' " *Atlantic* 221 (June 1968): 57–64.

Interviews

Benson, Steve, and Robert Solotaroff. "Talking Sense" (a radio interview with Robert Stone). KUOM, Minneapolis, 1 May 1992.

Bonetti, Kay. "An Interview with Robert Stone." *Missouri Review* 6, no. 1 (Fall 1982): 91–114.

Chapple, Steve. "Robert Stone Faces the Devil." *Mother Jones* 9 (May 1984): 35–41.

Karagueuzian, Maureen. "Interview with Robert Stone." *Triquarterly* 53 (Winter 1983): 249–58.

Ruas, Charles. *Conversations with American Writers*. New York: Alfred A. Knopf, 1985.

Schroeder, Eric James. "Two Interviews: Talks with Tim O'Brien and Robert Stone." *Modern Fiction Studies* 30, no. 1 (Spring 1984): 135–64.

Steinberg, Sybil. "Robert Stone." *Publisher's Weekly* 229 (21 March 1986): 72–74.

Woods, William Crawford. "The Art of Fiction XC: Robert Stone." *Paris Review* 27, no. 2 (Winter 1985): 26–57.

SECONDARY SOURCES

As of 1 January 1993, no books or monographs dealing exclusively with Stone's work had been published, and there are surprisingly few articles. Since most of the best criticism of his fiction has appeared in reviews, I am including below publishing information on what seem to me to be the most significant reviews of Stone's novels.

Alvarez, A. "Among the Freaks" (review of *CL*). *New York Review of Books* 33 (10 April 1986): 23–26.

Balliet, Whitney. "Good Ears" (review of *CL*). *New Yorker* 62 (2 June 1986): 23–26.

Beatty, Jack. "A Novel of Despair" (review of *FS*). *New Republic* 185 (18 November 1981): 37–39.

Capouya, Emile. "[Review of] *A Hall of Mirrors*." *Commonweal* 88 (5 April 1968): 79–81.

Clemons, Walter. "The Making of a Quagmire." *Newsweek* 98 (18 November 1981): 88.

Edmundson, Mark. "America at Sea" (review of *OB*). *New Republic* 206 (20 April 1992): 42–45.

Elliot, Emory. "History and Will in *Dog Soldiers, Sabbatical,* and *The Color Purple.*" *Arizona Quarterly* 43, no. 3 (Autumn 1987): 197–217.

Epstein, Joseph. "American Nightmares" (review of *FS*). *Commentary* 72 (March 1982): 42–45.

Furniss, David West. "Making Sense of the War: Vietnam and American Prose." Unpublished doctoral dissertation, University of Minnesota, 1989.

Garren, Samuel B. "Stone's 'Porque No Tiene, Porque Le Falta.' " *Explicator* 42, no. 3 (Spring 1984): 61–62.

Gray, Paul. "Flowers of Evil" (review of *DS*). *Time* 104 (11 November 1974): 111.

Hall, Joan Joffe. "*Dog Soldiers* by Robert Stone." *New Republic* 172 (4 January 1975): 31.

Karagueuzian, Maureen. "Irony in Robert Stone's *Dog Soldiers.*" *Critique: Studies in Modern Fiction* 24, no. 2 (Winter 1983): 65–73.

Ladin, Sharon Lee. "Lost in Space." In "Spirit Warriors: The Samurai Figure in Current American Fiction." Unpublished doctoral dissertation, University of California, Santa Cruz, 1979.

Leonard, John. "Leviathan" (review of *OR*). *The Nation* 254 (13 April 1992): 489–94.

McClay, Eileen Taylor. "Robert Stone: Some Sort of Religious Impulse." In "Images of Latin America in Contemporary U.S. Literature." Unpublished doctoral dissertation, George Washington University, 1987.

McConnell, Frank. "Transfiguration of Despair" (review of *FS*). *Commonweal* 72 (March 1982): 42–45.

Moore, L. Hugh. "The Undersea World of Robert Stone." *Critique: Studies in Modern Fiction* 11, no. 3 (1969): 43–56.

O'Haire, Hugh. "The Search for Transcendence in the Novels of Robert Stone." Unpublished master's thesis, City University of New York, Queens campus (no date).

Parks, John G. "Unfit Survivors: The Failed and Lost Pilgrims in the Fiction of Robert Stone." *CEA Critic* 53 (Fall 1990): 52–57.

Poirier, Richard. "Intruders" (review of *FS*). *New York Review of Books* 28 (3 December 1981): 37–39.

Prescott, Peter. "A Wasteland of the Heart" (review of *CL*). *Newsweek* 107 (17 March 1986):72–73.

Pritchard, William H. "Novel Discomforts and Delights" (contains review of *FS*). *Hudson Review* 35, no. 1 (Spring 1982): 159–76.

———. "Novel Sex and Violence" (contains review of *DS*). *Hudson Review* 28, no. 1 (Spring 1975): 147–60.

———. "Sailing over the Edge" (review of *OB*). *New York Times Book Review*, 23 February 1992, 1+.

Sale, Roger. "Robert Stone." In *On Not Being Good Enough*. New York: Oxford University Press, 1979.

Shelton, Frank W. "Robert Stone's *Dog Soldiers:* Vietnam Comes Home to America." *Critique: Studies in Modern Fiction* 24, no. 2 (Winter 1983): 74–81.

Strouse, Jean. "The Heebiejeebieville Express" (review of *CL*). *New York Times Book Review*, 16 March 1986, 1+.

Thorburn, David. "A Fearful and Mindless Violence" (review of *HM*). *The Nation* 206 (1 April 1968): 452–54.

Towers, Robert. "Navigating through Reefs" (review of *FS*). *Atlantic Monthly* 248 (November 1981): 86–88.

Weber, Bruce. "An Eye for Danger." *New York Times Magazine*, 19 January 1992, 19–24.

Index

The Author

Robert Solotaroff was educated at the University of Michigan and the University of Chicago. The author of *Down Mailer's Way* (University of Illinois Press, 1974) and *Bernard Malumud: A Study of the Short Fiction* (Twayne Publishers, 1989), he is a professor in the Department of English at the University of Minnesota and lives in Minneapolis with his wife and daughter.

The Editor

Frank Day is a professor of English at Clemson University. He is the author of *Sir William Empson: An Annotated Bibliography* and *Arthur Koestler: A Guide to Research*. He was a Fulbright lecturer in American literature in Romania (1980–81) and in Bangladesh (1986–87).